THE PRIVATE RENTED SECTOR IN A NEW CENTURY

Revival or false dawn?

Edited by Stuart Lowe and David Hughes

The POLICY PRESS

First published in Great Britain in September 2002 by

The Policy Press
34 Tyndall's Park Road
Bristol BS8 1PY
UK

Tel +44 (0)117 954 6800
Fax +44 (0)117 973 7308
e-mail tpp@bristol.ac.uk
www.policypress.org.uk

British Library Cataloguing in Publication Data
A catalogue record for this book is available from the British Library

ISBN 1 86134 348 5 paperback
A hardcover version of this book is also available

Stuart Lowe is Senior Lecturer in Social Policy at the University of York and **David Hughes** is Professor of Housing and Planning Law at De Montfort University Law School, Leicester.

Cover design by Qube Design Associates, Bristol.
Front cover: photograph supplied by www.third-avenue.co.uk

Printed and bound in Great Britain by Hobbs the Printers Ltd, Southampton.

Contents

List of tables and figures

Tables

Figures

Notes on contributors

A.D.H. Crook is Pro-Vice Chancellor and Professor of Town and Regional Planning at the University of Sheffield. He was elected a Fellow of the Royal Society of Arts in 1999. In 2001 he was elected to a Fellowship of the Royal Town Planning Institute in recognition of his distinguished contribution to town planning. Recent publications include: *Repair & maintenance by private landlords* (2000) (with J.M. Henneberry, J.E.T. Hughes, and P.A. Kemp), London: Department of the Environment Transport and the Regions; and 'The achievement of affordable housing policies through the planning system' (2000) (with C.M.E. Whitehead), in C.M.E. Whitehead and S. Monk (eds) *Restructuring housing systems: From social to affordable housing?*, York: York Publishing Services.

Hector Currie was Lecturer in the School of Planning and Housing, Edinburgh College of Art/Heriot-Watt University. Recently he has been appointed as Housing Policy Adviser for the Scottish Executive Development Department. He has published widely on housing management, most recently with his colleagues in a series of 'Good Practice' studies for the Scottish Executive. He has research interests in multiple occupancy, the private rented sector, the governance of housing, performance management, stock transfer and Registered Social Landlords.

Martin Davis is Principal Lecturer at De Montfort University Law School, Leicester. He publishes regularly on housing law and practice, and recently has conducted research on the law relating to student housing. Recent publications include: 'Students, academic institutions, and contracts' (2001), *Journal of Law and Education*, vol 13 no 1; *Housing law – cases and materials* (1999) (with David Hughes and others), London (CHECK): Blackstones; *Sourcebook on contract* (2000) (with David Oughton), 2nd edn, London: Cavendish.

Mike Ellison is a research student at De Montfort University Law School Leicester, examining the operation of Part 1 of the Housing Grants, Construction and Regeneration Act 1996. He has a wide experience of training and advice work on housing renewal grants, especially the test of resources, and social security law. He is a regular contributor to the *Disability rights handbook*.

Phil Hancock is Performance Manager but was previously Senior Housing Services Officer with Ryedale District Council. Previously he worked for the London Borough of Hammersmith and Fulham and the London Borough of Richmond, mostly in housing management. He is a member of the Chartered Institute of Housing. His research interest is focused on rural issues, particularly around housing.

David Hughes is Professor of Housing and Planning Law at De Montfort University Law School, Leicester. He was elected a Fellow of the Royal Society of Arts in 1994 in recognition of his work in relation to Environmental Law. He is Honorary Legal Consultant to the National Council for Housing and Planning. Recent publications include *Public sector housing law*, 3rd edn, (2000) (with Stuart Lowe), London: Butterworths; *Cases and materials on housing law*, (2000) (with Martin Davis and others), London: Blackstone. His main research fields are the Law of Housing, and Environmental and Town and Country Planning Law.

Peter Kemp is Professor of Social Policy, and Director of the Social Policy Research Unit, at the University of York. He was previously Professor of Housing and Social Policy at the University of Glasgow. Between 1990 and 1995 he was the first holder of the Joseph Rowntree Chair of Housing Policy, and founding Director of the Centre for Housing Policy, at the University of York. He has published extensively on the privately rented sector. His current research interests are housing benefit, social security and welfare reform.

Diane Lister is Research Associate at the Centre for Regional Economic and Social Research, Sheffield Hallam University. She recently completed her DPhil thesis at the University of York based on research into the socio-legal aspects of relationships between private landlords and young people. Her general research interests concern the private rented sector and housing and socio-legal issues.

Stuart Lowe is Senior Lecturer in Social Policy at the University of York. With David Hughes he is author of *Public sector housing law*, 3rd edn (2000), London: Butterworth's and has recently completed a new text book *Housing policy analysis: British housing in comparative context* (2002) Basingstoke: Palgrave. He has written on a variety of housing policy issues, most recently concerning low demand, and has an interest in housing policy in post-communist societies and more generally in housing and social theory.

Jill Morgan is Senior Lecturer at Norwich Law School, University of East Anglia. She contributes regularly to academic and practitioner journals on matters relating to housing law and landlord and tenant law. She is author of *Textbook on housing law* (1998), Blackstone Press.

David Rhodes is a Research Fellow in the Centre for Housing Policy, University of York. Since 1995, with Peter Kemp, he has been responsible for the preparation of the University of York Index of Private Rents and Yields. Other recent publications include: *The nature and impact of student demand on housing markets*, (with Julie Rugg and Anwen Jones), York: York Publishing Services (2000); *Chains or challenges? The prospects for better regulation of the private rented sector* (2000) (with Julie Rugg), Coventry: Chartered Institute of Housing and British

Property Federation. His general research interests are in private rented housing markets and the local impacts of national housing initiatives and policies.

Madhu Satsangi is Lecturer in planning and housing in the School of the Built Environment, Heriot-Watt University, Edinburgh. With a variety of colleagues his recent publications include: *Selling and developing land and buildings for rent and low-cost home ownership: The views of landowners* (2000), Edinburgh: Scottish Homes/Scottish Landowners' Federation; *Factors affecting land supply for affordable housing in rural areas* (2000), Scottish Executive Central Research Unit. His research interests are in private rental housing, land-use planning and the dynamics of rural housing markets and land reform.

Steve Wilcox is a Professor at the Centre for Housing Policy, University of York. He has now edited the Joseph Rowntree Foundation Annual *Housing Finance Review* for ten years, and has written many reports on housing finance and housing policy issues, for a wide range of national organisations. Recent reports have included *Housing benefit, affordability and work incentives* (1997) for the National Housing Federation, *Unfinished business: Housing costs and the reform of welfare benefits* (1998) jointly for the Chartered Institute of Housing, Council of Mortgage Lenders, Local Government Association, National Housing Federation and Joseph Rowntree Foundation, *The vexed question of affordability* (1999) for Scottish Homes, *Half the poor* (2000) for the Council of Mortgage Lenders and *Social housing, tenure and housing allowance: An international review* (2001) for the Department for Work and Pensions.

Preface

This volume has been produced by a truly collaborative effort. The editors have for many years enjoyed a close working relationship and have thoroughly enjoyed each other's company, albeit it that mostly this has been by phone call and latterly e-mail. Most of the contributors are known to one or other of the editors by a happy professional contact. Thus the production of this book, although hard work for all of us, has been in many ways a real pleasure.

The subject matter has its sombre side as will be readily apparent in the data presented at various points on the poor quality of a considerable part of the private rented housing stock, and the continuing scandal of shoddy management by some landlords. This housing sector offers some of the best and a very large part of the worst that is to be had in the British housing market. In a small way it is to be hoped that this collection will help all those concerned with both law, policy and practice in the private rented sector to understand more clearly the problems it faces and as a result to find a constructive way forward.

The editors wish to thank the contributors who have all made sacrifices of time and effort in busy lives to prepare their chapters. They range from a recently graduated doctoral student to a pro-vice chancellor, but all of them really know their field, a fact that makes the task of editing so much easier and rewarding.

Finally, David Hughes wishes to thank Sheila Brammall for typing his parts of the manuscript, Mr Harry Perry of Leicester Newarke Housing Association; and the Planning Department of Leicester City Council. Both editors wish to thank Dawn Rushen and the other members of The Policy Press office for their patience and courtesy.

Stuart Lowe and David Hughes
York and Leicester, April 2002

Preface

ONE

The new private rented sector

David Hughes and Stuart Lowe

Introduction

This book is written by policy analysts and legal specialists interested in the role played in the contemporary housing system by the private rented sector (PRS). The reason for bringing them together is because at the heart of the historic and contemporary position are cross-disciplinary issues, focusing principally on the nature of the tenant–landlord relationship. This relationship is encapsulated in complex and confusing statutory and judicial statements, although it is little understood by either tenants or landlords (Nelken, 1983). The policy context also involves this relationship but looks more widely at the macro-economic setting, the social security system (especially housing benefit), the role of local authorities, the housing market and changing demographic structures, which establish the parameters in which the PRS functions. Drawing on specialist knowledge within legal studies and policy analysis the book aims to provide an evaluation of this small but pivotal housing tenure as a new century dawns. The PRS was subject to dramatic changes at the end of the 20th century through long-awaited market liberalisation. The early years of the new century are, therefore, an opportune moment to draw together recent research and reflections on the newly deregulated PRS.

The Conservative governments in the 1980s signalled a strong intention not only to revive the long-declining PRS but also to change its ownership structure by bringing in more business-orientated landlordism to challenge the amateurism typical of the PRS's long history dating back at least to the 19th century. The 1988 Housing Act created a new form of tenancy, the assured tenancy, which set in train the deregulation of the sector by enabling rent increases and the limitation of tenants' security of tenure. These two elements shifted the balance in the landlord–tenant relationship very decisively in favour of landlords, bringing to an end a 70-year period in which the rights of tenants to enjoy their home were placed above the commercial interest and property rights of landlords. Subsequently assured shorthold tenancies became the norm for the sector under the 1996 Housing Act and these now account for three quarters of lettings.

'New' Labour has continued with the same agenda and has made no attempt to challenge the basic premise of the previous government that the future lay in the radical deregulation of the market. Having a 'healthy private rented sector' was promoted in Labour's April 2000 Housing Green Paper as a source of greater choice for people unable or unwilling to buy their own home (DETR, 2000). The declared policy objective aimed to "secure a larger, better quality, better-managed" private rented sector. There has thus arisen a bipartisan consensus on the need for a healthy PRS and the means to achieve it – namely, that higher rents would provide the incentive and the logic for better conditions and increased provision. The success of engineering market rents via the assured formula is not in doubt. The question, however, is whether the desired outcome of a bigger, better quality private rented sector has in practice surfaced out of this new regime? This in essence is the question addressed by this collection.

The purpose of this chapter is to provide a general background against which the more detailed and focused chapters can be read. It describes the decline of the PRS from its pre-eminent position during the early 20th century. Even as late as 1945 very nearly three in five households were tenants of private landlords (see Holmans, 1987, Chapter VIII; Kemp, 1993, 1997 for more detailed accounts). What happened to produce a slump to barely 8.5 per cent of households in the late 1980s? Why did previous attempts to deregulate the PRS fail so abjectly only to succeed, or appear to succeed, during the 1990s? What have been the consequences of deregulation for the long-term development of the sector? Who are its tenants and landlords? In short, what kind of housing sector has it become in the early years of the 21st century?

Decline and fall

From 1915, when rent control was first introduced, up to 1988, the Rent Acts constituted a significant interference with the property rights of landlords. For most of the 20th century legislation favoured security of tenure for private tenants, despite attempts to change it (notably in the 1957 Rent Act). People's homes were considered sacrosanct against the commercial interest of landlords. But this led to the progressive withering away of the sector. A brief commentary on this is needed to set the scene for the rest of the volume.

Following 1915 (and despite partial deregulation during the inter-war years) there was a steady decline in the traditional sector mainly due to landlords selling their properties to sitting tenants. The only exception to this long, inexorable decline occurred in the 1930s, due to favourable conditions arising from cheap labour and low interest rates, when nearly a million properties were built for private renting. These, however, were offered at the middle and upper end of the market. At the bottom end yields from rental income were simply too low to produce a corresponding investment surge.

The paradox was that rent control had made housing at the lower end of the market much more affordable to millions of households but apart from what already existed there was virtually no supply. It was this gap that subsidised provision (by local authorities) was designed to fill. Essentially the logic was the same after the Second World War. The difference was that the conditions in which the market operated were far worse than in the 1930s. Inflation increased sharply during the war and afterwards. Prices for consumer goods and services had risen 105 per cent between 1939 and 1951 and the price of building maintenance nearly trebled (Holmans, 1987, p 409).

During the inter-war period, the PRS witnessed a decrease of about half a million units, made up of losses due to sales to sitting tenants (1.1 million) and slum clearance (300,000) that were offset by the 1930s' new build of 900,000. In 1938 there was a stock of approximately 6.6 million privately rented units accommodating three in five households. By the mid-1970s this had been reduced by a combination of clearances and transfers to 2.9 million, just over 15 per cent of the total stock of housing, finally bottoming out at 8.2 per cent in the late 1980s. Such a dramatic reversal of fortunes was the consequence of patterns, policies and social changes already in place before the war. The severity of the circumstances created by the 1939-45 conflict intensified what were already structural and long-term pressures. It is doubtful whether anything could have been done to reverse these. By the time the 1957 Rent Act attempted to deregulate the sector it was already many decades beyond redemption. In post-war conditions for there to have been any major change in the fortunes of the PRS – at least seen from the viewpoint of likely investors - there would have needed to be an early separation between security of tenure and rent control.

The situation was not helped because rent control, imposed once again at the onset of conflict persisted for 12 years after the end of the war as a result of recommendations made by the Ridley Committee (in view of the chronic post-war housing shortage). Leaving controlled rents untouched meant large decreases in rental income in real terms due to inflation and building costs. With poor returns on capital invested, and price increases, yields fell (Kemp, 1997). It is hardly surprising that there was a dramatic acceleration in sales by landlords to sitting tenants or on vacant possession in most parts of the country. Property bought on the open market to provide accommodation suitable to the standards of the day, let alone built from scratch, required rents that were simply too expensive for millions of households. Even without rent control, "a system that permitted controlled rents to adjust to changes in the value of money" would not have stimulated new investment (Holmans, 2000, p 17). The Conservative government's housing policies in the 1950s were aimed mainly at overcoming the very great shortages of dwellings to households principally through promoting home ownership but also via subsidised council housing which was more easily planned and controlled than the PRS.

Deregulation, when it came via the 1957 Rent Act, was imposed by the simple expedient of linking increases in rent to rateable values using the (most recent) revaluation that had been conducted in 1939 as the benchmark figure. Decontrol took place for properties of gross rateable values above £30, the upper end of the market (£40 in London), and simultaneously ended security of tenure. Decontrol of lettings below that level was permitted only on vacant possession. For lettings remaining under rent control, rent increases were permitted and set at a level twice the gross rateable value. This system permitted a general increase in the order of 150 per cent compared to 1939 levels and the number of controlled lettings fell from about 4.3 million before the Act to about 1.75 million by 1964. (Holmans, 1987, p 414).

The most contentious part of the Rent Act was not the increases in rent but the implication of loss of security of tenure and the threat that unscrupulous landlords would exploit this loss, notably due to the 'Rachman' scandal of the early 1960s. Rachman was alleged to have intimidated tenants out of his controlled properties in order to gain vacant possession to let at higher rents, though most landlords were keen to get vacant possession to sell on into the owner occupier market. The greatest implication was for those properties that were not saleable. Before 1957 properties had to be let furnished if they were to be outside rent control but after the Rent Act they could be let *unfurnished* (the normal form for long-term lets) without security or rent control. The 1957 legislation, therefore, expanded very considerably the range of properties where landlords had an incentive to get rid of controlled tenants (Holmans, 1987, p 419).

In response to the Rachman scandal the 1964 Eviction Act, which became Part III of the 1965 Rent Act, attempted to address the problems caused by scurrilous landlords. The 1965 Act sought a wholesale restructuring of the rapidly dwindling PRS by the introduction of 'fair rents' and extended security of tenure to all tenants of unfurnished accommodation. The balance of advantage again swung in favour of tenants, which made the already untenable position for investment in the sector worse, and the PRS continued its inexorable decline. The 1957 attempt at deregulation was thus short lived.

The very considerable loss to the PRS of about one million properties through slum clearance should also not be forgotten in the overall pattern of post-war decline. These were mainly 19th-century terraces in poor condition having suffered from an inevitable lack of investment. In addition, landlords continued to sell to sitting tenants (apart from some areas in London). The PRS withered away reaching its lowest point, as we have seen, towards the end of the 1980s.

By the time the 1957 attempt at deregulation was implemented, the PRS was already many decades beyond restoration to anything like its former position in the British housing market. The logic of sales into owner occupation was not significantly altered by the 1957 Act. Deregulation on its own was not the answer to revival. The deregulation that has overtaken the PRS in the 1990s came about in very different circumstances, and directed to a much smaller sector consisting of a series of niche markets rather than a large-scale provider of general housing.

The current deregulation

The remaining sections of this chapter provide necessary context not covered elsewhere in the book to the liberalised market of the contemporary PRS. The current deregulation was the result of a conscious effort by the Conservative government to shift the balance of the relationship between landlord and tenant to favour landlords, and thus create conditions for increased investment. The new orthodoxy believed that the creation of the 'homeowning society' also required the existence of a healthy and functioning private rental sector and encouragement for the 'independently rented sector', that is, market responsive housing associations. Calls yet again for the 'revival of the private rented sector' rang out from government offices. But now there was an emphasis on changing ownership structures by bringing in large-scale investors. Deregulation was seen as the way to unlock corporate investment. As in the past the argument was that the difficulty faced by the PRS and the key to its revival was essentially a supply-side problem. Revival hinged on setting up the conditions favourable for new (and bigger) investors. Crook's chapter (Chapter Two) describes in detail the policy instruments used to underpin deregulation and designed to bring in corporate investors (schemes such as BES and HITs). Dave Rhodes and Peter Kemp (Chapter Four) demonstrate some of the practical difficulties corporate investors have in determining whether to enter this sector. They conclude that the outlook for rental yields remains unclear and institutional investors generally remain cautious and unwilling to commit themselves because of fears over relative risks and their lack of experience in the residential sector. Crook also discusses the factors which inhibit corporate investment in these terms, a fear of the unfamiliar and uncertainty about the long-term security of the market.

Madhu Satsangi's chapter (Chapter Four) continues the study of the attitudes and practice of investors in the context of rural landowners in Scotland; a significant factor in housing supply in that part of Britain. Small-scale private landlords predominate with the average owner having eight properties (80 per cent have fewer than ten, a finding close to Crook and Kemp's (1996a) data on England) but many of these properties appear to be tied to the estate and not freely available. House letting is a significant business activity, but for only a few does it count as a major source of income. Most landowners rent with a view to supporting estate activity and local communities. Satsargi's chapter provides a useful insight into what is on the minds of landowners and housing supply behaviour more generally.

Phil Hancock confirms these findings in the context of English rural housing markets. Again the pattern is shaped by small-scale landlordism and restructuring of the rural economy. The growth in the rural population (by nearly a quarter in the last 25 years) has been almost entirely made up of affluent town-dwellers moving into rural areas, a process closely associated with the displacement of less well-off and younger rural households. Relative to urban areas the PRS remains a more significant factor in rural communities, although a large proportion of formerly tied accommodation has been sold off. The pattern according to Hancock is one of a bifurcation of the rental market between affluent households choosing to live in good quality lettings, at relatively expensive rents (people who could well afford to buy if they chose to do so), and those in the 'traditional' stock of smaller properties in poorer condition let at low rent. As in Scotland there is a wide range of rural landlords with a variety of motives for being in the lettings market, but the vast majority of them operate on a small scale and few of them are dependent on their properties as a main source of income.

A first theme that emerges from these chapters is that the supply side of the PRS continues to be characterised, as Crook describes it, as a 'cottage industry' and has not changed in this regard since deregulation. Despite research evidence and a raft of government schemes to encourage and support corporate investors, fears about the long-term outlook and unfamiliarity with the property sector persist in inhibiting investment. Even rural landowners appear reluctant to develop new business ventures, beyond their parochial interests, despite the crisis in the rural economy. This evidence confirms previous work by Kemp and Rhodes (1994) that rural landlords in Scotland and quite likely elsewhere were less commercially orientated than their urban counterparts. A second supply-side theme also emerges from the consideration of rural versus urban markets, namely that the rural sector does not seem to have benefited to the same extent as urban areas from the growth of the 1990s. This would seem to reflect the different characteristics of the housing stock and the different circumstances of the urban and rural economies. However, unfamiliarity and doubts about the long-term security of property investment is a ubiquitous feature of the PRS, urban or rural.

The process of deregulation

What is not in doubt, however, is the scale and speed with which the PRS has been deregulated. The 1980 Housing Act began the process of re-engineering the relationship between landlord and tenant through the creation of the first version assured tenancies. A new scheme covered all new tenancies in the 1988 Housing Act and provided also for the creation of assured shorthold tenancies. The 1996 Housing Act, in effect, made assured shortholds the standard tenancy arrangement (with assured tenancies being enjoyed only by tenants of RSLs as a general rule).

Assured tenancies gave landlords much easier access to their property if tenants fell into rent arrears and gave them enhanced powers over possession issues, particularly on termination, and also over renegotiation of the rent. A landlord seeking possession of premises under an assured tenancy must still obtain a court order which refers to one or more of a list of 'grounds for possession' contained in the 1988 Act. Assured shorthold tenancies which now apply automatically (from March 1997) except where the tenancy agreement provides

Figure 1.1: Change in main letting types between 1988 and 1998/9

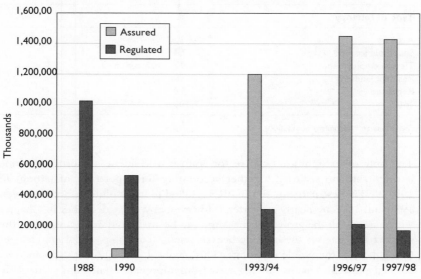

Source: McConaghy et al (2000)

otherwise (which will only very rarely be the case) give security of tenure for a limited fixed period – maybe as little as six months – after which possession may be easily gained, providing the landlord has followed the correct procedure in serving the notice to quit (see Chapter Eight).

Such was the advantage to landlords of the new tenancy types that as early as 1996 nearly three quarters of tenancies were, or had converted to, assured shorthold tenancies (see Figure 1.1). Currently (Spring, 2002) 90 per cent of new lettings in the PRS are of the assured or assured shorthold types. Shortholds accounted for 54 per cent of all lettings in 1998/99 compared to only 8 per cent in 1990, the first full year after the 1988 reforms. By contrast, *before* 1989 most tenancies in the PRS were 'regulated' under previous legislation. In 1988 nearly 60 per cent of tenancies were regulated but by 1998 this figure had fallen to only 8 per cent (a decrease from 1.1 million to only 190,000). Regulated tenancies mostly fell under the system of 'fair rents' by which landlords or tenants could apply to rent officers for registration of a fair rent – determined mainly on the size and amenities of the let not taking into account scarcity value.

As Table 1.1 shows, other forms of lettings make up a small proportion of the sector, notably tied accommodation, owned by employers and available only to their employees and their families. Health authorities, some universities, landowners/farmers and police authorities are typical landlords in this small sub-sector of the PRS. Together these closed lettings accounted for 17 per cent of all lettings in 1998/99, nearly two thirds of which were rent-free arrangements. This was a much lower proportion than in the past.

Table 1.1: Structure of letting types in the PRS as at 2000

Type of tenancy	%	
Assured	12	
Shorthold assured	54	
Tied to employment	17	(10% rent free)
Resident landlord	9	
Regulated	8	
Total	100	

Source: Source: McConaghy et al (2000)

The only other significant sub–sector consists of resident landlords and some lettings with no security, together accounting for 9 per cent of lettings in 1998/9. The restructuring of the PRS resulted in its absolute growth between 1988 and 1995 by nearly a quarter. However, as Wilcox describes in Chapter Three, nearly all the growth at that time can be attributed to the impact of the support available via the housing benefit system (covering, until 1996 changes to regulations, the whole rent cost). This involved, among others, low income council and RSL tenants moving away from unpopular estates, but particularly newly forming households moving into the PRS in greater numbers than before (notably economically inactive, young, single people). The availability (until 1996) of housing benefit to cover the costs of deregulated rents caused a massive increase in public spending. In real terms, housing benefit increased threefold between 1989 and 1995, to over £3.6 billion in 1994/5. In contrast the number of tenants in the PRS not supported by housing benefit stayed about the same (see Chapter Three). After the introduction of local reference rents (LRF) in January 1996 and single room rent (SRR) in October 1996 and other changes to regulations, numbers of PRS tenants in receipt of housing benefit have declined sharply and many landlords have withdrawn from letting to claimants. Nevertheless, at about 10.5 per cent of households the PRS has sustained a considerable expansion since before deregulation and despite housing benefit restrictions.

Profile of landlords

Crook's chapter looks in detail at the supply side of the sector, before and after deregulation. A brief profile of private landlords is required here by way of introduction.

Throughout its long history, the PRS in Britain has been owned and managed by large numbers of small-scale landlords and this remains so today. Crook and Kemp, (1996a) conducted a survey in the mid-1990s and found that over 60 per cent of landlords were private individuals. Only 15 per cent of landlords were private companies and these companies were not large, indeed the total of lettings by the business sector accounted for only 20 per cent of addresses.

Crook and Kemp found that 43 per cent of individual landlords owned only

Table 1.2: Types of landlord (%)

Private individual/couple	61
Partnership	5
Private company	15
Public company	5
Charity or charitable trust	4
Church or Crown Commissioners	1
Government department	3
Educational establishment	1
Other	5
Total	100

Source: Crook and Kemp (1996a)

one property, two thirds owned four or fewer and 82 per cent owned nine or fewer. Only 9 per cent of individual landlords owned a stock of more than 25 properties. Only one in seven individual landlords said that being a landlord was full-time job. All the rest were 'amateur', part-time landlords. Thomas et al (1995) referred to these types of landlords as 'sideline' landlords. This is overwhelmingly the most significant type of landlord, owning just under three quarters of privately rented addresses. Only 17 per cent of PRS addresses were owned by what broadly speaking could be called full-time landlords, with a further 10 per cent owned by institutions. All the rest, three quarters of landlords, were part-time, sideline landlords. Return on investment to these landlords was not a major part of their income – 70 per cent received a quarter or less of their income from property investment.

Evidence from the most recent *Survey of English housing* (SEH) in the post-deregulation years shows that most new investment was by sideline landlords. The number of tenancies let by individual landlords increased from just over 1 million in 1990/91 (53 per cent of all lettings) to nearly 1.7 million in 1998/99 (75 per cent of all lets) (McConaghy et al, 2000, p 228). There is no sign here of an influx of investment from the corporate sector, indeed virtually the whole of the new investment since the mid-1990s has come from traditional sideline investors. The individual ownership pattern of the PRS has been significantly underpinned, indeed enhanced, following deregulation.

Characteristics of tenants in the different sub-sectors

Who are the tenants of these 'sideline' landlords? The answer holds an important key not only to the issue of supply – as it always has done because affordability ultimately determines where in the market a household settles, which in turn impacts on the type and condition of the accommodation – but increasingly to the governance of the PRS, which is a core theme of the central cluster of chapters in this volume. A detailed introduction to this question is required here. Once again the SEH provides the most informed and up-to-date profile.

Referring back to the structure of the PRS described in Table 1.1, the SEH showed that there were considerable variations between the characteristics of tenants living in the different sub-sectors of the PRS. The dominance of the two types of assured tenancies (over two thirds of the market) means that these tenants strongly reflect the overall character of the contemporary PRS. Key features identified in the SEH were:

- 80 per cent of holders of assured tenancies were under age 45, including 20 per cent under 25. Tenants in the regulated sector and other small fragments of the PRS were older, but taken together over 70 per cent of all PRS tenants were under 45. Only 13 per cent of PRS tenants were over 65.
- 45 per cent of assured tenants were single, 19 per cent married and 16 per cent cohabiting

Table 1.3 shows the pattern of household types in the PRS as a whole. Single adults show up as the main type of household in assured tenancies, and a notably high proportion (11 per cent) of such households are headed by a single parent. By contrast nearly a quarter of tenants in the regulated sector are over age 60.

The SEH also shows that only half of PRS tenants are in full-time work, (although much better placed than social housing tenants, where the figure is only a quarter). Including part-time work 65 per cent of PRS tenants are in employment, with a mean gross weekly income (for the year 1999/2000) of £338 (compared to social housing tenants' mean weekly income of only £168).

In summary, the SEH reveals a typical profile of tenants who are young, are recent entrants to the assured lettings market, and mainly living in older, small properties. By contrast the smaller, rapidly dwindling regulated sector contains tenants who by definition were of long standing because no new Regulated tenancies were started after January 1989. These tenants were older (two thirds over 60), often living alone in unfurnished accommodation, and continuing to be protected by the 1977 Rent Act, with rent control and security of tenure. Over 60 per cent of regulated tenants had lived in the property for more than

Table 1.3: Private rental sector tenants, household types

Household type	All assured types	Other lettings	All
Couple, no dependent child(ren)	23	28	24
Couple with dependent child(ren)	12	16	13
Lone parent with dependent child(ren)	11	2	9
Other multi-person Household	18	10	16
One adult aged under 60	30	21	28
One adult aged over 60	5	24	10

Source: McConaghy et al (2000, table A4.1)

20 years. Taking the PRS as a whole, by 1998/99 only 16 per cent of tenants were aged over 60, a very large decease from earlier years: only ten years previously over-60s made up a third of all tenants. Different market niches were occupied by different types of tenants segregated by age and income.

The SEH shows that the PRS is very largely a tenure for mobile young people, catering for the upwardly mobile, but also containing a large number of badly disadvantaged, unemployed and otherwise vulnerable young people living in unsatisfactory conditions in bed-sits in Houses in Multiple Occupation (HMOs). It contains a disproportionately large number of single parents. About 625,000 (out of about 2.5 million) tenants in the PRS rely on housing benefit to pay all or part of their rent, a sharp fall from the 1.2 million in 1995. Restrictions on housing benefit payments since the mid-1990s have caused new strains between landlords and tenants in the deregulated market, as several authors in this volume testify (see Chapters Seven and Eight), and have caused a significant reduction in supply (see Chapter Three).

Mobility and turnover

One of the key features of the 'new' PRS is the speed of turnover both of people and properties. The accelerated rate of mobility has enabled the tenancy structure of the market to shift dramatically since deregulation (see Figure 1.1 above). The flows of people into and out of (and back into) the PRS is very revealing of its role as a ladder of opportunity, or tenure of last resort, depending on whether households are moving up or down the housing market.

From the mid-1980s to the mid-1990s there was a significant increase in the turnover of tenants. The proportion that had been resident at their current address for less than one year increased from 25 per cent in 1984 to 40 per cent in 1993/94 and has since stabilised about that level. It is noticeable, however, that in the under-30 age group the figure is 65 per cent and, measured by those who have been at their current address under three years, the figure increases to 93 per cent. The fact that this degree of mobility was apparent *before* deregulation of the market suggests that, at least initially, it was not the tenancy structure that caused this change. Almost certainly this mobility is explained by the increasingly youthful character of this sector of the housing market. The main function of the PRS has changed very rapidly to offer transitional and flexible accommodation to a highly transient population of younger people.

The SEH 1998/99 (McConaghy et al, 2000, pp 76-7) shows that of all tenants living in the PRS in 1998/99, 44 per cent had rented privately for less than a year and just over three quarters for less than five years. In the case of the relatively small number of tenants in the regulated sector 70 per cent had been private tenants for 20 years or more, mostly living at the same address. Mobility is very much associated with the large, youthful, assured sector of the market.

However, reasons for movements into and out of the PRS vary considerably as might be expected, depending on people's circumstances. Kemp and Keoghan's (2001) interrogation of SEH data showed that there was a 'reverse flow' of households *out* of social housing and owner occupation, as well as large numbers of newly forming households. Taking very recent movers (those who had moved into the PRS in the previous 12 months) they found that less than half the entrants were new households. While there were 356,000 new entrants to the PRS in the 12 months before the SEH interviews there were also 327,000 leavers (127,000 moving into social housing and 200,000 into owner occupation). Of the entrants most were young, leaving the parental home for the first time (Rugg and Burrows, 1999). Mostly they moved into furnished accommodation with low transaction costs. Typically this group were single and either lived alone or shared with other single people, and 20 per cent were students, reflecting the recent expansion of higher education. The revival of private renting in university towns and cities has to a considerable degree been stimulated by the growth in student numbers. What happens in any particular place is, however, subject to variation, depending on whether there is an adequate supply of PRS lettings and the economic strength of other tenant groups in local markets (Rugg et al, 2000). The situation in Leicester is outlined in detail by David Hughes and Martin Davis in Chapter Nine.

Tenants leaving social housing for the PRS were found to have very distinct social characteristics; a high percentage were unemployed or long-term sick or disabled and there was a high proportion of single parents. By contrast households leaving owner occupation to enter the PRS were mainly in work (86 per cent in full-time work compared to only 30 percent of social housing leavers) and nearly a quarter of them had moved to take up a new job, treating the PRS as temporary accommodation until they could buy. The other main issue affecting such entrants was relationship breakdown, with nearly 40 per cent saying this was why they left home ownership. Finding easy access, temporary accommodation in the short term was the key reason for the move.

The great majority of tenants leaving the PRS to move into owner occupation were in full-time employment and likely to be couples or couples with children. People leaving the PRS to enter social housing were a much more diverse group. They were mainly unemployed, retired, sick, disabled or otherwise economically inactive, and included a high proportion of single parents. The median income of leavers for owner occupation was over four times that of leavers for social housing (Kemp and Keoghan, 2001, pp 27-8).

There were thus considerable contrasts between the new households entering the PRS, households moving in from another tenure, and between leavers moving either into social housing or owner occupation. This underpins the notion of the current role of the PRS as a highly diverse and fluid tenure catering for transient populations moving up and down the housing ladder and in very different financial and social conditions.

A 'better managed' private rented sector?

A number of contributors to this book focus their attention on the theme of the governance of the PRS, especially changes in the balance of the tenant and landlord relationship arising from deregulation, and the fact that the contemporary PRS contains a large number of potentially vulnerable, mainly young and inexperienced people. The focus here is on the ambition in the government Green Paper *Quality and choice: A decent home for all* (DETR, 2000a) to create for the future a better-managed sector. The issue of harassment and problems caused by unscrupulous landlords has a long history. Harassment can take many forms but is not normally of the heavy-handed type. As Jill Morgan points out in her chapter, most harassment is not associated with commercial landlords but is very much the province of small landlordism. The low levels of knowledge both among landlords and tenants was a key theme to emerge from Nelken's (1983) classic study of tenant and landlord relationships. In the context of the 'cottage industry' tradition much of what happens is on an informal basis; tenants are not given rent books or written statements of the conditions of the tenancy. Where the relationship breaks down landlords turn to informal methods of redress. Morgan emphasises that harassment usually takes the form of sequences of small events, which makes it difficult to detect and to enforce a legal remedy. Local authorities often do not provide convincing evidence of an ability to investigate harassment and unlawful evictions and it is left to environmental health or homelessness officers to undertake such enquiries as do take place.

Rent increases and the end of security of tenure were argued for by the Thatcher governments as crucial to the revival of the PRS, a view not challenged by 'New' Labour. But neither of these in and of themselves convincingly explains the condition of the modern PRS. It was feared that liberalisation of the tenancy regime might lead to a wave of harassment and unlawful evictions, hence the 1988 Act also reworked the protection from eviction provisions of earlier legislation. This issue recurs in several chapters in this volume. Diane Lister's research into the relationship between landlords and young tenants under the age of 25 shows that landlords often operate in an unregulated fashion where the law is of peripheral significance. The amateur/part-time nature of landlordism is the principal culprit here and, she argues, is present at each of the stages in the relationship. The precontractual stage *legally* is predicated on the notion of freedom of contract and equal bargaining power but Lister's evidence shows that negotiations rarely go beyond 'take it or leave it' both for the terms of the letting and the rent. This continues throughout the tenancy life cycle. Landlords often see tenancies as a form of personal relationship and not as a legal relationship, although likely to cite 'the law' in support of their case even when ignorant of what it says. Few in Lister's sample seemed aware of the legal procedures for ending a tenancy, which as Morgan points out is a recipe for illegal repossession of property and for harassment. Indeed, as she shows, there is little incentive to behave properly because the legal system rarely penalises bad behaviour.

The dividing line between effective management and intrusion into tenants' rights is not an easy one to define. As Hughes and Davis point out in their chapter, in the context of student housing, corporate landlords can fail to be sufficiently disciplinarian by not stepping in to prevent nuisances to fellow students or to the local neighbourhood. Opposition to student lettings often stems from a failure to nip in the bud unacceptable behaviour. Effective management by corporate or institutional landlords could easily calm fears of students as nuisance neighbours, but what constitutes effective management and intrusion is not easily defined.

Regulatory issues have come to the fore in recent years, especially in the context of the government's aim to create a 'better managed' PRS. The Green Paper proposed the licensing of all landlords in areas of low demand as a method for stamping down on fraud and to encourage landlords to take part in area regeneration. A consultation paper on selective licensing of private landlords was published somewhat belatedly in October 2001 (DTLR, 2001). This follows consultation on licensing houses in multiple occupation in 1999, aimed at protecting the health and safety of tenants in the sector. The position in Scotland is very different as Hector Currie's chapter shows. Here discretionary licensing of HMO landlords by local authorities has been in operation since 1991 and was made mandatory in 2000. Currie's evidence shows that the discretionary scheme failed to overcome longstanding malpractices because local authorities taking up licensing had no clear strategic view of the role and place of HMOs in housing provision. Mandatory licensing raises several issues concerning the improvement of management in the PRS, in particular whether raising standards could lead to a diminution of the sector. As Currie observes, the justification for licensing, namely that landlords with licences will have an advantage in the market, may well turn out to have diminishing value as the scheme expands.

The English proposals are for a two-tier system, with licensing of HMOs operating in parallel with licensing of all private landlords in areas of low demand, principally in the north of England, although the Secretary of State could use existing powers to set up licensing schemes in other areas if there was compelling evidence that it was necessary. Given the Scottish experience that discretionary licensing does not work and the lack of evidence as yet that mandatory schemes do, it may be that general licensing in areas of low demand will make little impact. One of the main lessons from research on low demand is the extent to which normal housing market logic breaks down. Tenants are able to move quite freely between landlords whether public or private, so that licensing of private landlords is unlikely to have much impact in overcoming what are essentially structural problems in local economies (Lowe et al, 1999).

The governance of all rental housing is likely to undergo change following the Law Commission's proposals recently announced in a consultation paper. Their preliminary scoping paper, published in March 2001, was indicative of the Commission's determination to improve on the complex and anomalous legal framework of the current tenure structure built up on a piecemeal basis over many years. A key proposal is for a single status for all long-term tenants of social landlords, which might also be adopted by PRS landlords and would mark a radical change from the existing situation. The extent to which these changes are relevant to the PRS, given the essentially short-term and transitional nature of the vast majority of its tenants, is debatable. Short-term tenants would, under the Law Commission's proposals, continue to be covered by a tenancy similar to the assured shorthold currently governing the sector. Changes to legal status are not likely to affect the realities of the marketplace in the PRS, which have been transformed as a result of deregulation. The debate seems likely to come back to the question of whether it is desirable or necessary to protect, by a system of licensing, vulnerable tenants – students, other young people setting up their first homes, single parents, the unemployed and other claimants. And the wider debate about how far the revival of the PRS was driven by legal change remains open, although evidence of the role played by housing benefit in facilitating the initial growth and the increasingly mobile (and youthful) character of the sector both point to a number of overlapping factors rather than a single reason.

The recently published Law Commission proposals for the regulation of the sector are discussed in Chapter Thirteen.

The evidence overall is that the PRS has bifurcated with a relatively stable, good condition portion and a smaller but significant sub-sector (perhaps a third of tenancies) containing tenants who remain variously vulnerable due to lack of knowledge or financial resources, misinformation spread by ignorant landlords and subject to intimidatory behaviour such as frequent phone calls, lack of attention to repair work, a pattern of late night visits and so on. Local authorities have difficulty in determining names and addresses of such landlords while court cases take a long time to process, leading to further problems in recounting events that happened in the past and over a long period. This must lead to a general concern that the law is ineffective in protecting vulnerable young tenants who are those most in need of its support. As Jill Morgan puts it in her chapter, these people live under the blight of "legally sanctioned insecurity".

While reform of the law may be desirable in itself because currently it is a jumble of miscellaneous provisions and is cumbersome to use, law reform alone will not drive a revival of the PRS. Legal structures are in many ways simply a cosmetic dressing for a reality – characterised by ignorance, lack of training and potential vulnerability on the part of young and inexperienced tenants.

Housing conditions

The complementary chapters on the physical condition of the housing stock in the PRS, by Ellison and Crook, pursue the governance agenda by raising questions about responsibilities of landlords to maintain and repair properties. The PRS contains the worst housing of any of the major tenures. Ellison points out that the housing stock itself is relatively transient with property coming into and going out of the market quite rapidly. According to Ellison it was this turnover that accounted for a marked improvement in conditions in the PRS in the early 1990s. New properties were in better shape than those going out. Local authority grant aid has, on the other hand, had little impact on conditions. The question arises whether this recent improvement is a response to the ability of landlords to charge market rents and so provide both an incentive and finance for greater investment. Achieving better standards through market liberalisation crucially depends, as Crook points out, on the level of market rents. This means charging rents for property that reflect the attainment of socially desirable standards. Evidence from the *English House Condition Surveys* (ECHS) (DETR, 1998a) shows that a large part of the PRS stock is composed of smaller properties at the bottom end of the Council Tax bands (77 per cent are in bands A–C, the lowest level); and 40 per cent of PRS stock was worth less than half average house prices at the time of the last ECHS. Half the stock is more than 75 years old. It becomes very clear from both chapters that a large part of this sector, about a third of it, contains housing in very poor condition; 22 per cent have no central heating, two thirds are in urgent need of an external repair and 18 per cent are classified as unfit for human habitation. The results of the National Union of Students' (2001) survey of student housing found a widespread pattern of disrepair and worse: 16 per cent of student households reported accommodation infested with rats, mice and cockroaches; 40 per cent reported mould in kitchens, bathrooms or bedrooms; and almost half have never seen a gas safety certificate, which landlords are required by law to show them.

Repair and maintenance problems are mainly associated with HMOs – bedsits, shared flats and the like – and with pre-1919 terraces, all of which represent the bottom end of the market where returns are made by tolerating overcrowding and allowance of sub-standard conditions. Crook points out that young, mobile tenants may be more concerned about the 'white goods' and the state of decoration of the property rather than the state of the roof. Apart from in low-demand areas landlords can find tenants for properties and produce reasonable yields by following a strategy of low investment. Landlords thus have few short- or medium-term incentives to make improvements. Both Crook and Ellison conclude that at the bottom end of the market there is no rational economic incentive, even under the liberalised market, for landlords to raise standards. Once again this steers discussion towards issues of enforcement. The use of licensing in low-demand areas or mandatory licensing of HMOs, following the Scottish example, or any of a range of proposals (such as restricting housing benefit payments on sub-standard property) seem unlikely to alter the financial logic that if compliance increases costs, as it inevitably must, landlords may simply withdraw from the market. The evidence presented by Wilcox in Chapter Three shows clearly that the response of many landlords to restrictions on housing benefit was to withdraw from that part of the market.

Licensing in itself does nothing to overcome the financial barriers to improvement. This might not be undesirable if, as Ellison suggests, new property entering the market is in better condition. The problem is that such new property is almost certainly only available at higher levels of rent. The plain truth is that the contemporary PRS, as it always was, is bifurcated between a well-maintained, high rent sector and a poor quality sub-sector and nothing on offer in the current round of proposals seems likely to change that.

Main themes

Partly by design and partly arising from the common interests of the authors, several unifying themes weave their way though the chapters. First are issues concerning the traditional supply and demand balance. The supply-side of the PRS market consists, as it has done historically, of large numbers of small-scale landlords, and despite market liberalisation there seems as yet little evidence of corporate investment into the sector. The consequences of the 'cottage industry' character of the contemporary sector recur throughout the text. On the demand side it is clear that, unlike landlords, the characteristics of PRS tenants have changed dramatically, catering now for an overwhelmingly youthful, highly mobile market. This transformation dates from before the market reforms but is now a key feature of the sector. Young people, some upwardly aspiring, others relatively deprived and insecure, find their first independent homes in the PRS. Those with limited resources and little knowledge of the housing market are vulnerable to unscrupulous and/or badly organised landlords.

Young peoples' experience in the sector and the youthful character of the contemporary PRS link closely to the second theme of the chapters: the relationship between landlord and tenant. It is not insignificant that authors from both the 'policy' and the 'law' perspectives write about these issues because there is a crossover of general concern and disciplinary interest. Supply and demand meets legal prescription. As several authors show, the particular issue at the heart of this is that legal structures are complex and little understood by either by landlords or tenants. Indeed the strong implication is that legal structures are cosmetic: the reality is that the tenant–landlord relationship is conducted very largely on an ad hoc basis with little reference to the parameters established by the law.

This issue overlaps with the third theme, which can broadly be described as that of the governance of the PRS, the desire expressed in the Green Paper to create a 'better managed' sector. This involves the question whether and to what extent licensing of the sector could assist in creating better management, or whether it could drive landlords out of the market. Here an important series of issues focuses on the significance of the role of local authorities in monitoring and regulation. Prominent are the issues raised by the debate about licensing – a role that sits squarely in the lap of authorities – and the influence that authorities have in maintaining the physical quality of the stock, especially at the bottom end of the market through the renovation grant system. More broadly here is the influence that local authorities can bring to bear in planning provision for those households under stress through lack of adequate or affordable accommodation. It is readily apparent that local housing markets, incorporating of course both the social and the private rental markets, are symbiotic.

The themes of supply and demand, landlord and tenant relationships and governance are directly and indirectly present in all these chapters and together provide the main architecture of a text which inevitably is less unified than would be the case if single-authored. The editors believe strongly, however, that in this case the collective wisdom is far superior to the lone voice!

Finally, and not really a theme as such but an all pervading concern of every author, is whether, having become a more or less fully deregulated sector with the balance of advantage clearly in favour of landlords, a larger, better maintained, better managed stock of properties has emerged in the post-1988 years and can be sustained. Has deregulation created a revival of the sector or are we witnessing a false dawn? This is more than an academic question because the answer to it is bound up with issues that lie at the heart of national housing policy, of how to provide for the needs of low-income households. As Steve Wilcox points out in Chapter Three, given the constraints on social housing provision and the reduction in housing benefit to support households in all types of rental accommodation, there can be little doubt that serious housing stress is and will continue to be encountered. The contribution of the PRS in meeting housing need can only be judged by reference to the realities of the newly deregulated market.

TWO

Private renting in the 21st century: lessons from the last decade of the 20th century

A.D.H. Crook

Introduction

This chapter examines changes to the supply side of the private rented sector since rent deregulation in 1989 and speculates about likely trends in the first decade of this century. It focuses on the trend in overall supply, the extent to which there have been significant changes in ownership, and the extent to which landlords have been earning competitive investment returns.

There are six sections:

- government policy aims in relation to the supply side;
- the nature of the supply side in the two decades before deregulation;
- specific initiatives designed to increase corporate ownership and their impact;
- evidence about the way the supply side changed in the 1990s in general;
- evidence about rates of return;
- the implications of this evidence for the initial years of the new century.

Government policy aims

All main political parties now accept that the sector provides an important means of housing those who benefit from the flexibility that private renting can provide and those who do not want to tie up their savings in home ownership (Best et al, 1992). These include first time entrants to the housing market, including students and other newly formed households, as well as those who need to change their housing at short notice, such as job movers and people whose personal relationships have broken down. Flexibility can also improve the performance of the micro and macro economy by facilitating the movement of people into areas with labour shortages, and also by giving more housing choices to many young households who would otherwise have to borrow heavily to buy their own homes. If they buy instead, their high levels of indebtedness can significantly influence consumer demand when interest rates change, and hence amplify business cycles.

Recent changes in the labour market have increased the numbers of those who value this flexibility. Since the 1980s the proportion of heads of household aged under 30 who own their own homes has fallen. Greater proportions of tenants in the private rented sector are on above-average incomes than in previous decades. Although the private rented sector has always housed a wide range of households, its long-run decline up to the early 1990s was associated with the sector having an above-average proportion of households on low incomes and outside the labour market (Whitehead and Kleinman, 1986). Although rent deregulation was necessary to attract more (and reputable) investors, the low level of incomes prior to deregulation in 1989 meant that rent deregulation on its own was unlikely to be sufficient to raise returns to the level needed: higher rents were also needed. These recent 'demand-side' changes have therefore increased the prospects of investors being able to earn returns from better-off tenants within the labour market, and of thus being able to provide high-quality and reasonably secure housing at competitive returns – at least in principle.

The 1979-97 Conservative governments were convinced of these benefits. Their main approach to achieving this was to get the market to work by removing rent regulation and statutory security of tenure for new lettings. In addition to wanting to increase overall size, the Conservative government wanted to ensure there was a larger corporate sector.

The limited national survey research undertaken on the supply side before rent deregulation was introduced in 1989 showed that the majority of the sector was owned by individual landlords, with small portfolios which they managed themselves in their spare time (see below). Moreover, landlords who had invested for commercial reasons owned only a small majority of the sector. Many others had become landlords by accident (for example, through inheritance), or to house employees, or for a wide range of social and personal reasons. The net result was that landlords who were likely to respond on a strictly commercial basis to market signals, such as higher rents, owned only a small proportion of the sector. Furthermore, few landlords were large enough to realise economies of scale in management and maintenance: hence their costs per dwellings were high. Few were large enough to spread market risk through regional and market segment diversification. Finally, although the evidence was very limited, most of the landlords in the market at the time of deregulation were dependent on their own private equity and did not draw in investment funding from the main City institutions. Most landlords bemoaned the rates of return they were earning – less than half thought their rent adequate or that it was sufficient to cover repairs and give a reasonable return. The then Conservative government took the view that bringing in new corporate private landlords could help transform the sector.

Supply side in the two decades before deregulation

Evidence about the nature of the supply side before deregulation was very limited. Indeed debate was as much dominated by myth as by hard evidence. However, two large-scale social surveys, one undertaken in the mid-1970s and one in the mid-1980s, provide a baseline of data for measuring the extent of subsequent change in the 1990s (Paley, 1978; Todd and Foxon, 1987). The first survey covered the owners of a representative sample of all private lettings in the densely rented areas of England. The second survey was of the landlords of a representative sample of lettings made over the period 1982-84.

The surveys revealed the following key characteristics about landlords and their opinions and policies:

- Over half of all lettings were owned by individual landlords: 55 percent of all lettings in 1976 and 60 percent of lettings made between 1982 and 1984.
- Most landlords had small portfolios: 42 per cent of lettings in 1976 were owned by landlords who had fewer than ten lettings in all throughout England.
- Despite the long-term decline of private renting in preceding decades, a significant proportion of dwellings was owned by those who had become landlords in recent years: for example, 20 per cent of all lettings in 1976 were owned by those who had first become landlords in the previous six years.
- Similarly, a significant proportion of dwellings had been recently acquired by their current landlords: for example 30 per cent of all lettings made between 1982 and 1984 had been acquired since 1980.
- However, only a minority of lettings had been acquired for investment purposes: for example 36 per cent of lettings made between 1982 and 1984.
- Only a small proportion of lettings was owned by landlords who thought the law allowed them to charge a reasonable rent and adequately protected them against tenants (39 and 17 per cent, respectively, of the owners of lettings made between 1982 and 1984).
- Similarly, a small proportion of lettings had landlords who thought rents were adequate (for example, the landlords of only 39 per cent of lettings in 1976) or sufficient to cover repairs an give a return (the landlords of 17 per cent of lettings in 1976).
- Not surprisingly only a minority of lettings had landlords who would relet vacancies (only 40 per cent in 1976).

Government initiatives and the supply side of the sector

The Conservative government took a number of steps to achieve its objectives. To create a larger and market oriented private rented sector, rents of all new lettings were deregulated in 1989 and security of tenure was modified. These steps were designed to increase landlords' returns, by making it lawful to charge market rents. By improving liquidity and lowering risk generally, it was expected that the 'hurdle' rate of return that all types of landlord required would fall. Hence, more competitive returns would retain in the sector dwellings owned by then existing landlords and would also create a framework within which new landlords would have the confidence to invest.

The Conservative government also recognised that it would take time for confidence to be restored to an industry that had been in decline for most of the previous seven decades. To help speed up the revival of the sector and to provide a 'demonstration project' of what it hoped would be a profitable deregulated sector, the government used the Business Expansion Scheme (BES) to provide tax incentives to individual equity investors for a limited five-year period for the tax years 1988/89 to 1993/94 (Crook, et al, 1991, 1995). In effect, the government underwrote the risk that might otherwise have prevented investors entering the market.

The deregulation and tax incentive measures were introduced at a time when the housing market entered a recession, especially as far as the owner occupied sector was concerned. This had a major effect on the impact of deregulation and on the operation of the BES. Although the private rented sector expanded in the five years after deregulation (in England, from 1.8 million to 2.05 million dwellings), much of this can be attributed to the depression in the owner occupied market, as homeowners, unable to sell, temporarily let out their homes instead. About half the increase can be attributed to the recession (Crook and Kemp, 1996b). Over £3,000 million was invested in 903 assured tenancy companies under the BES scheme and these companies acquired 81,000 dwellings. However, many of these companies were launched in the anticipation of shareholders making significant capital gains through increases in house prices. These would be extracted by companies selling the houses they had acquired, once the minimum five-year letting period required to retain qualification for tax reliefs had expired. Hence many of these companies had only a short-term investment horizon. Although the subsequent fall in house prices meant that many were unable to realise their original objectives within five years, it was not expected that many of the lettings owned by BES companies would be retained in the sector in the long run, especially once house prices recovered from their nominal fall. Moreover, many of the BES companies did not acquire good quality housing. Significant proportions acquired stock possessed by mortgage lenders and sold on to BES companies as ways of placing this (often poor quality) repossessed stock off their balance sheets. Others acquired student residences from universities because the BES made it possible for the companies and universities to set up mutually advantageous sale and leaseback schemes. Meanwhile, the rental rates of return being earned by all these companies were not competitive. Although the largest companies achieved higher income (net rental) returns than the small ones (illustrating the presence of scale economies), these were below the benchmark returns required by companies for a long-term future (Crook et al, 1995).

Thus, the objective of having BES companies demonstrate to individual equity investors and also to financial institutions that private renting could provide competitive returns was not likely to be realised. Nor was the objective of establishing a larger corporate sector through this means.

In order to create a larger corporate sector and also to provide a basis for securing long-run equity and debt funding from the major financial institutions, the government launched a further initiative in 1996 designed to facilitate the securitisation of residential property investment. This is especially important because financial institutions are, with some exceptions, reluctant to own private rented dwellings directly (Crook and Kemp, 1999). Hence indirect investment vehicles are required to facilitate investment, with tax structures that are attractive to institutions, such as pension and other 'gross funds', who pay no tax on their income from directly owned property. Housing Investment Trusts (HITs) were designed to facilitate the involvement of City institutions in private renting, not through direct ownership, but through the purchase of shares, which would be subject to lower rates of corporation tax and to relief from capital gains tax. It was hoped that this would encourage the major institutions not only to buy shares in HITs but also to lend them significant sums of debt (Coopers and Lybrand, 1993, 1996).

However, HITs have not so far proved attractive to the institutions. This is for a wide range of reasons, although political risk is less of a barrier than in the past, given the commitment of the Labour government to deregulation (Crook et al, 1995; Crook and Kemp, 1999). Although there is much greater understanding of the sector and some willingness to provide equity and debt funding than in the past, important barriers to significant funding still exist. These include market risk, the small scale of existing portfolios and the difficulty of assembling new ones, the high costs and poor quality of property management, and the lack of market information. As a result, investors require a higher rate of return on residential than on commercial property – in part to reflect the higher risks and costs, but in part to reflect novelty. There are also difficulties connected to the specific structure of the HITs themselves, including the fact that they are not fully 'tax transparent' and are complex vehicles to structure. Moreover, some of the tax advantages that were designed to create approximate tax transparency were undermined by unrelated reforms made in 1997 to the structure of advance corporation tax. For all these reasons, no HIT has yet been launched (Crook, Hughes and Kemp, 1998; Crook and Kemp, 1999). Attempts have been made to set up indirect residential investment vehicles outside the HIT structure, including limited partnerships and property unit trusts, but there are very few to date.

Nonetheless, despite the difficulties so far of attracting major City funding into the sector and of creating a new corporate form of private rented ownership, the current government remains as committed to this, as was the previous government. Indeed, the Labour government has announced very clearly that it intends to make no changes to legislation for the deregulated sector nor to the general policy objectives about the sector (Armstrong, 1997). It has stressed its commitment to expanding the corporate sector and to fostering increased investment by major financial institutions (DETR, 2000a). While it has also stressed that it is willing to consider whether tax measures could help, it does not want to introduce tax breaks that would distort investment choices.

In the meantime, measures taken within the industry have succeeded in attracting finance into a new 'buy to let' scheme. This scheme was originally launched by the Association of Residential Letting Agents (ARLA) and a small panel of mortgage lenders, and was designed to attract individuals into the letting business. Debt funding has been provided by mortgage lenders at high loan-to-value ratios and with properties managed by professional letting agents. The intention is to enlarge the numbers of individual landlords by making debt funding available on attractive terms and by ensuring that they are relieved of the 'hassle' of day-to-day management and maintenance through engaging competent and professionally qualified agents. Recent evidence suggests that, by mid-2000, some £6,000 million of loans had funded about 80,000 of these buy-to-let mortgages financed both by the original panel and by other mortgage lenders (David Rhodes, University of York, personal communication).

Structure of ownership in the sector: current evidence

Despite the very limited success of the BES and HITs initiatives in creating a more modern form of private renting involving corporate ownership and institutional funding, the sector has grown very considerably since deregulation in 1989. In England, for example, the number of dwellings increased by approximately 25 per cent between 1989 and 1999 – from 1.8 million dwellings to nearly 2.3 million (similar rates of growth have been experienced in Wales; in Scotland growth has been less). There is evidence that this growth has a significant regional dimension, with that in southern England being greater than elsewhere. This variation is probably related to changes in both housing market (owner occupiers being unable to sell and renting out instead) and labour market (increased demand for labour on short-term and flexible contracts).

Despite the significant increase in the overall size of the sector since 1989, the most recent research suggests that the structure of ownership has not so far been changed. Indeed, evidence from key surveys in 1993/94 and 1998 shows just how little it *has* changed (Crook and Kemp, 1996a; Crook, Henneberry and Hughes, 1998; Crook et al, 2000).

The proportions in Table 2.1 are based on a categorisation of landlords that is related to their investment orientation. Business landlords are either corporate landlords or individuals for whom residential letting is their full-time occupation. Institutional landlords are organisations such as churches and educational institutions. Sideline landlords are individuals for whom letting is not their main occupation. These are subdivided into those who regard their lettings as investments and those who regard their lettings in other ways, such as letting to relatives and friends or for retirement.

The evidence from recent surveys of the landlords of representative samples of all lettings shows that only just over a half of lettings are owned by landlords with commercial motivations for owning them. For example, in 1994 only 17

Table 2.1: Classification of landlords: percentage of dwelling stock owned by types of landlords

Classification	1993 %	1994 %	1998 %
Business landlord	19	17	22
Sideline investor landlord	34	34	32
Sideline non-investment landlord	36	27	27
Institution	11	21	19
All	100	100	100
Cases	543	143	262

Sources: Crook and Kemp (1996a); Crook et al (1998, 2000)

per cent of dwellings in England were owned by business landlords and 34 per cent were owned by sideline landlords for investment purposes. These proportions are very similar for all three surveys undertaken in England in the 1990s. Moreover the surveys confirm just how large a proportion of the stock is owned by sideline landlords, for example 61 per cent in 1994 (Crook and Kemp, 1996a; Crook, Henneberry and Hughes, 1998; Crook et al, 2000).

Individual ownership still dominates the sector and has grown proportionately in scale. In 1976, 55 per cent of all lettings were owned by individuals. In 1993/94, 61 per cent of dwellings were owned by individuals and only 20 per cent by companies. The respective percentages in 1998 were 61 per cent and 22 per cent. The increase in individual ownership is by no means wholly explained by the numbers of owner occupiers temporarily letting out homes they had been unable to sell during the 1980s property slump.

Nor has the average size of portfolio grown. In 1993/94 it was seven dwellings. In 1998 it was still seven dwellings. Indeed, in 1998, 27 per cent of the stock was owned by landlords who owned only a single dwelling (a higher percentage than in 1994 when it was 24 per cent). Moreover, most dwellings are still managed by their owners themselves. In 1993/94 the proportion was 64 per cent. In 1998 it was 70 per cent. Nor have attitudes to ownership changed dramatically. In 1993/94 only 48 per cent of dwellings were regarded as investments, with returns coming from rental income and/or capital gain. In 1998, this proportion was 57 per cent. In 1998 only 23 per cent of dwellings had landlords who expected the rent to give them a return on vacant possession value, almost the same proportion (20 per cent) as in 1993/94.

This does not mean that there are no new landlords. Landlords continue to enter the sector, as they have regularly done over many decades. In 1993, 24 per cent of dwellings were owned by landlords who had started letting for the first time since deregulation. In 1998 the proportion was 25 per cent. Most new landlords were individual and sideline landlords, however, and were not companies. Most had a handful of lettings: the median ownership was one dwelling.

To summarise the evidence: although the sector has grown significantly in the last decade, this has mainly come from the growth of existing, as well as the entry of new, individual landlords. Thus after a decade of deregulation, it is still a 'cottage industry' owned and managed by small-scale individual landlords, few of whom have any qualifications in property, let alone in the letting business (Crook et al, 2000). Very few can achieve economies of scale in managing and maintaining their holdings, or manage market risk through a geographically and otherwise diversified portfolio. The picture in Scotland is similar to that in England. For example, half lettings in Scotland were owned by individuals and only four in ten were regarded primarily as investments (Kemp and Rhodes, 1994).

Despite the fact that the Conservative and Labour governments' objectives of increasing corporate ownership has not yet been achieved, deregulation does appear to have created much more confidence among landlords, with the majority holding generally positive views about letting. Landlords cited more advantages than disadvantages about new forms of letting, especially the ability to let at market rents and to obtain possession (Crook and Kemp, 1996a) and were much more positive about the legal framework for letting than in earlier decades (see above). For example, 67 per cent of lettings in 1993 had landlords who agreed that the law enabled them to charge reasonable rents and a half had owners who said their rent income was sufficient to cover repairs and give them a reasonable return (Crook and Kemp, 1996a).

Rates of return

Inevitably, the achievement of the government's aims depends on landlords realising competitive rates of return. That is, returns that are comparable with returns that can be earned in other alternative investments, allowing for risk and liquidity. Given that some key current objectives have not been achieved, it is important to establish if current rates of return are inhibiting progress. Historically, rates of return on private rented investments have not been competitive (Paley, 1978; Todd and Foxon, 1987). Survey evidence prior to deregulation suggested that returns were below landlords' requirements and that rental returns did not cover all their costs, let alone yield a return on investment. Moreover, survey evidence since deregulation in 1989 suggests that significant proportions of the stock in the deregulated sector are owned by landlords who still do not regard rental returns as adequate. Some estimates suggest that income (net rental) returns need to rise significantly – either through higher rents or through reduced costs. This appears particularly to be the case as far as new companies are concerned and in order to attract equity investment by City institutions (Crook et al, 1995; Crook, Hughes and Kemp, 1998; Crook and Kemp, 1999; Crook et al, 2000).

This does not necessarily mean, however, that it is possible to speak of one 'hurdle' rate of return. Rather it is likely that there will be several, ranging from those that encourage existing landlords to stay in the market to those that encourage new landlords, especially corporate landlords with City funding

(Crook et al, 2002). Returns required by companies (both existing and new landlords) will also be higher, *ceteris paribus*, than for individual landlords because the latter tend not to charge their own time to the costs of managing and maintaining their properties and do not incur the normal running costs of a limited company or partnership (such as the costs of auditing accounts and submitting company reports).

Information on current rates of return is crucial in identifying the size of the gap that may exist between actual and required returns. Information on the existence, size and reasons for that gap can help identify appropriate responses from within the industry as well as by government. The existence of such gaps does not necessarily require government subsidy or grant to bridge it. Simply providing more information about existing rents, costs and returns may be of itself important. Research suggests that the relative lack of information about existing returns being earned (compared with the information available in the commercial property sector) itself enhances required returns, since the uncertainty raises investment risks (Crook and Kemp, 1999). Hence producing reliable and regular data on such matters, on a basis that enables intra- and inter-industry comparisons to be made, is likely of itself to increase investment.

However, it is also important to note that existing returns may not be a guide to the future for a number of reasons. First, current rents may be set at levels which are explicitly set simply to cover the costs of the majority of landlords who have non-commercial reasons for being in the sector (and who look after their own property in their own time), rather than to also give them an investment return. Second, deregulation of the sector is only relatively recent and it takes time for newly emerging markets to mature; hence the rents being charged and costs being incurred may reflect residual market imperfection and be no long-term guide to rents and returns in the future. Third, operating costs are higher than for commercial property, but if more large companies emerge that are able to achieve economies of scale in management and maintenance, these costs should fall, so that current income (net rental) returns may be no guide to the future.

With these caveats in mind, the figures in Table 2.2 suggest that income returns from residential lettings in general perform poorly compared with other investments. The evidence comes from a survey of the landlords of a representative sample of all lettings in England (Crook et al, 2000) and from a further analysis of the data (Crook et al, 2002). The data includes the gross rent for all sample lettings, the management and maintenance costs for each letting, the purchase price landlords paid for each letting, and their estimate of vacant possession values. The data was used to calculate income (net rental returns) and total returns. The latter includes capital value increases as well as income returns. Capital value growth can be expressed in two ways: annualised real capital gains or nominal gains. Estimates of return from commercial property and financial investment use the latter basis for capital growth and this has been used in the calculations in Table 2.2.

The table shows that income (net rental) returns from deregulated lettings

Table 2.2: Income and total returns from residential lettings, other property and financial investments in 1998

Private lettings in England	Net (income) return %	Total (nominal) return %
Deregulated lettings[1]	7.3	10.6
Retail[2]	6.5	11.6
Office[2]	7.9	11.6
Industrial[2]	9.2	13.2
Equities[2]	2.8	13.7
Long dated gilts[2]	6.4	25.0 t
Treasury Bills[2]	7.9	7.9 t

Sources: [1]Crook et al (2002); [2]IPD (2000)

performed better than net income returns from retail property but worse than other property. It also performed better than equities and long dated gilts, but worse than Treasury Bills. As far as total (nominal) returns are concerned, deregulated lettings performed poorer than all other property and financial investments, with the exception of Treasury Bills.

Conventionally, residential lettings are seen as higher risk and lower liquidity than other property assets and all financial assets. If this is a correct assessment, residential lettings perform poorly on the basis of the above figures, since a higher return would be required to compensate for the greater risk and lesser liquidity. However, recent years have seen a reduction in the risk on residential lettings as the market has becomes more knowledgeable of the sector and has learned to better manage market and specific risk. Recent years have also seen a reduction in illiquidity since deregulation increases the certainty of landlords gaining vacant possession of property. Investment timing is important, especially in relation to capital growth cycles. Other evidence also suggests that most potential investors examine the manner in which assets contribute to their whole portfolio, rather than examining returns in isolation on a year-by-year basis. In particular, residential lettings are thought to provide additional diversification potential, since returns move in a different cycle from other property returns (Crook and Kemp, 1999).

Conclusions: prospects for the next decade

The evidence in this chapter shows that although the private rented sector has increased in size since deregulation, a significant part of this increase appears to have been due to the property slump of the early 1990s, while there has been no increase in corporate ownership or 'City' funding. Although landlords are much more confident about the lettings business than before deregulation, income and total returns do not appear sufficient to attract residential property companies backed by the major financial institutions with equity and debt funding. Government initiatives to stimulate this have markedly failed.

There appears to be little prospect of a significant change over the next few years. There seems little chance of significant corporate investment, but it is equally unlikely that the sector will decline in overall size. The remaining regulated sector will 'wither on the vine' and statistically is likely to be replaced by additional 'buy-to-let' investment made by individual landlords, primarily looking for capital growth and prepared to accept modest income returns, especially if they manage the properties in their own spare time. Hence the 'cottage industry' character of the private rented sector will remain largely unchanged, although it is likely to be more professionally managed, with the growth of more professionally accredited managing agents.

The fact that the sector has not drawn in more significant sums of corporate investment since deregulation is due to the lack of indirect investment vehicles for both retail and for corporate investors. At the moment, residential lettings provide a reasonably attractive investment for small–scale individual landlords, seeking capital gains and willing to look after property in their spare time. On the evidence of other surveys that suggests financial institutions look for total returns of 15 per cent (Crook and Kemp, 1999), the current market is not, however, providing what most potential corporate investors currently require. This suggests that the next decade is most likely to look much like the last.

Acknowledgement

This chapter draws on a section of Crook et al (2002) and incorporates additional material. The interpretations in this volume are, however, those of the author alone and not those of his co-authors of the other publication.

THREE

Housing benefit and social security

Steve Wilcox

Introduction

This chapter focuses on two topics related to the role of the private rented sector (PRS) in providing accommodation for low-income households. The first topic is the way in which the social security system, and the housing benefit scheme in particular, has provided assistance with the housing costs of low-income households over the decade since the 1989 deregulation of the sector. The second, related, topic is the relationship between government policies on housing benefit and the government view of the respective roles of the PRS and the social housing sector in meeting the housing costs of low-income households.

Benefit policy before 1989

However, before addressing those topics, it is useful to begin by briefly outlining some of the key developments in the evolution of the housing benefit scheme in the years before 1989, and the fundamental characteristics of the current housing benefit scheme, which have remained unchanged since the major social security reforms of 1988.

The current social security system in the UK has evolved from the national assistance and national insurance schemes introduced in 1948. While various important reforms over the ensuing half century were accompanied by changes in nomenclature (so national assistance became supplementary benefit and then income support and now, for pensioners, the minimum income guarantee) the current relationship between the contribution-based insurance scheme and the welfare safety net scheme still reflects the original relationship established in 1948.

One central factor is that the basic scales for the national insurance scheme were never set very much higher than those for welfare. While the national insurance benefits are not mean tested they have never been set to provide a sufficient income to cover household housing costs, and thus from the very beginning even households qualifying for national insurance benefits have usually had to rely on welfare benefits to top up their incomes to help with housing costs.

National help with the housing costs of low-income households was, until 1972, restricted to the unemployed, retired and other households that qualified for the basic welfare scheme. The actual housing costs for households, subject to maximum limits, were met by additions to the basic welfare scale rates, for households in all tenures. In addition in those early post-war years, the housing costs of low-income households in the council housing sector were kept low by general subsidies, while many councils operated a diverse range of rebate and other schemes to provide additional help to very low-income tenants (Parker, 1967).

The relationship between the national insurance and welfare schemes in the UK is in marked contrast to that in many other European countries, where the levels of contribution-based benefits are earnings related, and tend to provide levels of financial support significantly above the level of the welfare benefit schemes (Ditch et al, 2001).

In 1972 the various local council rebate schemes for council tenants were replaced by a national rent rebate scheme for low-income tenants not receiving welfare benefits (then supplementary benefit). In 1973 the rent allowance scheme was introduced to provide equivalent assistance to low-income households in the housing association and private rented sectors. Households in all tenures receiving supplementary benefit continued to have their rents met in full by additions to the basic welfare scale rates. The new rent rebate and allowance schemes were administered by local authorities, while the supplementary benefit scheme for help with housing costs continued to be administered by the local offices of the (then) Department of Health and Social Security.

A notable feature of the rent rebate and allowance schemes was that entitlement reflected rent levels as well as income levels. At the threshold income levels for the schemes, households were expected to meet 40 per cent of their rent, with the rebate or allowance covering the other 60 per cent. To reflect that requirement the threshold income levels for the rent allowance and rebate schemes were set at a higher level than the supplementary benefit scheme. Households with incomes above the thresholds had their rebate or allowance reduced ('tapered') by a percentage of the excess income; households with incomes below the threshold had their rebate or allowances increased by a percentage of the income shortfall.

This different structure of the schemes providing help with housing costs for households receiving and not receiving supplementary benefit resulted in anomalies, with households with identical incomes and household circumstances qualifying for different levels of housing help under the two schemes. This 'better off' problem was a practical concern, rather than just an equitable issue, for those households who could potentially qualify for help under either scheme. These included, for example, pensioner households who could opt not to apply for supplementary benefit. In their case an income based on state pension, plus a modest additional income from either savings or an employers pension, might result in a higher level of help through the rent rebate or allowance scheme.

Nonetheless, the two schemes operated virtually unchanged until 1983, when the administration of both were transferred to local authorities. However, while the reforms included some modification to the rebate and allowance schemes, and administrative measures to deal with the 'better off' problem, the main structural differences in the two schemes remained unaltered. These partial reforms fell well short of initial claims that they would introduce a "unified housing benefit scheme", and the introduction of the new administrative arrangements was poorly planned, leading to a chaotic period of transition in many parts of the country (Walker and Hedges, 1985).

A fully integrated housing benefit scheme was eventually introduced in 1988, and this is essentially the one that continues to operate, albeit with some important later amendments to the provisions related to the eligibility of private rents for benefit. While the scheme has continued to be administered by local authorities, the income thresholds for qualifying for maximum benefit have been fully aligned with the provisions of the welfare benefit scheme (now known as income support), with some limited exceptions.

Under the post-1988 scheme the maximum level of entitlement for housing benefit, for households with incomes at or below the level of the specified income thresholds, is initially based on the 'full' rent, regardless of whether the household is in or out of work, or whether or not they are also receiving income support. The scheme, however, places a number of important limitations on the maximum 'full' rent that can qualify for housing benefit, and those limits have become increasingly important with the deregulation of the private rented sector.

In all tenures eligible rents can be restricted if the dwellings are deemed to be larger than required for the households needs. Similarly, certain service charges, such as those for the cost of heating and hot water, are defined as ineligible for housing benefit. Most importantly for the private rented sector, in all cases where a fair rent had not been determined, the 1988 scheme requires rent officers to assess whether or not the private rent is in excess of a reasonable market rent for the dwelling concerned.

In 1992/93, for example, some 37 per cent of all the deregulated rent cases referred to the rent officer resulted in 'determinations' being made at a level below the referred rent (Department of the Environment, 1993). These cases included 7 per cent where the dwelling was deemed to be 'over-large', and the rent determined was lower than the referred rent. (In other cases a dwelling may have been deemed to be over-large, but with the referred rent nonetheless considered to be reasonable even after adjusting for size.)

Deregulation and the growth of the private rented sector

The deregulation of the private rented sector in January 1989 saw the end of the decline experienced throughout the earlier decades of the century. In the decade from the end of 1988 the sector grew by some 24 per cent, to 2,566,000 dwellings in Great Britain as a whole. In the process the sector grew to account for 10.5 per cent of all dwellings in Great Britain at the end of 1998; up from 9.2 per cent a decade earlier (Wilcox, 2001).

However virtually the whole of the growth in the private rented sector in the years from 1989 to 1995 can be attributed to a growth in the numbers of households in the sector supported by housing benefit. In contrast, the significant factor in relation to the numbers of households in the private rented sector not supported by housing benefit over that period is that they ceased to fall; not that they grew by any significant measure.

Precise figures for the numbers of households in the private rented sector receiving housing benefit in the years before 1995 can only be estimated from surveys. Only in 1992 did the Department of Social Security (DSS) begin to collect administrative statistics that distinguished between private landlord and housing association cases, and in the early years there are considerable doubts that all the returns from local authorities accurately reflected the distinction between the two tenures.

However, by May 1995 the DSS statistics suggest that some 1.16 million households in the private rented sector in Great Britain received housing benefit. Survey-based estimates suggest that in 1988 only some 650,000 private tenants were then in receipt of housing benefit. In other words the numbers of tenants in the private rented sector supported by housing benefit grew by some 80 per cent over the period of deregulation to May 1995.

Over the same period there was a small (4 per cent) growth in the numbers of housing benefit claimants in the council and housing association sectors. In all tenures the rise in numbers reflected in part the higher levels of claimant unemployment that prevailed in the early 1990s (albeit declining from 1993). However, the growth in the numbers of housing benefit claimants in the private rented sector was far greater than could simply be attributed to higher levels of unemployment, and the rise in numbers continued in 1994 and 1995 even after the numbers of claimant unemployed began to recede.

Part of the growth in the numbers of housing benefit claimants in the private rented sector can be attributed to low-income households moving from the council and housing association sectors to the private rented sector. In some cases those moves were voluntary, as households took the opportunity of the greater availability of dwellings in the deregulated private sector to move away from unpopular housing estates. While the rent levels in the PRS are generally (but not always) higher than those in the council and housing association sectors, in many cases those higher housing costs would be fully met by an increased level of entitlement to housing benefit; with no net costs to the household. In other cases the moves were prompted by council or housing association landlords taking possession actions for a range of reasons including rent arrears and anti-social behaviour.

While such moves out of the social housing sectors may have been significant in particular localities, data for England from 1993/94 show that in overall terms more households continued to move into the social housing from the PRS than moved in the other direction. While some 33,000 moved from social housing into the PRS, some 67,000 moved in the opposite direction (Burrows, 1997). The movements from the social rented sectors to the PRS were nonetheless a significant factor in areas such as Newcastle that had experienced long-term structural economic decline, and where the relatively low cost of private housing facilitated the residualisation of the social housing sector, with a related destabilisation of local neighbourhoods (Keenan, 1998).

Numerically more significant, however, were the moves of newly forming households into the private rented sector (almost 220, 000 in 1993/94), and moves of owner occupied households into the PRS (almost 100,000 in 1993/ 94). While in 1988 just 12 per cent of all newly forming households moved into the PRS (Department of the Environment, 1993), by 1993/94 almost two fifths of all newly forming households moved into the PRS. Relative to the newly forming households moving into other tenures, those moving into the PRS were disproportionately young, single and economically inactive (Green and Hansbro, 1995).

In effect, the combination of PRS deregulation and the structure of the housing benefit scheme was such that in the early 1990s it became much easier for lower income households, and newly forming low-income households, to access the private rented sector.

Rising costs of housing benefit

The increase in the numbers of housing benefit claimants in the private rented sector inevitably led to a substantial rise in the annual costs to government. However, the increase in costs was far greater than the increase in the numbers of claimants. The levels of deregulated rents eligible for housing benefit also rose, and over the years the numbers of deregulated tenancies supported by housing benefit grew, while the numbers of regulated tenancies (with lower 'fair' rents) declined. Between 1992 and 1995 the average eligible rent level for tenants in receipt of housing benefit rose by 32 per cent, from £43.90 per week to £57.90 per week. Inflation over that three-year period was less than 8 per cent.

Unfortunately the administrative data on rents and housing benefit payments for the years before 1992 do not distinguish between the PRS and the housing association sector. However, Table 3.1 below sets out estimates suggesting that over the first half of the 1990s, following the 1989 deregulation, the costs of housing benefit in the PRS rose more than fourfold in cash terms, to just over £3.6 billion in 1994/95. Even in real terms costs rose more than threefold.

The 1996 reforms

Largely as a response to the spiralling costs of housing benefit in the PRS the then Conservative government introduced new measures to restrict the levels

Table 3.1: Annual cost of housing benefit for private tenants in Great Britain, 1988/89 to 1994/95

Year	1988/89	1989/90	1990/91	1991/92	1992/93	1993/94	1994/95
£m (cash)	833	1,074	1,388	1,892	2,562	3,188	3,608
£m (1999 prices)	1,329	1,588	1,875	2,416	3,150	3,859	4,263

Source: Wilcox (2001)

of private rent eligible for housing benefit. Those new measures were largely adopted by the Labour government in its first term of office following the 1997 elections, not least because of the self-imposed constraint that flowed from the manifesto commitment to operate largely within the expenditure plans inherited from the previous administration. The new restrictions introduced in 1996 and 1997 only apply to tenants newly claiming benefit after those dates, and as a result authorities have to operate a number of rent limit policies in parallel, applying them to individual cases depending on the date of the benefit claim and the type of private tenancy, and according to other detailed regulations.

Under the new regulations the rent officers' decisions became the direct basis for housing benefit rent limits, with a far narrower measure of discretion for authorities to make payments in respect of rents above the level of rent officer determinations. In contrast for pre-January 1996 claimants' determinations only serve to limit the level of rent upon which benefit payments are supported by government subsidy. However, while it is for the authority to determine the maximum level of rent to take into account for the purposes of making benefit payments in those cases, in practice authorities have tended to follow rent officers' decisions in the great majority of cases.

The other key feature of the January 1996 regulations was the introduction of the 'local reference rent' (LRR) limits. Local reference rents are defined as average market rents for dwellings of the same size (or the size required if 'over-large') and in the same locality as the referred dwelling. This regulation, in effect, represented a tightening of the 'exceptionally high' rent limit introduced a few years earlier. Only 50 per cent of rents above the local reference rent, but below the reasonable market rent for the dwelling in question, are eligible for housing benefit under these regulations.

In October 1996 a new rent limit was introduced for new claims by most single people aged under 25 – the 'single room rent' (SRR). This tightened the space standards for young single people, from the already closely defined size limits that rent officers must follow in determining whether or not accommodation is 'over-large' for the requirements of the claimant household. The single room rent is based on a single room, with shared use of a kitchen and a toilet.

In October 1997 the regulations were further varied to remove the entitlement to have 50 per cent of the rent above local reference rents taken into account for dwellings where the reasonable market rent for the dwelling was above the local reference rent level.

The application of rent limits for deregulated PRS lettings under the housing benefit rules thus depends on whether the initial claim was made before January 1996, October 1996, October 1997, or at a later date, and whether the claimant was a young person subject to the single room rent rules. As at August 2001 there were 623,000 deregulated private tenants in receipt of housing benefit. Of those, 99,000 (16 per cent) had their rents assessed under the pre-1996 regulations, 93,000 (15 per cent) were assessed under the January 1996 LRR regulations, 418,000 (67 per cent) were assessed under the October 1997 LRR regulations, and just 13,000 (2 per cent) were assessed under the SRR regulations introduced in October 1996 (DWP, 2001).

The average rent eligible for housing benefit at August 2001 under the pre-1996 rules was £79.10, the average rent under the January 1996 rules was £72.10, and the average rent under the October 1997 rules was £72.90. The average eligible rent for the small number of cases subject to the single room rent limits (the October 1996 rules) was £44.20. However, it cannot be simply concluded from these figures that the introduction of the local reference rent rules have led to any significant reduction in the rents charged by private landlords to claimants, or that they have led to new claimants confining themselves to (even) cheaper properties within the wider private rented sector.

The DWP statistics do not distinguish between the size of dwellings subject to the different sets of rent restrictions, and there is some evidence that there is a more rapid turnover of smaller lettings. For example, a local survey of housing benefit cases in Brent found that larger (ie 2 or more bedrooms) dwellings accounted for 58 per cent of the cases subject to the pre-1996 rules, but just 50 per cent of the cases subject to the post-1996 rules. The same survey found no consistent relationship between the eligible rents of pre- and post-1996 cases when they were analysed by size of dwellings (Elsmore, 1998).

The post-1996 rent limit rules have also had an impact on the numbers of private tenants in receipt of housing benefit, with survey evidence suggesting that those rent limits have played a part in a number of landlords withdrawing from letting to claimants, particularly to young single people subject to the SRR restrictions. In February 1996 there were 1,167,000 private lettings to claimant tenants; by August 2001 the numbers had fallen by 38 per cent to just 727,000.

There was a particularly sharp fall in the numbers of young single people receiving housing benefit following the introduction of the SRR restrictions in October 1996. In November 1996 there were 114,000 young single people receiving housing benefit in the deregulated PRS, of which just 8,000 were subject to the new restrictions. By May 2000 the total numbers of young single people receiving benefit in the sector had fallen by more than two thirds, to just 31,000, of which 15,000 were subject to the SRR restrictions.

It should, however, be noted that overall unemployed claimant numbers also fell over that period, and this will also have contributed to the fall in the

Table 3.2: Annual cost of housing benefit for private tenants in Great Britain, 1994/95 to 2000/01

Year	1994/95	1995/96	1996/97	1997/98	1998/99	1999/00	2000/01
£m (cash)	3,608	3,867	3,777	3,522	3,229	3,082	2,928
£m (1999 prices)	4,263	4,416	4,212	3,809	3,376	3,173	2,928

Source: Wilcox (2001)

numbers of private tenants in receipt of housing benefit. Similarly, the introduction of the more generous working families tax credit scheme in October 1999 will have 'floated' a number of households off housing benefit.

Nonetheless, the post-1996 reduction in case numbers was largely unanticipated, and as a result housing benefit expenditure on private landlord cases fell by far more than estimated at the time that the LRR and SRR restrictions were introduced. In cash terms the costs fell from a peak of £3,867 million in 1995/96 by 24 per cent to just £2,928 million in 2000/01 (see Table 3.2 above). In real terms costs fell by 34 per cent over that period, but were still more than double the real costs in the last year before rent deregulation.

As a result of these falling claimant numbers and expenditures, over the four years to 1999/00 the overall out-turn expenditure on rent allowances came in some £3.5 billion lower than the estimated provision made in the 1997 expenditure plans that the Labour government inherited from their predecessors (see Table 3.3 below).

It should be stressed that the Cmnd 3613 (DSS, 1997) spending plans already took into account the anticipated savings from the new post-1996 restrictions. The only modification the new Labour government made to the rent limit plans inherited from the previous government was to drop the proposed extension of the SRR limits to single people aged over 25. To offset the anticipated costs of dropping that measure the government instead increased the level of 'non dependant deductions' applied to housing benefit households in all tenures. As the out-turn figures in Table 3.3 show the increased level of non-dependant deductions were entirely unnecessary.

Table 3.3: Estimated and out-turn expenditure on rent allowances since 1996/97

£ million	1996/97	1997/98	1998/99	1999/00
Cm 3613	5,887	6,005	6,550	7,200
Out-turn	5,810	5,681	5,665	5,815
Difference	−143	−471	−1,180	−1,730

Note: Estimated and expenditure figures relate to all rent allowances, including those paid to housing association tenants.

Source: Social Security Committee (2000)

Rent limits and housing benefit shortfalls

The most detailed published analysis of the post-1996 rent limit system was undertaken by the London Research Centre (1999). That research, however, focused solely on cases where the newer rent limits – the local reference rent (LRR) and single room rent (SRR) – had led to a restriction on the levels of rent eligible for housing benefit. , The research did not analyse the substantial numbers of 'post-1996 cases' where rent limits continued to be imposed, based on the continuing application of the earlier rules, without any additional restrictions resulting from the new LSS and SRR rules.

The LRC research found that some 40 per cent of all cases subject to LRR and SRR restrictions resulted in a shortfall of over £20 per week, although in just over two fifths of those cases some part of that shortfall could also be attributed to other restrictions, or other factors (such as excess income, non-dependant deductions, ineligible service charges). In cases where the shortfalls were solely attributable to SRR and LRR limits the LRC found that 34 per cent of the cases in the sample experienced shortfalls of over £20 per week, while 37 per cent experienced shortfalls of less than £10 per week.

However, these results must be seen on the context of the wider system of limits on eligible rents that continues to operate alongside the newer restrictions introduced in 1996 and 1997. Department of Transport, Local Government and the Regions (DTLR) data show that in 1999 53 per cent of all cases in England and Wales had determined rents below the level of the 'referred rents', with an average reduction of some £15.70 per week representing 18 per cent of the average referred rent.

The routinely published DTLR data do not show the additional impact of the LRR and SRR limits operating in conjunction with the pre-1996 limits for those cases where they also apply (DETR, 1999, 2001). However, DWP statistics show that in May 2000, 30 per cent of all the cases subject to the post-1996 rules had their eligible rents restricted by the new limits. In some cases the LRR/SRR limits would further reduce the eligible rent on cases that would, in any event, have been restricted to some degree by the pre-1996 restrictions. In other cases the LRR/SRR restrictions would restrict rents that would otherwise have been fully eligible for housing benefit.

Brent research

Recent London Housing Unit (LHU) research, based on a very large survey of just over a third of all Brent private sector housing benefit cases (at May 1999), examined all aspects of the new rent limit regime, and this brought out the continuing importance of the over-large, significantly high and exceptionally high rent limits, even in cases subject to the LRR and SRR rent limit rules (Elsmore, 2000).

The LHU report also showed the impact of the various rent officer limits in creating shortfalls, without including shortfalls arising because of non-dependant deductions, or of households with incomes above the levels of housing benefit allowances. For cases subject to the post-1996 rules the LHU Brent research found that 74 per cent of all cases faced a shortfall as a result of housing benefit rent limits, and of those cases:

- 6 per cent were affected by a single room rent limit;
- 17 per cent were affected by a local reference rent limit;
- 62 per cent were affected by a significantly high rent limit;
- 5 per cent were affected by a size-related rent limit;
- 10 per cent were restricted for other reasons (mainly ineligible service charges).

This more recent Brent study provides a useful reminder of the continuing importance and impact of the pre-1996 rent limits, and in particular the 'significantly high rent limits' that apply where the 'referred' rent is deemed to exceed a reasonable market rent for the dwelling in question. The more recent LRR and SRR limits are shown to add a further layer to the existing restrictions, but in Brent it is shown that they only result in a (further) rent reduction in just under a quarter of all the cases.

Current housing benefit policy issues

The April 2000 Housing Green Paper (DETR, 2000a) set out a range of radical options for reforming the housing benefit scheme. These included the option of introducing a system for defining eligible housing costs more like the scheme for rent allowances that operated from 1973 to 1982. Such a system would provide an element of 'flat rate' support, and then additional assistance based only on a proportion of the rent. Proposals along these lines have been set out in more detail in recent reports by Peter Kemp (Kemp, 1998a).

In practice the government decided only to proceed with a far more modest proposal to slightly broaden the definition of accommodation that forms the basis of the SRR limits (DETR and DSS, 2000). However, the government seemed subsequently to acknowledge that more radical reforms are required, and a renewed commitment to radical housing benefit reform appeared in the New Labour 2001 election manifesto. At the time of writing, however, detailed proposals have still to emerge

The critical issues that need to be addressed are the complexity of the current rent restriction schemes, their lack of transparency, and the impact of the substantial rent restrictions that apply to the majority of claimants in reducing the supply of private rented dwellings to low-income households. In principle a scheme along the lines proposed by Peter Kemp could provide the basis for resolving those concerns. However, the effectiveness of such a scheme would depend critically on the detailed way in which it was constructed and implemented.

Meeting the housing needs of low-income households

Over the last decade sundry reports have suggested the need for some 100,000 new social housing sector dwellings to be built (just in England) to meet the needs of newly forming households unable to secure unassisted housing in the private sector. Most notable of these have been the succession of reports by Alan Holmans (Holmans, 1995).

In practice government funding has supported a far lower level of investment in new social housing, partly because of concerns about the emergence of the phenomenon of 'low demand' for social housing in areas that have experienced long-term economic decline (Webster, 1998), and partly on the argument that the private rented sector could make a greater contribution to the provision of housing for low-income households, with the support of the housing benefit scheme. There was some substance to the latter argument in the earlier part of the 1990s, when the private rented sector was indeed providing accommodation for an increasing number of households supported by housing benefit. The argument, however, cannot be sustained in the context of the sharp decline in the numbers of households in receipt of housing benefit in the private rented sector since 1996. That decline in private sector supply has taken place at the same time as a decline in social housing re-let rates in areas of high demand, as house price increases during a rising economic cycle have sharply reduced the rate at which existing social housing tenants leave the sector to become home buyers. Together with the low level of supply of new social rented housing this has resulted in a resurgence in the numbers of households needing to be placed in bed and breakfast and other forms of often unsatisfactory temporary accommodation (Wilcox, 2001).

The numbers of new housing association dwellings funded through the Housing Corporation has continued to decline during the two terms of the New Labour government. In part this under-investment was permitted to continue because the new government accepted the argument that the private rented sector could make an increased contribution to meeting housing needs. This argument was also reflected in the assumptions embedded in econometric modelling commissioned by the (then) DETR, which suggested a far lower requirement for investment in new social housing (Department of Applied Economics, University of Cambridge, 1997). There are, however, serious questions about the assumptions and methodology of that modelling.

In particular the modelling assumed that all households needing assistance for a temporary period would be provided for by the private rented sector, and that only households requiring long-term support would be rehoused in the social rented sector. This is the sort of nonsensical application of economic theorising that gives economics a bad name. It envisages allocation policies that would be impossible to operationalise, and which are in any event at odds with the objective of promoting social inclusion and avoiding concentrations of wholly poor households in all too easily stigmatised estates of social housing.

The methodology thus effectively assumes away part of the effective demand for social housing.

Assessments of the need for investment in new social housing have to be coherently related to allocation policies and social policy objectives promoted by government. Those assessments need to be grounded in survey evidence of household movements into and between tenures; not on unfounded and inoperable economic theorising. There also needs to be consistency between a realistic housing policy view of the extent to which the private rented sector can assist in providing accommodation for low-income households, and housing benefit policies designed to ensure that private landlords are willing to meet the assumed level of supply. There is, at present, no indication of 'joined up' government thinking on these issues.

FOUR

Rents and returns in the residential lettings market

David Rhodes and Peter Kemp

Introduction

The Conservative governments of Margaret Thatcher and John Major introduced a range of initiatives aimed at breathing new life into the private rental housing market. These included one measure – housing investment trusts – that was specifically aimed at attracting investment in the market by financial institutions (DoE, 1995). Since coming to power in 1997, 'New' Labour has made clear that it too sees an important role for the private rental sector (PRS) and that it would welcome investment by financial institutions (DETR, 2000a).

While there has been a modest revival in the size of the PRS over the past decade (see Chapter One), there has been very little investment in the sector by financial institutions. Indeed, financial institutions currently own a negligible amount of private rental housing. There are a number of reasons why they have made no significant investment in the sector, but one of them is the lack of market information about the private rental market. In particular, very little regular and reliable information has existed about residential rents and rates of return (Crook et al, 1995; Coopers and Lybrand, 1996). This situation contrasts with the extensive market information that is available about equities, gilt investment markets and a range of commercial property market indices (Morrell, 1991, 1995). Likewise, there are a number of respected indices for house prices, including those developed by the Halifax Bank and the Nationwide Building Society.

If the financial institutions are to enter the PRS on a significant scale, market information about rent levels and rental yields is necessary to inform their investment decisions (Crook and Kemp, 1999). In considering whether to invest in the sector, fund managers for the financial institutions need to know how the returns from residential lettings compare with alternative investments, such as commercial property and equities. They will also need to know how the returns on the properties they have purchased compare with the average returns being made in the PRS as a whole. Market information of this kind makes it possible for fund managers to carry out performance benchmarking exercises to help inform their investment decisions.

This chapter is based on work undertaken to fill this information gap about rents and returns in the PRS. It discusses the difficulties of collecting information on private sector rents, considers alternative methods of index construction, describes the University of York Index of Private Rents and Yields, and presents some evidence on rents and returns based on that index.

Constructing an index for the residential lettings market

The principal reason why there has been a lack of information about rents and yields in the residential lettings market is the difficulty of constructing a reliable index. First, there is no centralised marketplace for residential property, which makes collecting data both difficult and costly (Morrell, 1991). Second, the ownership of residential lettings is divided up among a large number of people and organisations, many having only a small number of dwellings; more than half of all private landlords have less than ten lettings (Crook and Kemp, 1996a). This fact makes the task of obtaining data on the PRS more difficult than if the scale of ownership was larger. The extent of property *management* in the PRS is somewhat larger than that of *ownership* because about four in ten lettings in England (Crook and Kemp, 1996a) and about half in Scotland (Kemp and Rhodes, 1994) are managed by an agent rather than solely by the landlord. The number of managing agents is still relatively large in the residential lettings sector compared with the commercial property market.

As well as deciding which sources of information are to be used, there is also the question of the type of index to be constructed. Three main types of index for the PRS could be used: asking prices, valuations, and transactions. These different types of index have different strengths and weaknesses. It is important that these are considered because of the differing ways in which they can be interpreted and used.

Asking prices

Most previous attempts at charting housing market trends in rents are based on newspaper advertisements for private lettings. For example, the London Research Centre has for several years published a bulletin of private sector rents for London based largely on this method. In his study of rents in Edinburgh and Glasgow following deregulation, Gibb (1994) used advertisements as his source of information. Likewise, Bailey (1996, 1999) tracked market trends in rents in four Scottish cities using a database of newspaper advertisements.

Newspaper advertisements are often used because the information is readily available, even if time-consuming and laborious to collect. An important difficulty with this source of data, however, is that it provides information about *asking* prices; that is, the rents which landlords are seeking to obtain rather than the prices that are actually *achieved* (transactions). A discrepancy between asking prices and actual transactions may arise for a number of reasons. Some informal, 'sideline landlords', for example, are not well informed about market rent levels (Bevan et al, 1995). Moreover, in a rising market landlords might be able to let a vacant property at a higher rent than advertised. Equally, in a falling market they might have to accept a lower price than the one for which they advertised the vacancy.

As a source of information about asking prices, newspaper advertisements have certain other drawbacks. The amount of information provided in them is not consistent, making the compilation of reliable data difficult: advertisements can vary considerably in the amount of detail they provide on the letting itself as well as on its geographical location. Furthermore, some properties are advertised in a newspaper for several consecutive weeks, and the same letting may be advertised in more than one newspaper at the same time, which increases the scope for error due to double counting. In other cases, an advertised property may be withdrawn from the market without being let. Finally, many vacancies are not advertised in newspapers. Many lettings are advertised in newsagents' windows or in letting agents windows, and some are advertised on notice boards or on signboards outside the property. Other properties may be let by word of mouth or via employers and university accommodation offices.

Although none of these problems with newspaper advertisements as a source of data on private rents are insuperable (Bailey, 1999), they do limit their value for constructing a rent index on which the investment decisions by financial institutions could be based.

Valuations

Most of the commercial property market indices are based on valuations of properties made by chartered surveyors or experienced valuers. With this approach, a decision has to be made about whether the valuations should be carried out on actual properties or on typical, hypothetical properties. For example, the Investment Property Databank (IPD) indices for the commercial property market are based on valuations of the actual properties owned by their subscribers. In contrast, the Hillier Parker index is based on valuations of hypothetical property types (see Morrell, 1991).

With the PRS, there are several disadvantages to basing a valuations index on actual properties. First, there is the difficulty of identifying properties in different areas that would be similar enough to allow like-for-like comparisons to be made. A second and related point is that it would be difficult to generalise about the locality from a single property, as a range of specific and changeable market factors can affect rental value. Third, new rental evidence would only become available when the property was re-let or the rent renegotiated, thereby making the collection of regular market information difficult. Fourth, a specific property may cease to be let if the landlord decides to withdraw it from the market, which is something that may happen for a range of economic and non-economic reasons (Crook and Kemp, 1996b). There is in fact a history of movement of property between the owner occupied and private rented tenures in particular (Hamnett and Randolph, 1988; Kemp, 1998b), which raises the problem of continuity of the index if actual properties are used.

An alternative approach that avoids many of the problems with using actual lettings is to gather valuations on a panel of typical, hypothetical properties with prescribed characteristics. A particular advantage of taking this approach is the comparability of the valuations from one part of the country to the next, as well as over time. A further advantage is that the use of typical property types allows valuations to capture the generality of rents in the locality, rather than simply measuring rental variations on a specific property. A drawback with any form of valuation index, however, is the potential for 'valuation error'. This type of error refers to the potential for a difference between the 'true' market level and the actual valuation made. While such an error may occur, its existence or extent is difficult to quantify.

A specific feature of a valuations index based on hypothetical property types is that, because the open market valuations are based on many pieces of evidence in the locality, there is the potential for resulting trends to be artificially 'smoothed'. This situation presents the disadvantage that a single valuation will not reflect the diversity of rents in the locality, although use of a panel of differing properties can to some extent negate this limitation. In addition, provided that the valuations are made on the same basis at regular points in time, the generality of rents in the locality will be captured, which is a useful characteristic for benchmarking and monitoring trends.

Transactions

The third type of index that can be constructed for the PRS is one based on actual lettings transactions. Transaction-based indices provide information about the prices that have actually been achieved in the marketplace rather than on what landlords hope to achieve. Indices based on property transactions avoid many of the problems associated with asking prices. They also do not suffer from valuation error. Depending upon the source of information, a transactions index can be based on a consistent set of property attributes.

A particular disadvantage with an index constructed from transactions is that the composition of property types that are let will inevitably vary in differing parts of the country and at different points in time. The difficulty posed by variation in property mix is that comparisons between different parts of the country, and historically in the same locality, cannot readily be made on a like-for-like basis. On the other hand, this situation has the advantage that the transactions will reflect the nature of local housing markets and the changing mix of property types in the PRS marketplace over time. Regression analysis can be used to standardise transactions-based indices to create 'mix-adjusted' figures, which is an approach used with the house price indices produced by the Halifax Bank and the Nationwide Building Society.

The University of York Index

The University of York Index of Private Rents and Yields (hereafter, the UoY Index) was established to fill the information gap on rents and yields for the private residential lettings market. The aim of the Index was to provide regular and reliable open market information of value to a range of audiences, in particular the financial institutions. The Index was developed by the Centre for Housing Policy during 1995 and has been published quarterly since the beginning of 1996. It received seed-corn funding for three years from the Joseph Rowntree Foundation, with additional support from the DETR, but is now self-funded.

The inherent difficulties – outlined above – involved in constructing an index for the PRS partly explain why one has not been produced before. The problem of obtaining reliable market information of sufficient quantity was solved through establishing partnerships between the UoY Index and several organisations. These include the Association of Residential Lettings Agents, the Halifax Bank, the rent officer organisations across Britain, and the Valuation and Lands Agency in Northern Ireland. All these organisations are involved in providing the raw data from which the UoY Index is constructed.

Because of its severe limitations, an asking price index was rejected in favour of both a valuations and a transactions approach to index construction. In the UoY Index, the valuations and transactions indexes are completely separate from one another and utilise data from different sources.

The valuations index

The valuations index is based on a panel of six typical, hypothetical PRS property types (see Annex 1). Analysis of the 1991 Census identified the most commonly occurring property types within the PRS, which were then selected for inclusion in the index. Their specific hypothetical characteristics were devised in consultation with rent officers, who would be making the valuations. This approach was taken to ensure that the property types would be representative of the PRS and broadly applicable to all local authority areas.

Open market valuations of furnished and unfurnished weekly rents, and vacant possession capital values are made by rent officers for their local authority area during the middle month of each quarter. Rent officers are rental valuers who have an expert knowledge of the PRS in their locality, collecting market information from a wide range of sources, including letting and estate agents (Kemp and McLaverty, 1993) and are well placed to make valuations. In addition to the physical characteristics of the property types, rent officers are asked to assume that each is let to one household only on a single tenancy agreement. The rent officers indicate if they are unable to make a reliable valuation due to insufficient market evidence.

In compiling the index, the individual valuations are weighted at the local authority level to ensure that aggregate statistics are demographically representative. This process is necessary because each valuation captures many pieces of market evidence in a single figure, while the distribution of the specified property types varies considerably. London boroughs tend to have a much higher proportion of lettings in flats than most other areas of the country. Wales and many parts of England have higher proportions of lettings in terraced houses. The data used to weight the valuations is the same as that used to establish the most commonly occurring types of PRS property from the 1991 Census.

Using valuations provided by rent officers, *gross* yields in the valuations index are calculated on each property type by expressing the annual rent as a proportion of its vacant possession capital value. This approach does not allow for the 'discount' that usually accompanies the sale of *tenanted* properties, and which has been found to average two thirds of the vacant possession capital value (Crook et al, 1995).

It is also important that net yields are calculated to allow comparisons with yields on commercial property, which are commonly let on full repairing leases. *Net* yields in the UoY Index are estimated by using figures on average running costs derived from the representative survey of private landlords in Britain reported in Crook et al (1995). Analysis of this survey data showed that private landlords had an average total running cost of 43.1 per cent of the rent on furnished lettings, and an average of 29.4 per cent of the rent on unfurnished lettings. Included in these two figures are the costs of management and maintenance, rent arrears and rent lost due to voids. Estimated net yields are calculated, therefore, by making a deduction of 43.1 per cent from furnished gross yields, and a deduction of 29.4 per cent from unfurnished gross yields.

The transactions index

Two practical problems for a transactions index are that the scale of ownership in the PRS is largely small and the marketplace is fragmented – characteristics of the sector that present difficulties with obtaining a representative and sufficient quantity of cases. However, these problems were largely solved due to a partnership between the UoY Index and the Association of Residential Letting Agents (ARLA), members of which are involved in providing information on their letting transactions. Regarding the business of ARLA agents, the types of landlords who use them are representative of all private landlords, and the types of properties handled by the agents is broadly comparable with the national mix of PRS properties. However, self-contained flats tend to be slightly over-represented due to the concentration of ARLA members within Greater London (Rhodes, 1993; Rhodes and Kemp, 1996).

A sample of ARLA members was devised on the basis that their locality contained a high proportion of PRS lettings in order that their turnover of business would yield a sufficient number of cases. In addition, a random sample of agents in other localities was also included to help achieve a representative cross-section of lettings. The sample of agents provides details on the self-contained lettings transactions signed at their office during the middle month of each quarter. The details include the type of property, the number of bedrooms, the number of living rooms, the level of furnishings provided, whether the letting is a renewal of an existing contract or a completely new agreement for a new tenant, the letting's postcode, and the contractual rent.

Gross yields in the transactions index are estimated by using figures on vacant possession capital values from the Halifax Bank's mortgage transactions data. The Halifax data is made available in the form of an average capital value by property type, number of bedrooms, and postcode district (the first half of the full postcode). Thus, each letting transaction is ascribed an average vacant possession capital value for properties of the same type, size (in terms of number of bedrooms), and locality. Estimated gross yields are then calculated in the same manner as in the valuations index. Likewise, estimated net yields are also calculated by deflating the furnished and unfurnished gross yield figures by the same amounts as in the valuations index.

Use of two separate sources of data in the calculation of yields is not wholly ideal. However, both sets of data are based on transactions, which means that they are actual market values and not subject to valuation error. In addition, the time of exchange can be pinpointed to the signing of a letting agreement and the mortgage approval stage, which are less variable timescales than when a tenant takes up occupation of a letting or when a sale is completed, and both relate to when the price is agreed. A final point is that the Halifax is the largest financier of mortgages in the UK, and comparative research has shown that these were representative of all transactions financed by building societies (Flemming and Nellis, 1984).

Results

The valuations index is in essence pre-standardised, because it is based on a panel of identical property types in each local authority area. There will be negligible variation due to changes in property mix. One factor that might have a small impact, however, is variation in the availability of market evidence, making it not possible for all rent officers to provide valuations in every instance. Likewise, there may be changes in response rates from the rent officers (although the response rate has consistently been in excess of 90 per cent of all local authority areas). In constructing the time series in the valuations index, missing valuations are replaced by using the techniques of interpolation and extrapolation to adjust for missing data.

Figure 4.1 shows the trends in standardised valuations rents and gross yields for Great Britain as a whole. It shows that the standardised rent for the panel of self-contained properties together (that is, excluding bed-sits), increased by 20 per cent between the base quarter at the beginning of 1996 – when the index was set to 100 – and the first quarter of 2001. The standardised average weekly rent for the self-contained property types together increased from £92 to £111 over the same period.

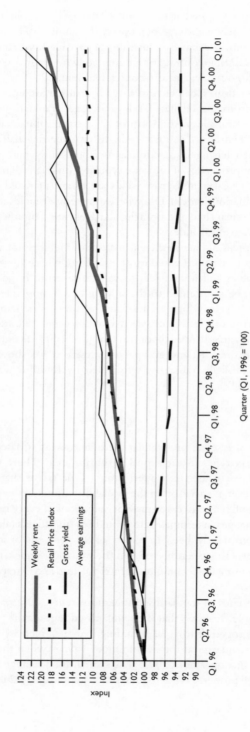

Figure 4.1: Trends in standardised valuations rents and gross yields in Great Britain, 1996-2001

Legend:
- Weekly rent
- Retail Price Index
- Gross yield
- Average earnings

Index

Quarter (Q1, 1996 = 100)

Table 4.1: Annualised total rates of return in Great Britain, 2000

	Net yield/Income return (%)	Capital growth (%)	Total return (%)
Residential lettings, UoY Index GB valuations index:			
Detached houses (4 beds)	4.1	5.9	10.0
Semi-detached houses (3 beds)	4.8	7.6	12.4
Terraced houses (2 beds)	6.0	8.6	14.6
Flats (2 beds)	6.9	8.2	15.1
Flats (1 bed)	7.2	8.8	16.0
All	5.7	8.1	13.8
Commercial property, IPD UK annual index:			
Retail	6.2	0.4	6.6
Office	7.4	8.1	15.5
Industrial	8.4	5.4	13.8
All	6.9	3.5	10.4
Other assets:			
Equities (all share)	2.1	-8.0	-5.9
Gilts (long dated)	5.2	4.0	9.2
Cash (Treasury bills)	6.2	-	6.2

Figure 4.1 also shows that residential rents have risen at a faster rate than consumer prices over the five-year period, as measured by the Retail Price Index excluding mortgage interest payments (RPIX): 20.2 points compared with 12.5 points in the RPIX. In fact, rents have kept pace with growth in average earnings, which typically increase at a faster rate than prices over the long run.

Despite increasing rent levels, the standardised gross yield index had dropped to 94.1 by the first quarter of 2001. This gradual slide in rental yields occurred because vacant possession capital values rose at an even faster rate than rents over this period. This substantial rate of increase may be a cyclical phenomenon, reflecting the recovery from the sharp recession of the late 1980s and early 1990s when house prices fell in both nominal and real terms (Forrest and Murie, 1994).

As well as rents and yields, the UoY Index contains figures on total rates of return. This is calculated by taking the sum of the current net yield and the annual percentage change in vacant possession capital value. These figures, annualised for 2000, are shown in Table 4.1 along with annual figures for the commercial property market and other forms of asset. During 2000, residential total returns compared favourably with the returns on commercial property as well as on other types of asset.

The total rates of return were particularly competitive on the smaller property types: a feature connected to the higher net yields on the smaller properties, and particularly on the one- and two-bedroom self-contained flats. During 2000, however, the capital growth component exceeded one half of the total return on each hypothetical property type, and additionally the increases in capital values throughout 2000 were slightly greater on the larger property types. Thus the total rate of return on one-bedroom, self-contained flats was 60 per cent greater than that on four-bedroom detached houses, whereas the net yield alone was about 75 per cent greater than the net yield on detached houses.

An important difference between the valuations index and the transactions index is that the latter is based on data comprised of the individual characteristics of lettings rather than on a fixed set of attributes. This type of information lends itself to forms of analysis that can be used to explore the factors that have a significant influence on rent variations. One such method is multivariate regression analysis. This method can be used to analyse variations in a dependent variable in terms of a range of independent variables. In this case the dependent variable is weekly rent, and the independent, or explanatory, variables are the characteristics of the individual lettings. Thus the analysis considers rental variations not in terms of a letting as a whole entity but rather for the set of attributes possessed.

Table 4.2 shows the results of a regression analysis on the transactions recorded throughout 2000. The independent variables that were available for the analysis are listed in the order in which they entered the regression model, and all were highly significant ($p < 0.005$). They include: the property type; whether a letting was a renewal of an existing contract or a completely new agreement for a new tenant; whether a letting was fully furnished, partly furnished, or unfurnished; the number of bedrooms; the number of living rooms; and standard region (derived from the letting's postcode). Examination of the relationship between the dependent and independent variables found that the model of 'best fit' was with the weekly rent figure recorded in natural logarithm form. Regarding the independent variables, the number of bedrooms and number of living rooms were recorded as continuous variables, while the other characteristics were entered into the analysis as dummy variables. The reference categories for the dummy variables are the South East region, unfurnished lettings, lettings that were renewals of an existing agreement, and terraced houses. The explanatory power of the model as a whole was very satisfactory, the adjusted R^2 being 0.72 (an R^2 of 1.0 would indicate a completely positive linear relationship between the exponential of weekly rent and the collection of independent variables).

Table 4.2: Multiple regression analysis of the predictors of variations in weekly rent

	B	Beta
Greater London	.826	.523
Number of bedrooms	.279	.395
Yorkshire & the Humber	−.538	−.232
Flats	.169	.120
Northern Ireland	−.620	−.148
Furnished lettings	.149	.106
Number of living rooms	.009	.085
East Midlands	−.379	−.123
West Midlands	−.300	−.099
Wales	−.408	−.083
Scotland	−.207	−.084
North West	−.190	−.077
South West	−.197	−.059
New lettings	.071	.045
Detached houses	.093	.035
North	−.271	−.027
East Anglia	−.080	−.026
(Constant)	(3.993)	

Notes: adjusted R^2 = 0.72; all independent variables significant at p>0.005

The partial regression coefficients (B) for each variable are adjusted for all the other independent variables in the model, and indicate their relative importance when the model is considered as a whole. The beta values, on the other hand, are standardised coefficients measured on the same scale (z-scores), and which indicate the independent impact of each explanatory variable while controlling for the others in the model. Thus the beta coefficients of the individual independent variables can be directly compared with one another. The beta coefficients quite clearly show that the location of a letting within the Greater London region has the largest single influence on variations in the exponential of weekly rent (0.523). The second most important predictor of weekly rent is the number of bedrooms within a letting (a beta coefficient of 0.395).

The remaining regional dummy variables all had smaller, but still statistically significant, impacts on rental variations. With the exception of Greater London, the coefficients for the regional dummy variables were negative, indicating a downward influence on rent levels relative to the South East (the reference for the regional dummy variables). In contrast, the number of living rooms had a positive influence on variations in rent, as did lettings that were furnished compared with those that were unfurnished (partly furnished lettings had no significant influence on variations in the exponential of weekly rent). Likewise, lettings in flats and detached houses had a positive influence in rent variations compared with lettings in terraced houses (the dummy reference property type), as did lettings that were completely new agreements compared with those that were renewals of existing contracts.

An alternative method for examining the factors that influence rental variations is CHAID analysis (Chi-Squared Automatic Interaction Detector method [Kass, 1980]), which can be used to explore the hierarchy of interactions between the independent variables. CHAID analysis performs segmentation modelling by dividing a population into different categories (or segments) in terms of the most significant predictor of an independent variable, which in this case is the actual weekly rent figure (rather than the exponential of weekly rent). The method then splits each of these categories into smaller sub-groups based on other predictor variables. This process continues until there are no more statistically significant predictor variables left in the analysis. As CHAID analysis does not require the use of dummy variables, the standard region, level of furnishings, whether a letting was a renewal or not, and the property type were all entered into the analysis as categorical variables. The numbers of bedrooms and living rooms were again recorded as continuous variables.

Figure 4.2 contains the first stage of the CHAID analysis of all the transactions recorded throughout 2000. The total number of cases before any segmentation has taken place are shown at the top of the tree diagram (4,716), with an average (mean) rent of £204.27 per week.

The CHAID considers which of the variables in the analysis is the most strongly correlated with variations in weekly rent, and this turns out to be standard region. In terms of the weekly rent figures, the analysis finds no statistically significant difference between the regions of the North, the North West, the West Midlands, the South West, and Scotland, and hence groups them together. These regions collectively had an average weekly rent of £120.52, and accounted for 28.7 per cent of the total number of cases. Likewise, the analysis finds no significant difference between the two regions of Yorkshire and the Humber, and Wales, which together have an average weekly rent of £83.35. The East Midlands and Northern Ireland together had an average weekly rent of £98.16; and East Anglia and the South East together an average rent of £137.05 per week. The Greater London region was singled out as being significantly different in its own right, and for which the average weekly rent was £438.99.

The CHAID analysis then considers which of the remaining variables most strongly correlate with variations in weekly rent, and these differed in order of

Figure 4.2: CHAID analysis of predictors of weekly rent: first segment by standard region

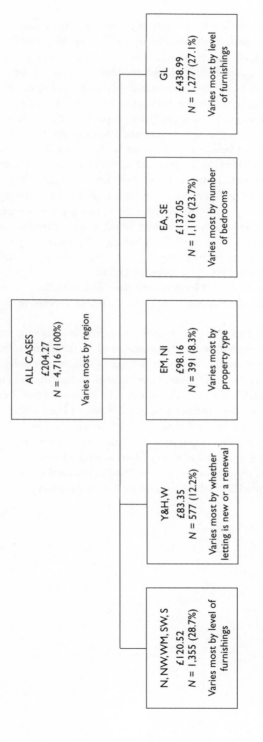

ALL CASES
£204.27
N = 4,716 (100%)

Varies most by region

N, NW, WM, SW, S
£120.52
N = 1,355 (28.7%)

Varies most by level of furnishings

Y&H, W
£83.35
N = 577 (12.2%)

Varies most by whether letting is new or a renewal

EM, NI
£98.16
N = 391 (8.3%)

Varies most by property type

EA, SE
£137.05
N = 1,116 (23.7%)

Varies most by number of bedrooms

GL
£438.99
N = 1,277 (27.1%)

Varies most by level of furnishings

Key to standard regions

EA = East Anglia
EM = East Midlands
GL = Greater London
N = North
NI = Northern Ireland
NW = North West

S = Scotland
SE = South East
SW = South West
W = Wales
WM = West Midlands
Y&H = Yorkshire and the Humber

importance within the five regional segments. In the collective regions of the North, the North West, the West Midlands, the South West and Scotland (Figure 4.3), the most significant predictor of weekly rent was whether a property was let fully furnished, or partly furnished or unfurnished together (unfurnished may include carpets and curtains only, whereas partly furnished also includes white goods). The average rent for the fully furnished lettings within these regions was £131.70 per week, and for the partly furnished and unfurnished lettings it was £110.55 per week. Fully furnished lettings are then further segmented by the number of bedrooms. Lettings with one bedroom had an average rent of £97.92 per week, and which did not vary significantly among the other predictor variables. Lettings with two bedrooms had an average rent of £137.43 per week, and this figure varied significantly between lettings in flats (£143.12 per week) and those in all the other property types together (£111.88 per week). Likewise, the furnished lettings with three or more bedrooms (£166.71 per week) also varied depending on property type, with detached houses and flats being grouped together (£185.72 per week), and all the other property types being grouped together (£146.93 per week). Partly and unfurnished lettings varied most by property type; and, with the exception of detached houses, there was further significant variation according to the number of bedrooms.

Taking another example, Figure 4.7 shows that variation in weekly rent within Greater London again depended primarily on the level of furnishings, but in this instance on whether a letting was unfurnished (£605.86), or fully and partly furnished together (£384.80). Among the unfurnished lettings, the most significant predictor of weekly rent was the number of bedrooms, the average rent for one and two bedrooms together being £278.88, and the average for lettings with three or more bedrooms being £939.17 per week. The fully and partly furnished lettings were first segmented according to property type into studio flats (£179.85), flats and bungalows (£368.19), and all types of house (£539.45). The segments for all houses, and for flats and bungalows together were then further segmented according to the number of bedrooms.

Figure 4.3: CHAID analysis of predictors of weekly rent for the North, North West, West Midlands, South West and Scotland

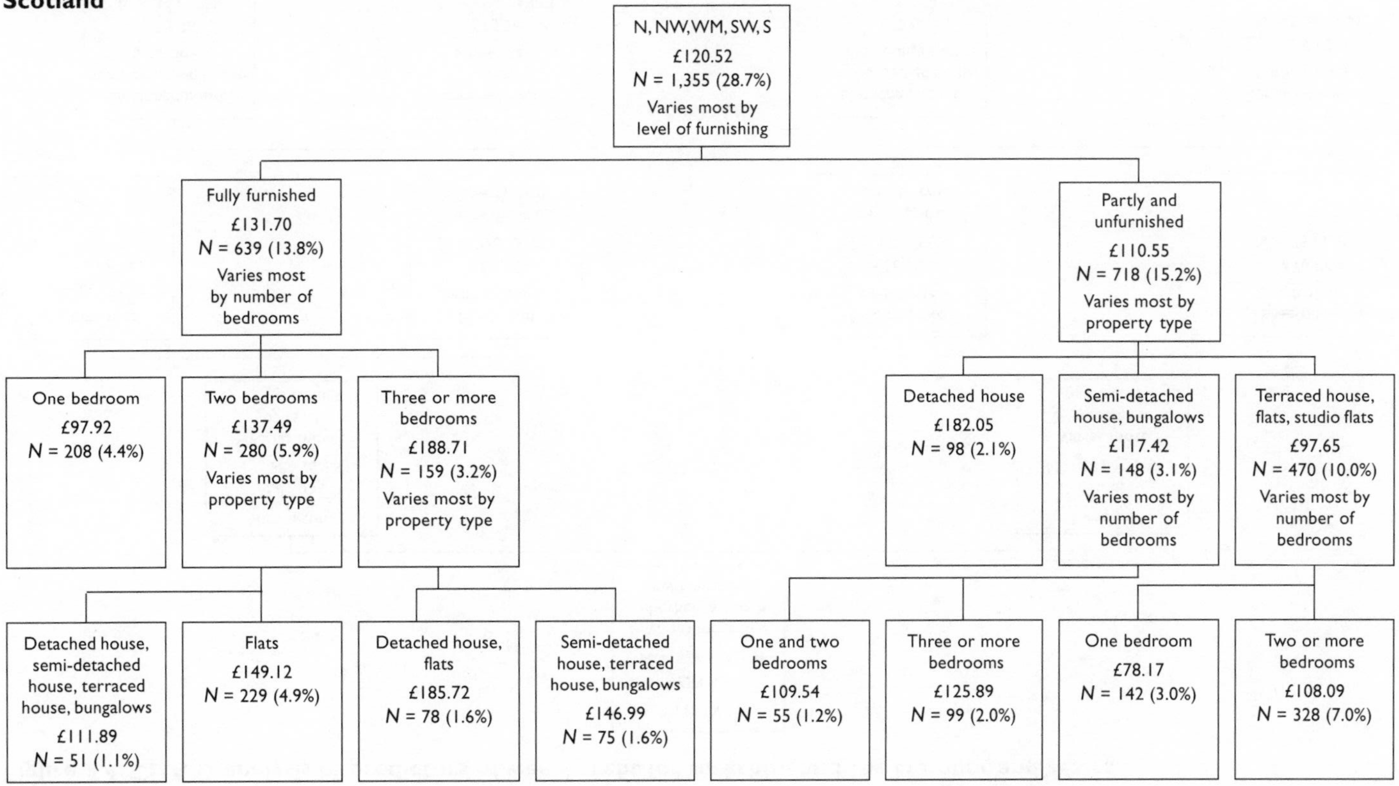

N, NW, WM, SW, S
£120.52
N = 1,355 (28.7%)
Varies most by level of furnishing

Fully furnished
£131.70
N = 639 (13.8%)
Varies most by number of bedrooms

Partly and unfurnished
£110.55
N = 718 (15.2%)
Varies most by property type

One bedroom
£97.92
N = 208 (4.4%)

Two bedrooms
£137.49
N = 280 (5.9%)
Varies most by property type

Three or more bedrooms
£188.71
N = 159 (3.2%)
Varies most by property type

Detached house, semi-detached house, terraced house, bungalows
£111.89
N = 51 (1.1%)

Flats
£149.12
N = 229 (4.9%)

Detached house, flats
£185.72
N = 78 (1.6%)

Semi-detached house, terraced house, bungalows
£146.99
N = 75 (1.6%)

One and two bedrooms
£109.54
N = 55 (1.2%)

Three or more bedrooms
£125.89
N = 99 (2.0%)

Detached house
£182.05
N = 98 (2.1%)

Semi-detached house, bungalows
£117.42
N = 148 (3.1%)
Varies most by number of bedrooms

Terraced house, flats, studio flats
£97.65
N = 470 (10.0%)
Varies most by number of bedrooms

One bedroom
£78.17
N = 142 (3.0%)

Two or more bedrooms
£108.09
N = 328 (7.0%)

57

Figure 4.4: CHAID analysis of predictors of weekly rent for Yorkshire and the Humber and Wales

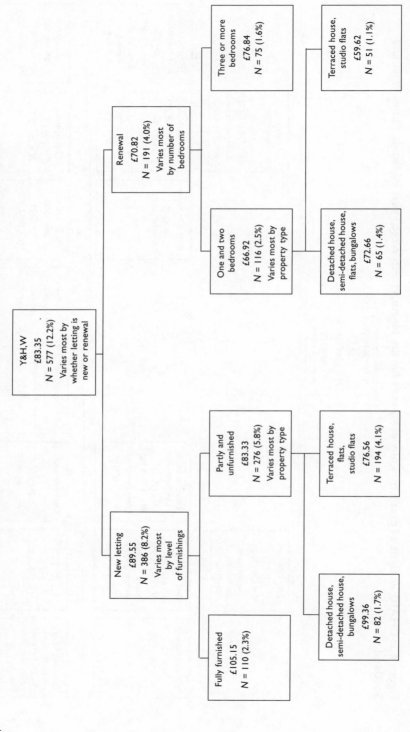

Figure 4.5: CHAID analysis of predictors of weekly rent for the East Midlands and Northern Ireland

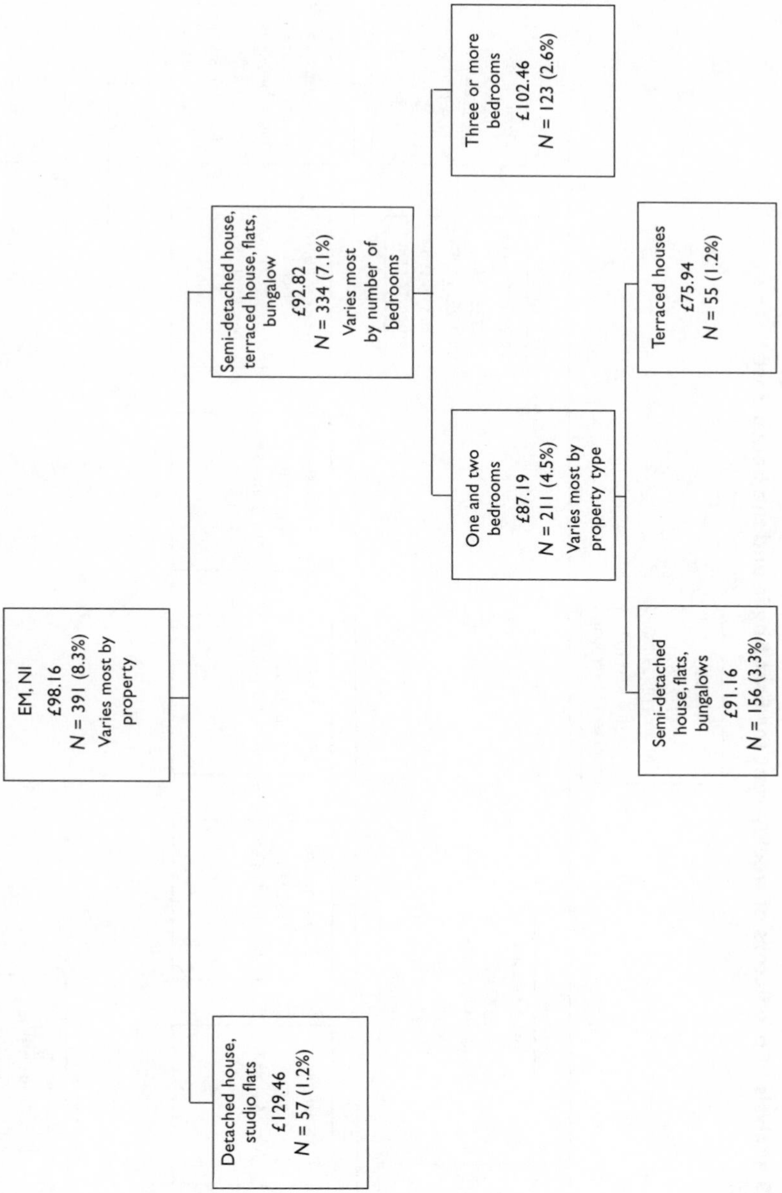

EM, NI
£98.16
N = 391 (8.3%)
Varies most by property

Detached house, studio flats
£129.46
N = 57 (1.2%)

Semi-detached house, terraced house, flats, bungalow
£92.82
N = 334 (7.1%)
Varies most by number of bedrooms

One and two bedrooms
£87.19
N = 211 (4.5%)
Varies most by property type

Three or more bedrooms
£102.46
N = 123 (2.6%)

Semi-detached house, flats, bungalows
£91.16
N = 156 (3.3%)

Terraced houses
£75.94
N = 55 (1.2%)

Figure 4.6: CHAID analysis of predictors of weekly rent for East Anglia and the South East

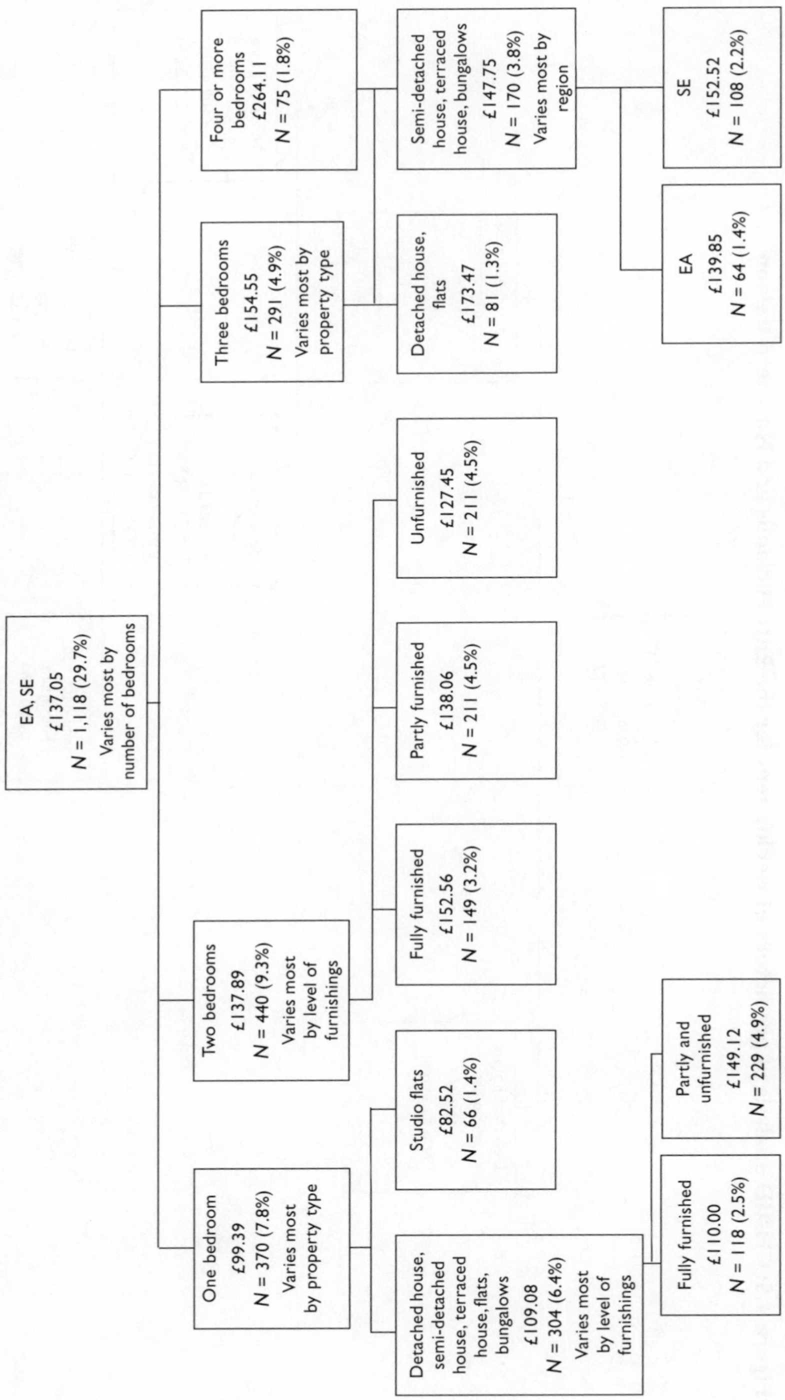

Figure 4.7: CHAID analysis of predictors of weekly rent for Greater London

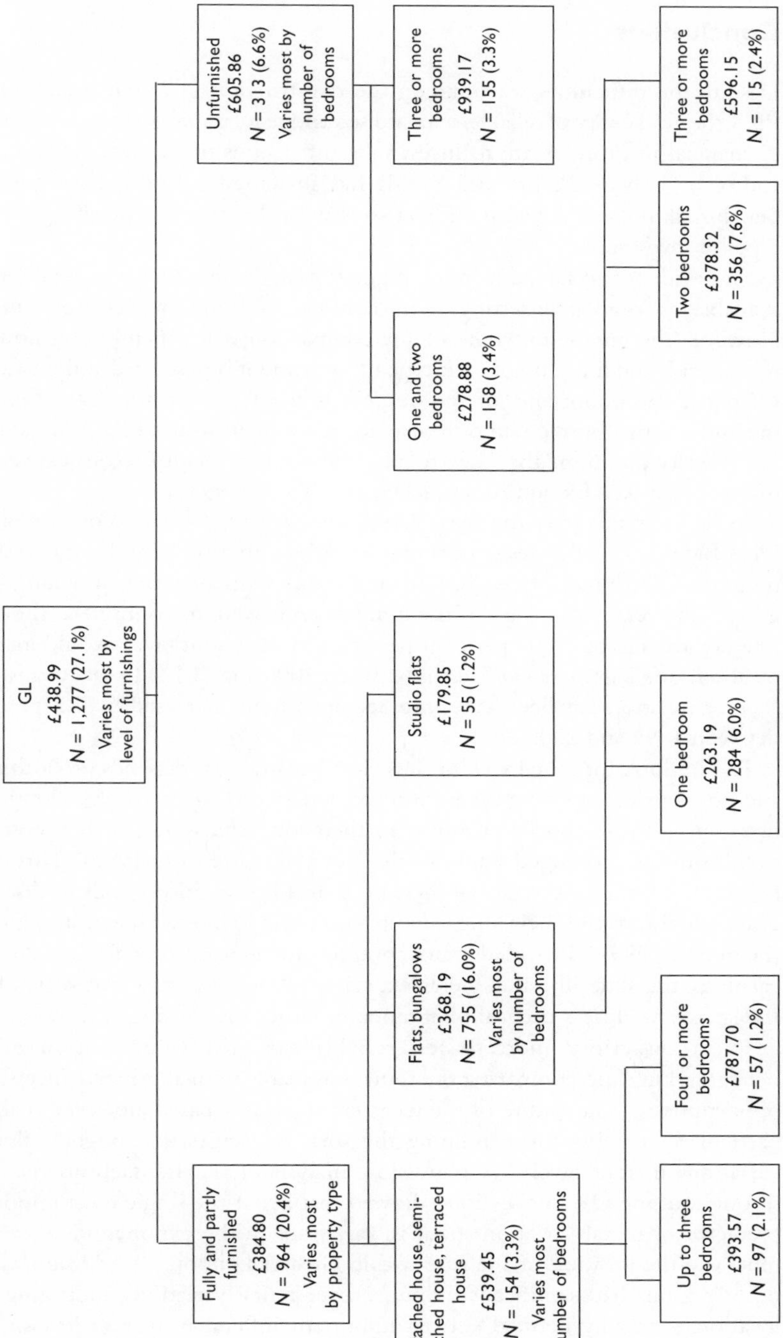

GL
£438.99
N = 1,277 (27.1%)
Varies most by
level of furnishings

Fully and partly
furnished
£384.80
N = 964 (20.4%)
Varies most
by property type

Unfurnished
£605.86
N = 313 (6.6%)
Varies most by
number of
bedrooms

Detached house, semi-
detached house, terraced
house
£539.45
N = 154 (3.3%)
Varies most
by number of bedrooms

Flats, bungalows
£368.19
N= 755 (16.0%)
Varies most
by number of
bedrooms

One and two
bedrooms
£278.88
N = 158 (3.4%)

Three or more
bedrooms
£939.17
N = 155 (3.3%)

Up to three
bedrooms
£393.57
N = 97 (2.1%)

Four or more
bedrooms
£787.70
N = 57 (1.2%)

Studio flats
£179.85
N = 55 (1.2%)

One bedroom
£263.19
N = 284 (6.0%)

Two bedrooms
£378.32
N = 356 (7.6%)

Three or more
bedrooms
£596.15
N = 115 (2.4%)

Conclusions

Despite the difficulties surrounding the construction of a rent index for the PRS, the availability of reliable, standardised and regular information is important if financial institutions are to invest substantial sums in the sector. The UoY Index of Private Rents and Yields has provided a useful new tool for benchmarking and drawing comparisons with the returns available on other types of investment.

The evidence so far from Index suggests that, during 2000, the total returns available on residential lettings were competitive with alternate investments. However, the precise outcome of any comparison will depend upon how the relative risk and liquidity of each type of investment is perceived and measured. Of particular importance is this respect is the fact that, for some financial institutions, the 'hurdle rate of return' for investment in the PRS is inflated by the 'novelty premium' that they require due to their lack of recent experience of the sector (Crook and Kemp, 1999).

So far as trends over the five years from 1996 to 2000 are concerned, the UoY Index shows that residential rent levels have increased by about two thirds more than consumer prices (RPIX), and at approximately the same rate as the growth in average earnings. If the trend in rents were to continue at the same rate (an average of +4.04 per cent per year), average rent levels would increase by about one half in *nominal* terms between 2000 and 2012. In real terms (that is, after inflation has been take into account) rents increased by 7.7 per cent between 1996 and 2000.

The outlook for rental yields is less clear because that depends on both rents and house prices. During the period covered by this chapter (1996–2000), real house prices rose at a faster rate than their long-run trend, as they bounced back from the prolonged slump of the late 1980s and early 1990s. This event reflects the fact that the rate of increase in real house prices tends to fluctuate quite widely around their long-run upward trend in line with earnings growth (Hamnett, 1999). Provided rents continue to increase broadly in line with earnings, the slide in rental yields experienced over the first five years of the Index may well be a cyclical phenomenon rather than a long-run trend.

The transactions index is less reliable than the valuations index for benchmarking and comparing the returns available with alternative investment opportunities. The nature of the data on which it is based, however, makes it particularly suitable for examining the sorts of factors that might influence variations in rent levels. A regression analysis of the transactions recorded throughout the UK during 2000 showed that by far the single most important predictor of rental variations (that is, variations in the exponential of weekly rent) was the location of a letting within Greater London. In addition, all the other regions had significant influence over rental variations, indicating that location – broadly defined – is an important influence on rent levels. Not surprisingly, the number of bedrooms within a letting was also strongly correlated with variations in rent levels.

A CHAID analysis of the letting transactions also found that the most statistically significant predictor of weekly rent during 2000 was location, as indicated by standard region. The first stage of the analysis produced five regional segments. Four were groups of regions that did not significantly differ from one another with respect to predicting weekly rent. Greater London was the only region to be identified as being unique in its own right in predicting weekly rent. The CHAID analysis then disentangled the factors within each regional segment that provided further explanation of variations in rent levels. These factors differed within each of the regional groupings, suggesting that the market values property characteristics differed slightly according to regional location. This differential operation of the markets should not be over-emphasised as it may, of course, be to do with what is available as much as with the nature of tenant demand. Additionally, although the predictors of rent within the regional segments were dissimilar, the same collection of predictors, but in differing order of importance, usually had significant impacts.

Annex 1: hypothetical property types included in the valuations index

ONE-ROOM BED-SIT in the most representative private rented sector locality in the local authority area. Mid-terrace two-storey house: comprising four bed-sits; built c1900; good decorative order; improved to fitness standard; central heating; furnished accommodation; shared use of kitchen, internal bathroom/wc, front door/entrance hall, stairs.
Valuations: furnished weekly rent for one bed-sit (including service charges, such as lighting for communal areas), vacant possession value for whole house.

ONE-BEDROOM SELF-CONTAINED FLAT in the most representative private rented sector locality in the local authority area. Mid-terrace two-storey house: converted into two flats; built c1900; good decorative order; improved to fitness standard; central heating; exclusive use of one bedroom, one living room, kitchen, internal bathroom/wc.
Valuations: furnished weekly rent for one flat, unfurnished weekly rent for one flat, vacant possession value for one flat.

TWO-BEDROOM SELF-CONTAINED FLAT in the most representative private rented sector locality in the local authority area. Mid-terrace two-storey house: converted into two flats; built c1900; good decorative order; improved to fitness standard; central heating; exclusive use of two bedrooms, one living room, kitchen, internal bathroom/wc.
Valuations: furnished weekly rent for one flat, unfurnished weekly rent for one flat, vacant possession value for one flat.

TWO-BEDROOM HOUSE in the most representative private rented sector locality in the local authority area. Mid-terrace two storey house: built c1900; good decorative order; improved to fitness standard; central heating; entrance hall, two bedrooms, two living rooms, kitchen, internal bathroom/wc.
Valuations: furnished weekly rent, unfurnished weekly rent, vacant possession value.

THREE-BEDROOM HOUSE in the most representative private rented sector locality in the local authority area. Semi-detached two-storey house: built c1930; good decorative order; central heating; entrance hall, three bedrooms, two living rooms, kitchen, internal bathroom/wc.
Valuations: furnished weekly rent, unfurnished weekly rent, vacant possession value.

FOUR-BEDROOM HOUSE in the local authority area either within ¼ of a mile of the centre of a market town or suburban area, or on the outskirts of a large town on an exclusively residential estate. Detached two-storey house: built c1965; good decorative order; central heating; entrance hall, four bedrooms, two living rooms, kitchen, internal bathroom/wc, garaging.
Valuations: furnished weekly rent, unfurnished weekly rent, vacant possession value.

FIVE

The private rented sector in rural areas

Phil Hancock

Introduction

Is the rural private rented sector any different from its urban counterpart? If it is, why should it be of interest? Part of the answer lies in the changed policy agenda introduced by New Labour since they came to power in 1997.

Rural concerns are higher on the national policy agenda now than they have ever been in recent years. The BSE crisis, the debate over hunting and the foot and mouth outbreak have successively grabbed the national headlines. Housing has also been pushed up the national agenda, albeit quietly, because of its links to broader social, economic and environmental issues. However, many housing professionals, if asked, are likely to say that the 'rural voice' is still largely ignored by what is seen as an urban–oriented government. Even when rural issues are debated housing is seen as marginalised within that debate (Brown, 2000). This lack of attention is reflected in the somewhat limited research undertaken on housing in rural areas generally and of the private rented sector's role in such areas in particular.

The government's publication of both a Rural White Paper (DEFRA, 2000) and a Housing Green Paper (DETR, 2000a) may have done little fundamentally to change the views of housing professionals. Both documents outlined a range of measures around housing issues, some new, some not so new but few revolutionary in nature. Those proposals contained in the Rural White Paper are now being carried forward through the newly formed Department for the Environment, Food and Rural Affairs Implementation Plan (DEFRA, 2001). Action on the measures set out in the Housing Green Paper have been incorporated in *The way forward for housing* (DETR/DSS, 2000). This policy agenda needs to be seen against a backdrop of social and economic change in the countryside. As Shucksmith (2000) argues, "The economies and societies of rural areas of Britain are changing rapidly in the face of globalisation, economic restructuring, migration and other social and policy changes". What is the role and experience of the private rented sector in rural areas in this changing world? (For a specifically Scottish perspective see Chapter Six.)

This chapter looks first at definitions of what is rural and the implications that lie behind such definitions. It goes on to offer some comparisons between rural and urban areas. An examination of the position and role of the private rented sector within rural housing markets then follows. Available research on the rural private rented sector is then summarised to give a more detailed picture. The chapter ends by drawing together some thoughts and conclusions on its future.

How are rural areas defined?

It seems a simple enough question but how can rural areas be identified from their urban counterparts? Robinson (1998) acknowledges that the division between rural and urban is an arbitrary one but he recognises that the different ways of defining a rural area puts more emphasis on some features or aspects than on others. How rural areas are defined also has important implications for the distribution of government resources and for the collection and use of statistics.

The government's pre-eminent rural body, the Countryside Agency, inherited a definition of rural areas from its forerunner, the Rural Development Commission. The Commission, using local authority boundaries, defined most of England outside the major conurbations (London, Birmingham, West Yorkshire, Greater Manchester, Teeside and Tyneside) and outside other major urban centres (Bristol, Norwich, Brighton, York and so on) as rural. In essence, Council areas in their entirety were considered to be either urban or rural. The Countryside Agency's intention is to devise a more sophisticated definition by using settlement structure, population density, land use and land cover, but so far they have not been able to do so because relevant data remains unavailable.

Government agencies and academics have typically defined rural areas through the use of population densities. Chapman et al (1998), in their examination of poverty, used postcode areas that have a population of less than 3,000 as defining a rural area and those between 3,000 and 10,000 in population as semi-rural. For the purposes of allocating funding to housing associations for the provision of new housing, the Housing Corporation (1995) considers settlements with a population less than 3,000 as rural but particularly targets resources at those settlements with under 1,500. Such definitions have been considered arbitrary and some discussion in government circles has suggested that the Housing Corporation's definition be amended to include market towns with populations up to 10,000 (Inside Housing, 2000).

Other researchers have taken a different approach. Bevan and Sanderling (1996) in their examination of private renting in rural areas used a categorisation of census wards according to their constituent proportions of urban and rural enumeration districts. Shucksmith et al (1995), dissatisfied with existing classifications of rural England, devised a more complex classification focusing on rural housing markets, also at census ward level. This classification provides a national overview of rural areas using measures of land supply, demand for housing, and access to housing for households on low incomes. DTZ Pieda (1998) subsequently used this classification in a selection of five areas for their study on rural housing markets. However, one of the key conclusions of that study was that rural housing markets were not self-contained but were strongly influenced by nearby urban areas. In this sense, can there ever be a truly rural private rented sector or is it merely private landlordism that happens to operate in a rural area? Whatever the answer to this question it seems clear that, while at the extremes there are significant differences between urban and rural areas, there are also large areas of quasi–rural/urban settlement. What are these differences as they specifically relate to housing?

Rural and urban comparisons

The difficulties of defining rural areas gives some cause for concern when looking at available data on them. It is as well to consider that there may be as much variation within rural areas as between rural and urban areas. Rural areas can include declining former coal mining areas, expanding commuter villages, areas with a mixture of market towns and small villages, as well as areas such as the more sparsely populated National Parks.

Nevertheless, surveys of public opinion show that most people in England would live in the countryside if they could and this has been borne out in practice. Over the last 25 years the population of rural England has risen by 24 per cent, four times the rate of growth for the country as a whole. In each year since 1981 roughly 80,000 people have migrated from urban to rural areas in England with a similar trend reported for Scotland. Phillips (1993) has demonstrated that this migration has been socially selective with gentrification of the countryside occurring over time. His analysis indicates that affluent people have migrated in to the countryside and displaced less affluent groups primarily through the competition for scarce housing. What has been the impact on the rural private rented sector of this change?

In rural areas the most visible activity is agriculture, but agriculture is no longer the countryside's principal economic activity. Agricultural workers continue to live in housing tied to their employment and as such can be classed as part of the private rented sector. But agricultural employment has been in long-term decline (see also Chapter Six). Less need for agricultural workers means less need for tied housing for them. It also means that such housing can be freed up for other uses if demand exists. Between 1981 and 1996, agricultural employment declined from 6 per cent to 4per cent of total employment, but overall rural employment has grown faster in rural than non-rural areas. Although agriculture still employs just over half a million workers nationally most people in the countryside now work in commerce, services, industry and the public sector.

Apart from agriculture the rural economy now broadly mirrors that of urban areas. Rural areas have shared in the national shift to a service-based economy. Some of that shift is likely to reflect the fact that many people living in the countryside commute to work in nearby towns and cities, most particularly in those areas with good transport links.

The role of agriculture in the wider economy has also steadily diminished. It is estimated that total income from farming in the year 2000 fell to its lowest level in 25 years, while agriculture's direct contribution to the national economy in 1999 declined to less than 1 per cent (Countryside Agency, 2000). The foot and mouth crisis has drawn attention to the small contribution agriculture now makes nationally but nevertheless underlined the important role it plays in underpinning the rural economy.

Persistent unemployment tends to be less but low pay greater in rural than non-rural areas but employment in agriculture and in tourism is generally seasonal and insecure. It has become more widely recognised by rural local housing authorities and by others that in many rural areas even those households on moderate but steady incomes experience real difficulty in being able to afford to buy a home (Chapman et al, 1998; Market Research UK Ltd, 1999; Murie et al, 1999; David Couttie Associates, 2001). Those in seasonal employment are likely to suffer even greater difficulty in securing accommodation. However, rural areas do not all share the same characteristics: some are prosperous while others are not; some have better access to services, facilities and higher levels of employment (Cabinet Office, 2000). All these issues impact on rural areas and on the role the private rented sector performs in such areas.

Proportionately, rural areas have fewer single person households of working age (9 per cent compared to 14 per cent in urban areas, derived from Ford et al, 1997) but more couples, with or without children (68 per cent compared to 58 per cent). This may reflect the simple fact that rural areas have few colleges and

Table 5.1: Proportion of stock of businesses by standard industrial classification

	Rural (%)	Non-rural (%)
Agriculture, hunting and forestry	15	2
Fishing	0.5	0.5
Mining and quarrying	0.5	0.5
Manufacturing	7	8
Utilities	0.5	0.5
Construction	11	10
Wholesale and retail	19	22
Hotels and restaurants	6	6
Transport, storage and communication	4	4
Finance	1	2
Real estate, renting and business	23	30
Public administration and defence	0.5	0.5
Education	1	1
Health and social work	3	4
Other social and personal services	8	10
Total	100	100

Source: Countryside Agency (2000)

universities. Rural areas may also be perceived to offer better primary and secondary school education and so attract families with children, or those thinking of starting a family. There are also proportionately more, larger families in rural areas (75 per cent compared to 46 per cent in urban areas) and fewer small terraced houses and flats (22 per cent compared to 47 per cent in urban areas). In numerical terms, of course, there are fewer of all types of property in rural areas than in urban areas.

With regard to housing tenure, owner occupation is clearly more dominant in rural compared to urban areas (73 per cent against 66 per cent) and there are relatively fewer council houses (13 per cent compared to 20 per cent). The private rented and tied housing sector together is almost as large as the council sector in rural areas (12 per cent compared to 10 per cent in urban areas). Reasons for this will be discussed later. While these figures give an interesting snapshot of rural areas they fail to reveal some of the social processes that have been taking place over time.

Changes in rural housing markets

Clark (1990), in his work for the Rural Development Commission, observed that many employers in rural areas provided tied housing with jobs. Country estates also retained rented housing for local families, including their own retired staff, in recognition of the difficulties of obtaining housing in those communities. He also observed that over time substantial changes to the nature and tenure of the housing stock in rural England had taken place.

Clark found that many local authorities had built up a stock of rented council housing in villages from before the First World War. With the general decline of the private rented sector this programme of local authority building gained impetus in the years after 1945. However, this building programme had been eclipsed by the later growth of owner occupation, both through new build and by transfer through the sale of rented property.

Between 1981 and 1988 Clarke estimated that around half a million homes had been built in rural areas but of these 90 per cent went for owner occupation. Around 50,000 council and housing association homes had also been built, but significantly, over the same period, about 400,000 thousand rented homes had transferred to owner occupation. Half of these properties had become owner occupied through the opportunity given for purchase by council tenants. Before 1980 some rural authorities gave discounts of up to 20 per cent of the market value to council tenants. The process gathered pace following the introduction by the Conservative government of the statutory right to buy (RTB) for council tenants in the 1980 Housing Act, offering significantly higher discount. The other 200,000 properties had transferred through private landlords sales to sitting tenants or by sale on the open market.

Many of Clark's findings are echoed in DTZ Pieda Consulting's more recent study on rural housing markets (DTZ Pieda Consulting, 1998). The report looked at five rural areas. In each the stock of rented accommodation had declined, including both local authority and tied accommodation. However, there had been a similar but less marked decline in the stock of privately rented accommodation. The research evidence suggested that the number of hidden households and the scale of involuntary out-migration from these rural areas were small. Inward migration, however, was significant, with most households moving for job reasons. The overall decline in the stock of rented housing had been significant, particularly during the 1980s following the introduction of the RTB.

Rises in local house prices were found to have had a significant effect on accessibility and affordability. If existing owner occupiers were excluded, between 19 and 37 per cent of all households in the study areas were defined as being unable to purchase. A similar analysis confirmed that the majority of households in social housing (local authority or housing association property) could not afford to rent without subsidy in the private rented sector. This emphasises the important role housing benefit and its effective administration performs in sustaining poorer households in rural areas.

DTZ Pieda Consulting also found that the option to rent in these rural areas was in decline. Tied accommodation was typically sold for owner occupation or was rented privately. There was a less marked decline in the number of private rented properties, possibly through the transfer of property from being tied to employment to being made available for rent. In some areas a new phenomenon was identified, that of the 'dual market'. The dual market consisted of an 'upmarket' sector providing good quality accommodation for people who could purchase if they wanted, and the 'traditional' rented sector of smaller, often poor-condition properties let at comparatively low rents. Where this dual market had emerged, the opportunities for low-cost renting had declined further than implied by the overall reduction in the stock of privately rented dwellings.

The growth of a two-tier market potentially reflects a change in attitude to owner occupation but also to the operation of the whole housing market. Anecdotal evidence from estate agents in one district of North Yorkshire indicates that households moving from outside were selling their home first, moving initially into rented accommodation in the area and being in a good position to buy when the right property came along. Some households moving to take up employment in the area for a year or two may also choose to rent. Other households not in a position to buy may see the benefit of renting on a long-term basis from an estate or other farming landlord. In this way they can secure the type of property and the 'lifestyle' they are unable to afford through owner occupation. Evidence from the Cumbrian district of Eden suggests that the private rented sector is meeting a large part of in-migrant demand and is also providing short-term housing solutions in the absence of available social rented housing (Market Research UK Ltd, 1999).

The nature and role of the private rented sector in rural areas

Just as it is difficult to characterise and define rural areas so it is also difficult to do the same when looking at the rural private rented sector. Research on the private rented sector has tended to look at it as a whole rather than focus specifically on rural areas. Similarly, where rural research has been undertaken this has sought either to answer a specific question or has been part of a wider study of rural housing or of rural areas generally. This section summarises some relevant research on the private rented sector and also that relating specifically to rural areas. It also draws on some of the author's own research on and experience of the private rented sector within North Yorkshire.

Size of the sector

Studies have revealed the relatively small-scale nature of private landlordism in Britain. Thomas et al's (1995) research indicates that there are a surprisingly wide variety of people who are landlords and they have a range of motives for letting property. Over a half of all lettings are estimated to belong to individual landlords owning only one or two properties. This applies to rural as much as urban areas. In one of the most rural districts of North Yorkshire, for example, there are estimated to be 3,600 households living in the private rented sector with around 800 landlords receiving housing benefit on behalf of some but not necessarily all of those tenants. Whilse a handful of landlords own a hundred or more properties it is clear that the vast majority will own only one or two.

While the size of the private rented sector is proportionately almost as large as the social housing sector in rural areas both have been in long-term decline compared to the owner occupied sector. Evidence suggests that the sector will decline still further or at best remain fairly static.

Bevan and Sanderling's 1996 study of private renting in rural areas found that while most landlords expected to maintain their existing portfolio of lettings, only a few intended to increase them and equally a few expected to reduce them. At the time of the study some landlords were considering transferring to the holiday market as 'safer' than letting to tenants. The precarious nature of this business has been demonstrated by the recent foot and mouth outbreak but the attraction of letting property for tourism may still assert itself in the long term. Other landlords thought they might sell if and when the general housing market improved.

Bevan and Sanderling also found that very few landlords had specifically acquired their property in order to let it on the open market, which suggested that there was little potential for new growth in the sector. This was mirrored in the evidence given by landlords in North Yorkshire (Hancock, 1999).

Chapman et al's (1998) research indicated that private renting in rural areas had declined rapidly during the period 1991-96 (8.9 per cent to 6.9 per cent in the five years), as had tied accommodation (4.6 per cent to 3.3 per cent in the five years). The rural sector did not appear to have shared in the growth experienced by urban areas. This was contrary to the stated intentions of large landowners in rural England as found in Bevan and Sanderling's study. However, part of the explanation for this contradiction may lie in the fact that Bevan and Sanderling's study was of traditional country landowners who may not generally consider selling property that sits among the land they farm. These landlords may well wish to retain control of such property to prevent interference in their everyday activities from incoming owner occupiers who may not be used to, let alone put up with, the noise, smells and long working day associated with farming activities.

In Scotland research on rural private landlords by Kemp and Rhodes (1994) found that they were much less commercially oriented than their urban counterparts (see also Chapter Six in this volume). However, there was some evidence that the 1988 Housing Act provisions that created assured shorthold tenancies had given many rural landlords more confidence in letting their property on the open market and at full market rents. Separately, there also appeared to be some evidence of a growing trend away from estates providing rent-free accommodation to workers on retirement (Henderson et al, 1991). The research by Chapman et al (1998) indicates the possibility that a similar situation could be occurring in rural areas in England and Wales. The expectation of estate landowners may be that the social housing sector should accommodate their retiring employees, helping them to boost their return from letting property in order to maintain the viability of the estate at a time when agricultural income is declining.

In North Yorkshire some large-scale landlords have continued to emphasise their traditional role of providing accommodation for their employees as well as for the rural community at large. However, one landlord reported that while some five years ago most applicants would be personally known to the estate's staff, this was now no longer the case. In their view many applicants were now people who were moving into the area, often from some distance away, while local applicants were much fewer in number (Hancock, 1999).

The reasons for this change were not examined but there could be a number. Local people generally on low incomes could see that better opportunities existed for them or their children in local towns or cities. The rent local landlords asked could also be too high or there was other, cheaper property available through the increased competition from housing associations. The local council in this area had sponsored housing associations in providing over 600 new homes in the previous eight years, some for single people and couples, a group not previously catered for.

Some of these estate landlords continue to offer accommodation where no social housing provision exists at all. But such housing in small rural communities may be very isolated. There is a lack of public transport, limited shops, no local schools, and a lack of access to jobs. Evidence suggests that the ability to run a car or several cars may be a necessity that is difficult to achieve on a low wage (Rugg and Jones, 1999; Pavis et al, 2000; Storey and Brannen, 2000). While households may appear to be living in idyllic surroundings they may nevertheless be trapped in poverty. As a result these households may wish to move to local towns, as is suggested by housing waiting lists, to be replaced by those who can afford the costs of rural living. However, there is evidence to suggest that for some low-income households who do have access to local support networks this is less of a problem (Hancock, 1999).

In order to maintain the availability of their stock for rent, estate landlords may need encouragement. The development of the 'dual' market, identified in the DTZ Pieda Consulting study, may intensify as more households search for the rural lifestyle that they cannot afford through owner occupation but can afford by renting on a long-term basis. Estates seeking to maximise their income will inevitably let at higher rents if there is demand, thus pricing low-income households out of that market.

Access to the private rented sector

Just as in urban areas many low-income households of necessity seek housing in the private rented sector to which access can be difficult. As in urban areas obstacles to entry into accommodation include the availability of financial resources for rent, deposits, legal fees and so on, the attitudes of landlords; and the local administration of housing benefit. These are all issues that must be addressed by local and national policy makers if the private rented sector is to continue to provide accommodation for these households.

Several national studies of the private rented sector (Crook et al 1995; Thomas et al, 1995) identified the difficulty that people in receipt of housing benefit have in finding and securing accommodation. Most landlords preferred not to let to those on housing benefit, generally because of the undesirable image they had of them and the administrative difficulties they associated with the scheme. More recent evidence from North Yorkshire supports this view and suggests that problems arising from changes in housing benefit regulations, such as the payment of benefit in arrears, and a failure to process claims quickly can deter some landlords from letting to low-income groups. Tenants themselves also felt that housing benefit rules were complex and the process of application stressful. There was little evidence of negotiation over the rent possibly because households do not pursue tenancies they do not feel they can afford (Hancock, 1999).

Crook et al (1995), in their national study, found that as many as two out of five landlords said their least preferred household type was young single people, yet these were the largest demand group. Three quarters of landlords preferred their tenants to be in work. They least preferred to let to the unemployed and to students. However, qualitative research suggests that landlords judge each prospective tenant as much on appearance as on whether they are in some particular category of household. This seems to be the position in rural areas also. Nevertheless, there are examples in the smaller communities of rural areas of individuals, particularly young people who were not in work, who were labelled as problematic and thereby found their access to the sector impossible, necessitating a move away.

As has been indicated previously significant issues were found to exist around the availability of affordable housing in rural areas. Analysis of advertised lettings in local newspapers revealed that few properties could be considered 'affordable'. Only 48 family lettings were advertised in 1998/99 with rents that could be considered affordable. Nevertheless, over the same period the local council received 30 homelessness applications and 57 enquiries for accommodation from households with children (Hancock, 1999). A more recent study of the district indicates that the position has deteriorated still further. The private rented sector within that same district is now judged to make little contribution to access to affordable housing (David Couttie Associates, 2001).

Rhodes and Bevan, in their 1997 study, specifically addressed the extent to which the private rented sector nationally could house the homeless. The government at that time had proposed that councils should house homeless people in the private rented sector rather than in social housing. The study concluded that the ability of the sector to house the homeless varied significantly across the country. The number of homeless acceptances in comparison with the annual flow of lettings in the private rented sector was most favourable in deep rural areas and in mixed rural/urban areas rather than in urban or metropolitan areas. However, since the Rhodes and Bevan analysis was undertaken it has been suggested that there has been both significant growth in and under-reporting of homelessness in rural rather than urban areas (Rural Development Commission, 1998).

Bevan and Sanderling (1996) had already suggested that the rural private rented sector might be accommodating a proportion of households who would, if living in an urban area, be housed in the social rented sector. Indeed, in North Yorkshire the examination of the housing histories of people approaching one council indicated that some had previously been council or housing association tenants in urban areas. Their moves, however, were not associated with them fleeing from large, rundown inner city estates but from suburban housing and for a variety of reasons but generally related to a relationship breakdown (Hancock, 1999). However, their initial move undoubtedly created a vacancy within that housing market that could form part of a hierarchy of moves that could eventually lead to the phenomenon of difficult-to-let estates and abandonment. Further detailed research would be required to establish this link.

In North Yorkshire some households that were becoming homeless appeared to 'choose' the private rented sector partly because of the processes and responses of local councils and also because of the pressures placed upon them through having children. Those households interviewed were not generally willing to stay in temporary hostel accommodation because the continuity of their children's schooling was seen as a priority (Hancock, 1999). However, local councils are unlikely to change the nature of their provision since the homelessness legislation is a 'safety net' for households that have no other alternative.

Some households were not prepared to wait on the housing list for the offer of a housing association home. They did not want to move their children from the school they were attending or away from their friends and family. Others indicated that they did not want the stigma of moving to the council's hostel.

Those households that did access the private rented sector did not spend long periods living in it. Households indicated significant feelings of insecurity, preferring social housing because of the security it offered and the ability for them to personalise their home without fear of its loss. Generally, although properties in the sector were affordable to them, as a result of housing benefit, in relatively good condition and well managed, households still saw the sector as a transitional tenure because they lacked security (Hancock, 1999).

Those households surveyed spent anything between six months and five years in a private rented property, although the average was just under two years. Some of these households were starting out in their housing 'careers'. Some moves occurred as a result of relationship breakdown or households moving in with partners, rather than landlords requiring a property back. At least four out of ten lone parent households considered that they could continue to reside in their properties for an indefinite period. Any analysis of these housing histories is plagued with ambiguity. However, there was some evidence (Hancock, 1999) of households making forced moves, sometimes multiple moves, within the private rented sector as a result of landlords serving notice rather than by tenants own choice.

Chapman et al (1998) used the British Household Panel Survey 1991-95 in order to identify household movement between different tenures in rural areas. They found that the majority of households surveyed started and ended the year in the same tenure. The highest percentage level of movement was out of the private rented sector and into owner occupation, with a lower percentage moving from the public sector to owner occupation. In such circumstances, if the size of the private rented sector remained static within those years, it is clear that there would be considerable opportunity for new households to enter the sector. If the sector had expanded this would suggest that the opportunities to rent were even more substantial. Interestingly, the percentage of households leaving the private rented sector for the social sector is similar to that of households in the private rented sector moving to the social sector. Some local councils have become concerned that the private rented sector is a source of demand for social housing in their area from households constantly moving through it. But it would equally appear that the sector is also a destination for many social housing tenants. What is not clear is the extent to which such movement causes difficulties for the local housing market generally but more specifically for the social housing sector either through the creation of low or high demand. Much depends on the characteristics of the area as to which may come forward.

The explanation for such dominant movement probably rests with a number

Table 5.2: Transitions between housing tenure in any year by percentage for those who lived in rural areas throughout the survey period 1991-95

From/to	Owner occupied	Public rented	Private rented	Total
O/O at start of year	99.04	0.2	0.76	100
Public rented start of year	3.92	93.73	2.35	100
Private rented start of year	8.71	2.4	88.89	100
Total	78.93	9.71	11.36	100

Source: Chapman et al (1998)

of factors. First, that first time buyers are most likely to set up their first home in the private sector. Second, that the public sector is largely a residual sector of households who cannot afford to buy. Third, that the private rented sector is a tenure that is easy to access for those who can also afford to buy.

The issue of movement within and between the private rented sector is significant and appears to have grown year on year. In 1984, 1.8 million households moved home but by 1996/97 this had increased to 2.3 million. In 1996/97, 40 per cent of all private renters, 13 per cent of social renters and 6 per cent of owners had moved in the previous year. Significantly, there was also a high turnover of the privately rented stock. This could partially explain the high turnover of private tenants as either they died or they were forced to seek other accommodation when their tenancy was brought to an end (Green et al, 1999). With such large movements of both stock and tenants, the private rented sector can rapidly change in nature necessitating ongoing research.

Conclusion

In many ways the rural private rented sector can be seen to mirror its urban cousin. Rural landlordism remains small in scale with large numbers of landlords owning only one or two properties. For those on low incomes access into it is difficult. However, the sector has a stronger presence in rural areas, where it is seen by some commentators to act as a form of social housing. This is particularly the case where estate landlords have maintained their commitment to their employees and to their local communities. There is also evidence that commercial considerations are becoming more significant for these landlords perhaps reflecting a wider trend towards economic diversification in the face of a weaker agricultural sector. That diversification could see the further transfer of rented housing for second homes or for tourism.

The identification of a two-tier market indicates that some households are willing to pay extra for the opportunity to live in rural areas and there is evidence that landlords are responding to this demand and letting their property at higher rents. This change is perhaps evidence of a feeding through of demand for the rural lifestyle desired by so many. As such it is further evidence of the part that the sector plays in the gentrification of rural areas. For the future we may see more and more estate and other farming landlords letting their property to households unrelated to the estate or farm, or to the local community. Other landlords may decide to sell but where such a sale could interfere with their farming business this is unlikely. The profitability of the sector and continued government support in the form of housing benefit will clearly influence decisions.

In the 21st century the rural private rented sector appears at worst to be in decline and at best to be static in the face of competition from owner occupation. This contrasts with the private rented sector generally, which saw substantial growth during the early 1990s. The development of the flexible labour market has led to an increase in demand for private renting, especially from younger people who are yet to establish themselves. The state of the rural economy will undoubtedly influence the future of the sector. Leisure and tourism are strong in many rural areas and it is these sectors of the economy that employ young, casual labour. It is this group that is likely to continue to generate demand for private rented accommodation in rural areas but they may have considerable difficulty in accessing what might be available. Rural local authorities may need to take up the full range of policy initiatives set out by 'New' Labour both to improve the private rented housing that is available but also to encourage new landlords into the market.

Where the sector continues to survive it appears to be seeing competition from a wider range of groups wishing to secure the desired rural lifestyle either by using it on a temporary or a more long-term basis. Rural areas and rural households are more dynamic than at first sight might be supposed and the rural private rented sector clearly plays an important role in this increasing dynamism. Overall, it seems likely that without national and local intervention the rural private rented sector may become at best static in overall numbers but the households it accommodates may well need to become wealthier in order to live in it. Improving our understanding of the complex role the private rented sector plays in contributing to or in combating the socially selective process of rural gentrification in this new century remains a significant challenge for academics, for researchers and for policy makers wherever they may work.

SIX

Rental housing supply in rural Scotland: the role of private landowners

Madhu Satsangi

Introduction

This chapter looks at the supply of private rented housing in rural Scotland. In particular, it focuses on the role played by private landowners. Rural Scotland houses about a quarter of the nation's population. Rural land is predominantly privately owned and rural rental housing is predominantly privately supplied. This means that the views and housing market behaviour of rural landowners are extremely influential. The chapter draws on research recently completed for Scottish Homes and the Scottish Landowners' Federation (Satsangi et al, 2000)[1].

The first section sets the context by looking at the literature relevant to rural private renting in Scotland and by drawing attention to recent national policy debate. It then looks at new national evidence on the role of private renting. Section three examines the local scale, looking at evidence on landowners' motives from eight rural housing markets. The final section draws some conclusions.

Rural housing markets

From even the most cursory look at the geography of Scotland, it is clear that there is no homogeneity to rural areas. From readily obtainable data a variety of distinctions can be made including: lowland against upland; peri-urban against remote; relatively economically buoyant against relatively fragile. The same distinctions have important repercussions for housing demand and supply characteristics: availability, affordability, choice and constraint.

In terms of the way that housing systems work, and on a more general level, numerous classifications of rural areas have been made over the past decade (for example, Shucksmith, 1990; Departments of Geography and Land Economy, 1996; and, in England, Shucksmith et al, 1995. Using the characterisations of demand and supply pressure that these suggest, with some descriptions of local housing markets (see Scottish Homes, 1998a), it is possible to reach a functional typology of rural Scotland's housing systems:

- 'Buoyant' areas where population, economic activity and housing pressure are all increasing, while supply is constrained. Examples include the Inner Moray Firth and much of West Lothian.
- 'Pressured' areas where population and housing pressure are increasing, some with indigenous economic growth. These are areas with demand increasing from external sources, notably second and holiday home ownership (well known examples are: Badenoch and Strathspey; Skye and Lochalsh; Lochaber; Wester Ross) and commuting (for example, parts of the Lothians and Forth Valley).
- 'Fragile' areas with limited economic growth, having seen emigration of young people but with continuing pressure on rental housing supply (examples include: North West Sutherland; the Outer Hebrides; much of Argyll and Bute).
- 'Regeneration' areas, with lower demand-side pressures, but problems of deprivation and land dereliction (including West Fife and North Lanarkshire).
- 'Intermediate' areas, with pockets of deprivation or pressure (including parts of Fife, the Mearns, East Perthshire).
- Areas that have mainly buoyant but some fragile markets (such as Orkney).
- 'Transitional' areas, recovering from the loss of traditional economic activity (including parts of Argyll).

All available recent sources on national rural housing trends concur in their broad descriptions of the characteristics of rural housing systems at the local level and in defining the nature of housing problems that these characteristics may pose for some people (see, for example, Scottish Parliament Information Centre, 1999; Shucksmith and Philip, 2000). The principal issues can be summarised as follows. Rural areas tend to have a relatively high rate of home ownership compared to the country as a whole. Lower rates of social rental housing provision, with low rates of turnover, mean that there can be access difficulties for people on low or seasonal incomes (see Chapter Five for matching evidence on the rural PRS in England). Studies have pointed to particular concerns for young people looking to gain their first independent home (Pavis et al, 2000; Satsangi et al, 2001). For rural markets in relatively economically buoyant areas (for example, Perthshire, East Lothian and Stirlingshire) and those close to prosperous cities (Aberdeen, Edinburgh and Inverness), house price inflation may exacerbate difficulties. In many other areas of the country, including those that are more remote from major settlements, supply difficulties may be exacerbated by holiday and second home ownership (for example, in many parts of Argyll, Inverness-shire, Ross-shire, Sutherland, Berwickshire and Dumfriesshire). Associated with this is a relatively high house vacancy rate. At the national level, rural areas also show a disproportionately high incidence of poor physical housing condition, as defined by the Tolerable Standard (see Scottish Homes, 1997).

The literature also suggests that rural housing supply faces a series of constraints, varying in magnitude for different local markets (with more recent research presented by Satsangi et al, 2001):

a) Infrastructure and location. In this class of constraint are considerations relating to access to land, costs and difficulties in site assembly, site servicing and the transport of labour and materials and "... landowners' fears that [affordable housing] development may reduce the attractiveness of adjoining sites for more lucrative development" (Scottish Homes, 1998b).

b) Building material availability.

c) Accessibility.

d) Land and development costs.

e) Land use and the planning system. Some important criticisms have been made of the land-use planning system for hindering or putting brakes on housing development (for example, Shucksmith et al, 1993, 1994; the Scottish Landowners' Federation, 1998; Shelter Scotland, 1998).

f) Land ownership. The general issue here is that variations in land ownership have implications for land availability and owners' willingness to sell.

Land ownership, land tenure and land reform

MacGregor (1993, cited in Wightman, 1996, p 15) comments that "... in many areas of rural Scotland, large landowners play a crucial role in local development: they are the local planners". Wightman (1996) has expanded the argument, commenting that the wide range of types of landowner that own the country encompass diverse backgrounds, rationales and levels of wealth and interests, ranging from private enjoyment to profit maximisation. He notes that a landowner may be 'old' or 'new' money; a charity; absent; or a farmer working the estate. Each type of owner may have quite different views on and reasons for or against the provision of housing on their land. A national study conducted in the early 1990s, though limited by a relatively poor response to a postal survey of landowners, estimated that rural landowners own about 25,000 houses across the country. It was not able to clarify what proportion of owners let houses, nor to investigate fully landowners' motives in letting houses (System Three Scotland and Housing and Planning Consultants, 1992).

The principal representative body of landowners, the Scottish Landowners' Federation (SLF) has argued that "... many farms and estates meet some form of social need through their housing enterprises ... [they] admit to an allocation policy which aims to 'help local housing needs' or 'keep supporting the local school or shop'" (SLF, 1998). This argument is consistent with evidence from Kemp and Rhodes (1997) on the non-profit maximising behaviour of landlords (rural and urban) across Scotland. It also tallies with analysis of rural private landowners' behaviour south of the Border (Bevan and Sanderling, 1996; see also Chapter Five in this volume).

The Federation points out that the private sector contribution to meeting housing needs in rural areas is commonly overlooked or underestimated and that, given the appropriate incentive, private landowners could do more. In some respects, the Housing Green Paper (Scottish Office, 1999) opened the door to this prospect in suggesting that it may be appropriate to widen eligibility to mainstream public grants. The Housing (Scotland) Act 2001 made no direct provision for this, though the Scottish Parliament is open to the prospect of (public) grants being made to private landowners where circumstances indicate that it is appropriate as a way of meeting rural housing needs.

This enabling of a modification to general procedure comes at a time when the country is also witnessing other sorts of evolution in property rights. The most significant parts of this are land reform and the abolition of feudal tenure. An early action of the then newly elected UK Labour government was to establish, through the Scottish Office, a Land Reform Policy Group to identify and assess proposals for land reform in rural Scotland. Its work has led, in Scotland's post-devolution coalition government, to a draft Land Reform Bill (Scottish Executive, 2001) to be brought to the 2001/2002 Parliamentary session. Wightman (1999) notes that the debate around reform has been wide-ranging, covering both land reform *sensu stricto* "... the nature and distribution of power over land" and land policy "...government or public policy towards how land is used and managed" (p 51). As summarised by Lloyd and Danson (2000), the issues that have received attention are associated with "... a concentrated pattern of land ownership, the effects of an out-dated land tenurial system, the sustainability of crofting, and the relationship of land to wider processes of rural development" (pp 214-15). Looking at each of these points in turn:

a) *The pattern of ownership*. Wightman (1999) notes that 88 per cent of Scotland's rural land is privately owned, with a half of this being in the hands of only 343 owners. Dependent on ideology, this concentration might be argued to be iniquitous. Independent of ideology, conventional economic analysis tends to suggest that ownership dispersal is both economically and socially more efficient than concentration.

b) *Land tenure*. The country's land laws were, until the passing of the Abolition of Feudal Tenure (Scotland) Act in 2000, feudal in origin in the 11th century). Over time, that highly hierarchical system had become increasingly complex and liable to delay development.

c) *Crofting*. Crofting developed as a distinct form of land tenure following the 1886 Crofters' Holdings (Scotland) Act, which ensured the protection of agricultural tenants' rights in the seven crofting counties (covering the Highlands and Islands except Nairnshire). Its major impact has been the retention of people in some of the most economically fragile areas of the country though it has been criticised for its lack of provision to those without land (cottars) and for having retarded agricultural development (Wightman, 1996).

d) *Land and development.* In addition to the comments at the start of this section, it is worth bearing in mind the Scottish Office Land Reform Policy Group's (1998) judgement that "...housing in rural Scotland interacts with land tenure, ownership and use in many ways, few of which are well understood".

Attitudes toward housing supply: the national picture

The next two sections present recent evidence that can help formulate an answer to the challenge identified by the Land Reform Policy Group's judgement. The data are drawn from research funded by Scottish Homes (the government's National Housing Agency) and the Scottish Landowners' Federation. The research was designed to describe the scale of rural landowners' current involvement in housing provision, to identify what new housing opportunities (conversion and new build) there were on private rural land, what barriers there were to realising those opportunities and how those barriers might be overcome. Its data were drawn from a questionnaire survey of over 750 landowners or their factors, covering about 30 per cent of Scotland's privately owned rural land, and case studies of eight rural housing markets (see Satsangi et al, 2000 for the full research report).

Looking first at the overall scale of housing provision, the research estimated that landowner members of the SLF own approximately 21,000 houses (not including owners' principal residences) across rural Scotland. But the majority of landowners do not have many dwellings – a sixth of landowners have no houses other than their own, and four owners in five have ten or fewer. The 'average owner' has eight houses. Echoing the common urban picture, therefore, the new research confirms that rural private landlordism is generally a small-scale activity (Kemp and Rhodes, 1997).

The full-time renting out of housing to people other than those with a direct connection to the estate is an important housing activity of landowners and landowner members of the SLF let out approximately 10,000 houses across rural Scotland. The linkage of housing to other estate activities is important as there are approximately 5,300 tied houses in rural Scotland. Holiday lets are rarely numerically important with three quarters of landowners having under 2 per cent of their stock used for that purpose.

The importance of rented housing within a landowner's range of business activities is a factor that helps explain current and past investment behaviour and owners' thinking about future housing supply. Across the country, one landholder in four said that they earned at least a fifth of their total business income from (gross) house rents (and 10 per cent of owners earned at least half of their total business income). The median figure was 5 per cent, with a third of landowners receiving 2 per cent or less (and 29 per cent between 0.5 per cent or nothing). As might be expected, higher percentages were recorded in estates with more houses, a greater proportion of dwellings being let full-time, a greater proportion of houses used as holiday lets and a lower proportion being tied housing or being tenant crofts. Taken together with the data on ownership, these figures are supportive of two broad generalisations: letting houses forms a significant business activity for the majority of landowners; and only for a minority is it a major source of income.

Turning to how much housing stock was vacant, there was again a wide range of circumstances – from none to 200 habitable vacant dwellings reported. However, three quarters of respondents indicated that they had no habitable empty properties, with one being the median number of those who had any. A third of the owners reported having uninhabitable houses – with one being the median number for those who had any. Approximately 40 per cent reported having had houses vacant for two months or longer – with one again being the median number for those who had any. Of those owners who indicated reasons why their dwellings were vacant, by far the most common were poor dwelling condition or an absence of services (water, gas, electricity and the like), and the cost of installing them, each mentioned by two fifths of respondents. A tentative estimate would be that across the country there are 2,000 habitable vacant houses owned by SLF members and a further 2,500 that are considered uninhabitable due to being in poor condition or lacking basic services or both.

For the first time, data at national level on rural landowners' motivations in letting houses are provided . Respondents were asked to rate the importance of a series of different objectives on a scale from 0 (not an issue at all) to 5 (a very important motive). Table 6.1 shows the pattern of responses, excluding those landowners who had no houses apart from their principal residence.

What these data show is that owners can be divided into:

- the majority, whose prime concern is covering their costs, if not making a surplus, with support for the community a valuable secondary issue;
- a smaller group for whom connection with estate activities is the primary motive, with the viability of housing less of an issue than estate viability as a whole.

Does the significance of different possible rental housing investment motives have any bearing on the ways in which stock is used? Owners with property let on a full-time basis attach a high importance to 'earning a surplus', especially

Table 6.1: Motives for letting houses

Motive	Response pattern
Covering costs	Very important 40%, not an issue 37%
Connection with estate activities	Very/quite important 8%, not an issue 72%
Earning a surplus	Very important 38%, not an issue 38%
Following family practice	Very important 5%, not an issue 74%
Support for local community	Very/quite important 19%, not an issue 53%

those with a greater proportion of stock let full-time. None of the other motives shows a clear correlation with that figure. There is also a clear association with all owners between a high degree of importance attached to 'connection with estate activities' and a higher proportion of housing stock being let to current or former employees. The data also show a significant, strong negative correlation between the proportion of stock let on a full-time basis and the proportion of stock used as tied housing. These data were probed further in the more qualitative case study phase of the research (see below).

Owners' motives for renting housing also correlates with the level of rent charged. Most commonly, a distinction is made between the rent that is levied on houses let to 'local people' and the 'market rent'. In one sense, the terminology applied here (owners' own) suggests a clear form of segmentation of market rents, in another it implies that 'local rents' are not market rents. In most places local rents are about 75 per cent of market rents. Owners earning more of their income from housing tended to have greater differentials between local and market rents for three-bedroom houses. Owners with higher rental incomes rated more highly the importance of covering costs, earning a surplus, supporting other estate activities and supporting the community, and lower ratings to the significance of following family practice.

Another comparison can be made between private and public sector rents. Table 6.2 presents national and sub-national (generally local authority) data. Bearing in mind the different economics and finances of the two landlord types, the broad similarities in figures might be interpreted as indicative of the private sector adopting affordable housing rent policies.

The study was designed to produce evidence on development opportunities and constraints. These were investigated with respect to both conversion of non-residential buildings and new building. Half of those responding said that their holding contained buildings that were suitable for conversion into housing. Landowners estimated that these could provide numbers of homes ranging from 1 to 50, though active consideration to conversion had been made by about three landowners in ten. Most commonly this was consideration of the conversion of one building, which would provide one or two homes. Nationally, the data suggest active consideration of around 750 buildings that would convert into approximately 1,800 houses.

For all owners with suitable buildings, the major constraint to their redevelopment was financial viability (noted by 71 per cent). Planning restraint was recorded by two in five, and service provision and access or the location of the building by one owner in five respectively.

If financial support were available, 64 per cent of owners would consider providing low-cost housing from buildings surplus to requirements, for local people. It can be assumed that a number of owners with buildings in non-housing use might be keen to explore alternative, more profitable, development opportunities. Of the owners who expressed a preference, the vast majority said that they would rather make housing available for rent rather than for home ownership.

Table 6.2: Private landowners' local rent levels and council housing

Area	3-bedroom houses		2-bedroom houses		Local authority housing*
	Median rent £ per month	Number of owners £ per month	Median rent £ per month	Number of owners	Average rent 1999-2000 £ per month
Western Isles	218	6	140	3	166
Ross & Cromarty[1]	284	13	160	18	178
Caithness /Sutherland[1]	200	15	200	23	178
Aberdeenshire/ Kincardineshire	300	65	160	75	138
Renfrewshire /Ayrshire[2]	200	31	250	13	147
Inverness-shire[1]	230	74	250	30	178
Argyll/ Bute	200	29	200	24	158
Perthshire/Angus[3]	250	141	243	134	191
Central/Fife[4]	350	88	303	86	148
Orkney/Shetland	180	5	130	3	167
Dumfries + Galloway	220	95	180	66	149
Lothian[5]	300	36	225	54	135
Borders	200	103	180	86	137
Moray/Banff/Nairnshire[6]	200	26	250	45	153
Scotland[7]	249	734	200	652	152

Notes: All local authority figures are weekly rent figures, multiplied by 52/12; the averages (arithmetic means) are not adjusted for local authority house size.

[1] Local authority figure is that for Highland Council.

[2] Local authority figure is the average for East Ayrshire, East Renfrewshire, Inverclyde, North Ayrshire, Renfrewshire and South Ayrshire Councils.

[3] Local authority figure is the average for Angus and Perth and Kinross Councils.

[4] Local authority figure is the average for Clackmannanshire, East Dunbartonshire, Falkirk, Fife, North and South Lanarkshire, Stirling and West Dunbartonshire Councils.

[5] Local authority figure is average for East, Mid- and West Lothian Councils.

[6] Local authority figure is the average for the Highland and Moray Councils.

[7] Local authority figures excluding Aberdeen City, Dundee City, City of Edinburgh and Glasgow City Councils.

Source: Satsangi et al (2000, Table 3.7)

Incentives to make conversion and subsequent rental viable could take a number of forms. Owners declaring an interest in conversion were asked to rank the attractiveness of possible mechanisms, these being:

- Capital grant assistance
- Repair and improvement grants
- Treating house rental as a business, eg with respect to Schedule D and inheritance tax provisions

- Depreciation allowances
- Tax relief on capital gains
- Easier repossessions

The result was that owners had a very strong preference for direct capital grant.

Around one owner in ten said that they had sold some of their land for residential development during the last decade. A large purchase by one individual accounted for half of the sales. Sales to developers were five times as popular as sales to housing associations. Although there was some evidence of sale of land having been more likely on bigger holdings, there was no correlation between the amount of land sold and the size of the holding. It was estimated that land sales have resulted in the development of some 4,000 houses over the past decade.

Rather more landowners, however, indicated that their holdings had surplus land on which housing could be built. The responses showed that rural landowners might supply up to 26,000 acres of land for housing across the country. The main constraints on them doing so were planning restraint (46 per cent), financial viability (23 per cent) and service provision (19 per cent).

Owners were asked whether they thought there was a problem in the local availability of low-cost housing and 54 per cent thought that there was. Comparing responses with landowners' motives for renting housing, there was a clear association between the perception of a problem and 'support for the local community'.

Local housing market evidence of supply behaviour

Case studies were undertaken in order to examine with landowners, their agents and local housing bodies, issues regarding local rural housing markets and the behaviour of local landowners in relation to housing and land supply. Professional planning and housing staff were also approached for their views and for information on local provision, areas of housing need and opportunities and constraints on local housing provision.

To understand the opportunities and constraints for developing land and building supply the research sought to distinguish between different types of rural situation. Four area contexts were chosen so as to reflect diversity in housing demand conditions and to distinguish between accessible and more remote areas:

- *Type 1:* an accessible rural area, experiencing some indigenous and higher commuting economic growth pressure, with constrained land supply.
- *Type 2:* an accessible rural area, experiencing commuting economic growth pressure, with a stable/declining indigenous economic base.
- *Type 3:* a remote rural area, experiencing housing market pressure from second and holiday home-ownership, with a stable/improving economic base.

- *Type 4:* a remote rural area, with static/declining economic base, with housing market pressure from second and holiday home-ownership.

Eight case study areas were chosen, with two case studies fitting each of the four types identified above. The areas chosen were:

- *Type 1:* West Aberdeenshire, Speyside and Nairn
- *Type 2:* Borders, Lower Nithsdale
- *Type 3:* South Skye, Oban and Lorn
- *Type 4:* Mid Ross, Lochgilphead

The case study areas only partially coincide with local authority local administrative area boundaries, although reference is made to such boundaries in the discussion of the context for housing markets in the case study areas.

This section is a discussion of the similarities and differences between the case studies in the four areas. Key themes are identified that relate to local rural housing markets, and the behaviour of local landowners in relation to housing and land supply. The material is analysed in two sub-sections: the first takes each pair within each area type and discusses the similarities and differences between them; the second is a summary of the main points arising from a comparison of the four area case studies.

Looking at the case studies as pairs

Type 1

Both case studies featured communities where commuting and income levels were comparatively high, and other areas where local industries were less buoyant, and where local wage levels were relatively low due to dependence on the primary sector and on seasonal tourism. Both areas featured high demand for both expensive and 'affordable' housing, both rented and bought.

It was surprising to find a high degree of support from local landowners for providing affordable rented accommodation for local people. Even though landowners could, theoretically, rent their properties at higher prices, they often chose not to do so in order to privilege access for local people, particularly if they had families. This reflected landowners' concern for the maintenance of local continuity and the role of local families, and those of new residents, in keeping community facilities such as the local school open. They were also aware of difficulties for locals in low-income brackets in entering the home ownership market where prices were inflated by influences beyond the local economy; however, they were cautious of subsidising home ownership in these circumstances as the buyer could then sell on the open market.

Landowners unanimously said they preferred letting to people in employment, although this was not the only criterion in choice of tenants. In Speyside, and closer to Cairngorm, there was a particular problem for temporary, migrant, and low-paid workers in the tourism sector.

Landowners in Type 1 were markedly more aware than others of the local economic and housing situations, especially in pockets of intense growth pressure. Most were interested in developing in a cautious way income from house rental or land sales, against the common rural backdrop of decline in the agricultural sector.

Most landowners had been approached by local housing bodies, as well as by individuals seeking housing. They were keen to provide land and housing and to explore new ways of working in partnership with agencies, especially for new build projects. It was found that most estates in Type 1 had already thought through and explored development and grant possibilities, and that the empty properties remaining on their estates required much higher rates of capital and other grant support to make it financially viable to renovate them. Virtually all Type 1 area landowners were clearly aware of land that could be developed, and were prepared to allow the building of affordable housing in return for planning permission and support for housing development. This matched Type 1 landowners' expectations of a higher rate of net return from housing investments. However landowners in this group were also more critical of 'restrictive' local authority housing and planning policies.

Most Type 1 area landowners also wished to retain influence in allocation of local affordable housing, and in property development rights. Few had the capital resources to build for new so preferred to supply land and to maintain ownership of that land.

All were critical of policies that allowed the sale of public housing stock, especially if housing/land was acquired which was sold for lower than market prices. In conclusion, while mindful of estate business priorities, landowners in Type 1 areas were informed about local supply difficulties, had explored grant mechanisms, and made some provision for lower paid and local populations, and were willing to participate in affordable housing provision programmes providing their business interests were not compromised at a later date by housing and land speculation.

Type 2

Landowners were well aware here of locally depressed employment sectors and wage levels, and of buoyancy created by better waged commuters. This resulted in no homogenous view of how estates could develop housing possibilities. Landowners realised that commuters were likely to wish to buy properties, but problems had been widely experienced by estates in getting planning consent to renovate such properties for sale and some expressed disagreement with planning policy for rural housing. Landowners were also faced with the dilemma of whether to sell or rent out good estate accommodation; they did not want to be left with only poor quality housing, as there was perceived to be little market and grant structure to help with the substantial costs of renovating poor stock.

Landowners were aware of pressure for accommodation from lower income groups and generally they were supportive of keeping estate accommodation tenanted, especially by local people and by families, because of perceived links between their 'social responsibilities' and support for local facilities and populations. Many landowners had already carried out minor repairs on letting properties, but most had mainly properties that required serious financial input, and in the absence of a buoyant, high-priced rental market, this was seen as uneconomic.

All landowners were concerned about the downturn in the agricultural sector, and this resulted in a tension between supporting local, low-paid populations and developing the estate as a more diversified business, charging higher rents. Landowners however were less aware than Type 1 landowners of grant mechanisms, partly because they had no pressing need to access them, and partly due to a lack of approach or information from the local authority. But some landowners did express strong interest in developing housing for rental, particularly given the downturn in the local economy and limited opportunity and prospects to develop the economy. Landowners agreed that there was adequate subsidised housing.

Type 3

In both areas the 'improving local economic base' was in fact strongly related to tourism activities and other generally low-income jobs. This meant a supply of low-paid jobs and resultant pressure on low-cost home options of renting or buying. Tourism also brought in second or holiday home ownership, further exacerbating the low availability of affordable housing. Estate owners were well aware of local housing problems. They reacted by supplying their own estate workers with housing first, to ensure labour supply. Landowners expressed a preference to let to local people where possible, especially if they were in employment. Rents were reported to be set for locals at lower levels than market prices, and circumstances were frequently taken into consideration in both letting decisions and rents. Estates were willing to bring derelict stock back into the housing rental market, but lack of substantial grants meant that major improvements were uneconomic.

Landowners were also willing to sell land for home ownership. Again, they were interested in low-cost provision of homes, but were keen to retain land rights so that the estates did not pass on the development value of their property to another individual, especially when the local building plot and housing markets were very buoyant.

All the landowners had discussed housing provision with local housing bodies. In Skye no grants had ever been received. In Oban and Lorn only one landowner had successful obtained a repair grant. In Skye local housing bodies have proactively approached estate owners regarding land and housing provision. In both areas such bodies and estate owners have reached a good compromise, where one opportunity to develop is sanctioned if another low-cost opportunity was made available. As in the Aviemore area of Speyside, intense pressure in Sleat has resulted in proactive approaches to landowners, with signs of success. In Skye, Highland Council has implemented its Empty Homes strategy, and progress is beginning in this.

Type 4

As in the other areas Type 4 area estates are strongly affected by the agricultural sector decline. This has in some cases increased the business focus of estates on diversifying income sources, to include letting properties for market rent. However, all landowners rented property to locals at lower rates; this was a key feature of Type 4 area estate housing policy. This resulted, however, in lower improvement and investment in housing stock, because rental income was reduced.

Landowners were aware of pressures created by second and holiday home ownership; in Mid Ross the winter let problem was exacerbated by the influx of winter let 'victims' from other areas. Many estates commented that summer lets did not generate sufficient income to support local people at locally affordable rents. Estates reported lower expectations of return on their housing portfolios, with rates of return down to 2 per cent in one case.

Some landowners had accessed grants, but thought them insufficient to develop dilapidated housing on estates. Much interest was expressed in a better grants system and in better information on grant support. Landowners thought that the majority of capital costs of redevelopment should be met through grants.

Landowners had sold land for private development by individuals. All of them said they were keen to support affordable housing, but the trade-off would be to have choice in selecting tenants and a ban on resale for profit.

Looking at the case studies overall

Common to all four area types is their rural situation, a history of dependence on the primary sector, and a related historical link with large, feudal landed estates. Population and local wealth in the population largely depends on diversification of businesses so that they overcome problems such as distance from markets, educational and work opportunities for different age groups, shortage of skilled labour, training, and a lack of social amenities. Housing development, and landowners' positions regarding their involvement in the provision of low-cost home options, is clearly related to economic opportunity. Agricultural decline has led to an increase in most areas of properties requiring extensive renovation; but such renovation, along with new build, is not feasible for estates if economic prospects and markets are depressed, capital is difficult to access, and returns are not guaranteed. Increasingly, estates are run as businesses that seek to cover costs, if not make a profit; and while this creates potential for affordable housing development through partnerships with agencies and better grant systems (and landowners are actively supporting local communities), it is still the landowners' view that the onus is on public agencies, not landowners, to plan more generally for society.

The rural nature of all of the areas above makes them popular with tourists. There are also in all four areas high rates of second or holiday home ownership and dependence upon seasonal, low-paid and often part-time work opportunities. Where local income is low, this dependence on tourism is particularly negative in terms of a resulting lack of affordable, year round housing opportunity and of land affordable development opportunities.

The most significant variation between the areas was the nature of local housing markets, but they all had pockets of depression and, to varying degrees, of 'boom', or at least of activity spurred by high demand. Types 1 and 2 differed from 3 and 4 in the degree of presence of economically active and comparatively high income residents: they, it seems, could swim in the tides of home ownership with greater ease and get higher quality accommodation than could those people more typically found in 3 and 4, who relied on low-cost housing. In Type 1 areas landowners were perhaps more likely to be aware of specific local needs, were more likely to be interested in development and already involved in this, and were more likely to have thought through development opportunities and grants. They were also more likely to have been proactively approached by housing development bodies, especially when economic development depended upon better, appropriate housing supply.

What is particularly striking about all four areas is that landowners as a group are almost universally positive towards local people and the local area, and are keen to be socially responsible people, not just towards estate employees and tenants but towards the wider community. Allocation policy in most cases makes local tenants equally if not more desirable. Rents are never privileged over general issues of reasonably low thresholds of affordability. Landowners share the need to diversify estate income away from traditional forms of agriculture to, for example, the rental or housing plot market.

Landowners are willing in all cases to participate in affordable housing schemes, but not in cases where low-cost homes can be sold on and therefore removed from the affordable homes market. They prefer the option of renting buildings to developers of housing rather than the option of outright sale of buildings or land, especially in areas of demand. They also wish to retain some of their traditional influence over who tenants are in new affordable housing projects on their estates. Given their vocal support above for accommodating local and low-income new residents, as well as private home owners, this is not perhaps such an unfair request as it might at first seem, particularly if allocation can be agreed in partnership with public housing bodies.

There was a big variation in views of the potential of proposed land reform legislation on estate objectives and their role in housing provision. One view was that estates had to be viable businesses; another view was that agricultural coverage was a major issue and if this were to be changed significantly the estate as a unit could not continue. It was generally felt that the proposed land reform legislation was not (at least yet) a significant factor in encouraging landowners to develop their estate's role in the provision of housing. A strong sense of social responsibility and stewardship continues, despite major changes in the nature of rural communities.

Conclusions

It is clear that across rural Scotland, exemplified in our case study areas, a relatively high percentage of rental housing is owned privately rather than by public or social landlords. This means that landowners' housing supply decisions are particularly significant. Landowners providing rented housing to employees, former employees or others with no direct connection to an owner's main business have an extremely important role in local communities. Across the country, our survey and case study data show that many landowners would concur with the view that "... housing is ... the single most important issue in the sustainable development of rural Scotland" (Scottish Office, 1998, p 41). At the same time, however, as housing to rent is rarely the *major* source of business income for landowners, it quite clearly forms an important source for many.

This point has important resonances across the country (and in England; see Chapter Five). Constant across rural Scotland, for each of the area types, has been a decline in primary sector employment – in arable and cattle farming over a period of decades, in forestry rather more recently. A concern for all estates has been to bolster the profitability of their prime activities, or to adopt a deliberate policy of diversification of income sources. In less remote areas, estates have been able to use the combination of high locally generated demand and demand from commuting and in-migration to develop rental housing as one income source. All estates recognise tourism, employment-related and holiday home pressures on the housing market. Across the areas, however, there is a degree of reticence to reliance on income from housing. In the more remote areas, estates have had greater difficulty developing income from letting houses. It is important for all of the estates, particularly those with higher proportions of tied housing, that housing development should not detract from their prime activities. It remains to be seen, however, whether, or in what amended form, estates can survive sustained recession.

Maintaining and encouraging the development of local communities is most strongly exemplified in the clear preference among owners to let housing to local people. Very commonly, rent levels for local people are lower than open market rents. This shows that most landowners' behaviour towards rental housing does not fit with idea of the profit maximising investor. In this respect, this study corroborates other research, that a complexity of behavioural factors underlies private rental supply decisions (Kemp and Rhodes, 1994).

Generally landowners regard their housing role as being complementary to the social housing agencies rather than being a substitute for them. Landowners invest a significant amount of time in finding suitable tenants, in many cases to create social balance, often so that school rolls can be maintained, in some cases to fill fairly remote houses, and generally to reduce management and maintenance problems. There is no evidence that landowners or factors fail to meet the equal opportunities standards that are incumbent on social landlords. But it is clear that there is a reluctance to let housing to benefit-dependent households.

Across Scotland, housing development opportunities are available through upgrading vacant houses, the reuse of surplus/redundant buildings and the development of surplus land. This study shows that lack of financial viability is the major constraint on redevelopment, and many owners in higher demand contexts have canvassed support from local housing providers. In lower demand situations, it is acknowledged that redevelopment for housing is unlikely to be a viable option. Much more attractive would be development to facilitate local enterprise growth and improve housing quality. The evidence suggests that given changes to grant regimes, new supply could be encouraged. In addition, the study points to willingness on the part of landowners to consider local partnership arrangements with public or voluntary agencies.

The evidence clearly suggests that owners are not averse to considering land sales or development. Indeed, a significant number of owners have made recent sales. The fact that these have been small scale probably suggests that any future sale or partnership development may be small scale too. The net effect of new development in small communities may, nevertheless, be significant. The inability of estates to finance development from their own resources is a major constraint. In addition, the postal survey and case study interviews both highlighted a perception that local planning policies were overly restrictive.

The study has added to the slim body of research evidence available on private landowners' housing supply behaviour. New research questions will inevitably arise from land reform, particularly whether a more diverse ownership structure will lead to different attitudes towards housing and community development.

Acknowledgement

I wish to express my thanks to Scottish Homes and the Scottish Landowners' Federation for having funded the research and for consenting to quotation from the published research report. The views expressed in this chapter are my own and may not coincide with those of the sponsors.

Note

[1] Since the completion of the research, Scottish Homes has been replaced by Community Scotland.

SEVEN

The nature of tenancy relationships: landlords and young people

Diane Lister

Introduction

This book is concerned with the private rented sector (PRS) in a new century. However, the focus of this chapter is upon 'the oldest, most common, and perhaps because of it, the most neglected of contractual relations' (Englander, 1983, p 4) – those between private landlord and tenant. This chapter is specifically concerned with current relationships in the PRS between the main providers of accommodation, that is, individuals operating on a small scale for whom landlordism is not their main occupation, and the main consumers of accommodation – young people under the age of 25. The discussion presented here, rather than exploring exceptional or extreme behaviour in the sector, centres upon the typicalities of day-to-day relationships between the parties and how they manage interactions and exchanges with each other.

The role that the PRS has played in accommodating British households has changed significantly during the 20th century. At the beginning, the PRS catered for generalised housing need with 90 per cent of the population renting privately (Kemp, 1992). However, the sector has declined considerably over the century. The reasons for this decline are widely documented elsewhere (see, for example, Kemp, 1997) and it is not within the scope of this chapter to detail the trend other than to highlight that in 1998/99 the sector comprised approximately 10 per cent of all households (McConaghy et al, 2000) and now performs a specialised role in providing accommodation to young and mobile households, particularly those on low incomes (Kleinman et al, 1996; Rugg, 1999).

Following successive deregulation in the 1988 and 1996 Housing Acts, the PRS has become increasingly regarded as a transitional and residual sector (Rugg, 1999) particularly in association with its role of housing single young people and vulnerable households. Although the sector is small, it nevertheless performs a crucial role in providing accommodation for young people who have become "the key demand group" (Kemp, 1993, p 72; see also Chapters One and Two in this volume). Secondary analysis of the Survey of English Housing 1996/97

at this point are likely to set the general tone of the relationship and affect its relative success. In addition, this stage is, in some instances, the only time where landlords and tenants meet together face to face to discuss issues relating to the property and the terms of the tenancy relationship.

Interactions and exchanges between the parties at this stage, although outside of the scope of legislative provisions, are underpinned by a number of key legal assumptions. Classical liberal conceptions of contractual relations assume that each party is able to negotiate on equal terms and enter into relationships as legal equals, having successfully reached an agreement that satisfies the interests of both parties. These claims receive further support from the provisions of the 1988 Housing Act, which deregulated the PRS with a return to free market conditions and placed the role of negotiations at the centre of relations. Since the 1988 Housing Act came into effect private agreements free from the dictates of excessive statutory regulation can now be entered into while the parties, during their discussions, aim in theory to "maintain an equitable balance between the[ir] respective interests" (*Hansard*, House of Lords, 24 October 1988, col 1343). However, it does not automatically follow that relationships are constructed in circumstances that provide for equality. These assumptions of equality are based upon an idealised conception of behaviour which fails to recognise the social context of relationships encompassing power differentials, personal abilities, bargaining skills and inequalities in the market – factors which affect young people, given their age, inexperience and financial resources.

During this formative stage of tenancy relationships a number of legal, social and financial issues need to be clarified and confirmed through discussions and negotiations – for example, the terms of letting agreements, rent levels and arrangements for repairs services. The outcomes of these discussions provide the basis for the evolving relationship between the parties. However, the views expressed by both young people and landlords suggested that, in practice, levels of participation in the bargaining process were limited and relationships were not entered into equally, based upon the product of fruitful discussions. Instead, legal, social and financial arrangements were rarely negotiated or discussed. This was hardly surprising considering that for the most part landlords and young people rarely sought information or advice prior to entering into legally binding arrangements (Lister, 2001). As a consequence, they entered into relationships with incomplete knowledge of the legal framework and a lack of awareness of their basic rights and responsibilities and so failed to realise that the terms of the tenancy relationship itself, including rent levels and the contents of letting agreements, were open to discussion and negotiation rather than being 'fixed'.

The research revealed that both financial issues and those relating to the contents of letting agreements were rarely discussed or negotiated by the parties. In terms of financial arrangements, both landlords and young people regarded the initial payment of a deposit and a month's rent in advance as an inevitable feature of the setting up phase of the tenancy. Landlords simply assumed that young people would comply with these financial requirements and did not expect them to negotiate. Indeed, negotiating the amount or the method of payment was not common among young people, and landlords' requirements were generally accepted without question even where financial hardship was evident. Young people commonly stated that they did not contemplate negotiating because landlords did not appear amenable to discussions and that "it was pretty much set in stone, the rent, so there was no room to manoeuvre on that really".

The views of landlords supported the perceptions of young people in that they were loathe to negotiate on rent and deposits because "you'll let it anyway", and they expressed the attitude that having already told prospective tenants what the rent was "there's no need to go into further discussions about it because it's already been sorted out". Where tenants attempted to negotiate with landlords, it was perceived as denoting financial insecurity and a potential risk. As one landlord stated: "I'd be gravely suspicious if they hadn't got that amount of free money, they probably couldn't afford it anyway". In addition, where landlords felt they were being altruistic and, for example, required less than a market rent and/or a low deposit, or where the rent included bills, negotiation was out of the question as "they [tenants] know where they are well off, don't they? They're not going to negotiate anything".

Similarly, the statements made by both landlords and young people suggested that the latter rarely had an active role or a direct influence upon the contents of letting agreements – none of the young people interviewed had negotiated the contents with landlords. The main reason cited by young people for failing to negotiate was that they were not given the opportunity to do so as the agreement was "fixed" or the landlord simply "presented it" and "we just took what he'd laid down". Landlords expressed unyielding and inflexible "take it or leave it" attitudes and expected that young people would simply accept the terms of agreements, and "if they're not happy they don't sign it" and were free to find alternative accommodation.

In addition to landlords' uncompromising attitudes, young people also recognised other factors affecting their ability or willingness to discuss and negotiate important issues. A number stated that their financial circumstances constrained them. This was particularly the case for those in receipt of housing benefit who often had little choice but to accept landlords' terms in a competitive rental market where they struggled to find a 'sympathetic' landlord who would accept them. Other factors mentioned, which prevented young people from entering into discussions with landlords, included the length of time spent viewing the property, the circumstances in which the viewing took place, as well as forgetfulness as a result of 'feeling stressed'. The data also indicated that although tenants had the opportunity to ask questions they did not always possess the confidence or the appropriate skills to do so. Furthermore, where they were able to articulate their concerns, they were often reluctant during the initial sensitive stages of relationships because they were unsure of the responses they would receive from a landlord.

A number of factors, such as shyness, embarrassment and the personality of the landlord also contributed to hampering discussions. In addition, tenants often found it difficult to articulate their queries effectively, during face-to-face meetings. This was evident with young people, including students, seeking accommodation individually or in groups, where communication skills and social capital were not automatically transferable from one sphere of relations to another. Lack of knowledge and foresight about points to clarify with landlords were evident, particularly with inexperienced renters. A student explained his experience of viewing a property for the first time, where group solidarity did not facilitate confidence or skilled discussions:

> "We didn't know what to ask. We wrote a list of what we were going to ask the landlady and on the evening I don't think we asked any of them. It's not good practice. We were all nervous, there were five of us and we were all trying to talk to her at the same time and we didn't really make much sense of any of it."

The bargaining process fails to take into account the personal, social and economic circumstances of individuals and severely limits the choices available to young people by reducing relationships to "a private matter with which they are expected to deal on their own and as best they can, no matter what their age or capabilities" (Harvey, 1964, p 12). In spite of optimistic legal assumptions that parties to a contract are free to negotiate on an equal basis, however confident and skilled young people appeared to be, they were evidently not in circumstances where they were free or able to negotiate with landlords on egalitarian terms. A prominent feature of this stage of the relationship was the non-negotiability of the terms of lettings. Shared understandings were reached between the parties only in relation to financial aspects as a result of landlords' assumptions and tenants' acceptance that these issues were non-negotiable. In this sense the setting up phase of the relationship is founded upon the basis of economic exchange, a minimal role for the legal framework and an enhanced role for social relations. Instead of relationships based upon mutual exchanges between the parties, landlords closely regulated and controlled the terms and conditions of young peoples' entry into the PRS, highlighting the importance of social practices over legal codes.

Tenancy relationships

Following on from the setting up stage, the prominence of social practices over legal codes was evident as landlords continued to exercise control over tenancy relationships through the frequency and quality of their interactions with tenants, in addition to controlling the circumstances in which interactions took place. Given the parties lack of knowledge of the legislative framework and the social construction of relationships, landlords were able to adopt a number of idiosyncratic management practices to ensure that tenants conformed to their perceptions of 'good behaviour' and used property appropriately. These practices inevitably varied depending upon landlords' orientations to letting, with some landlords becoming highly involved with tenants and their use of property.

The findings from the research indicated that throughout the duration of tenancy relationships, landlords were able to adopt a number of overt and covert strategies to control and regulate young people and their use of property. However, these strategies often conflicted with the few basic legal rights tenants possessed. A central, often unacknowledged, legal precept of all tenancy relationships is that landlords grant tenants' rights to 'exclusive possession' of property. This provides tenants with the legal right to exclude others from the property, including the landlord. Another, often unacknowledged, condition of tenancy relationships is that landlords promise to leave tenants in 'quiet enjoyment' of the property and, therefore, should not interfere with its use. In spite of the legal situation, tensions often existed between tenants' *possession* and landlords' continuing *control* of property. Although tenants pay for possession of property (Allen and McDowell, 1989), landlords nevertheless retain rights of ownership and can assert rights of control over the property and its use. The tensions exhibited between tenants' possession and landlords' control were symptomatic of the unwillingness or inability of landlords to fully relinquish their property to tenants, often still regarding it as a "personal possession" (Allen and McDowell, 1989, p 52) to be dealt with accordingly, without regard for the rights or well-being of tenants.

A key issue to emerge from the data was that "control rather than use is the essence of ownership" (Ryan, 1982, p 57). The basic rights that tenants acquired legally and by virtue of economic transactions were merely rights on paper as, in practice, they can be overridden by landlords. In addition, tenants cannot easily exercise or enforce their rights given their lack of security of tenure and the fear of loss of their accommodation, as well as the inaccessibility of the legal system, both financially and practically, to obtain redress. A relatively common feature of relationships was landlords "close surveillance of property" (Allen and McDowell, 1989, p 46) which took a number of forms, both overt and covert. Both forms interfered with tenants' use and enjoyment of property and proved equally problematic for young people to deal with successfully. Overt strategies of control took the form of landlords' direct interference with tenants' 'exclusive possession' of property and rights of 'quiet enjoyment' by repeatedly visiting the property without giving tenants warning. As a tenant described, "he'll come round like two or three times a week, just knocking on the door, in fact, at the beginning he even used to let himself in".

This type of unpredictable behaviour was often combined with attempts to control and regulate the ways in which tenants lived in the property, for example, by leaving notes and instructing tenants to clean it. Furthermore, landlords often perceived and described their young tenants as 'children' or 'boys and girls', and acted in loco parentis towards them, regarding them in a similar manner to their own children. Accordingly, where young people were perceived in this way, landlords had scope for a level of control that was unavailable in relationships with older tenants. Landlords were able to adopt a disciplinarian attitude and/or a supervisory role with young people, which was often based upon how they treated their own children, with the focus upon correcting tenants' conduct. One landlord described the nature of such disciplinarian management practices:"I don't believe in a distant landlord. I like to be involved. I like getting involved and I'm not frightened to get involved, it's just all part and parcel. If they do something wrong I play bloody hell".

Similarly, a number of landlords stated that they felt their 'role' was to 'train' and correct young peoples' behaviour so they would "learn the social skills that they'll need later in life". These attitudes highlight the coercive aspects of social exchanges between the parties. However, according to the accounts of the young people interviewed, such excessive levels of control and interference with their lifestyles did not contribute to their overall well-being and instead caused considerable distress and resentment. In addition, the conflicting priorities of the parties were evident, highlighting the difficulties faced by young people in achieving a relationship that 'works both ways' when landlords were able to misuse their authority in such a way that threatened tenants' basic rights

Landlords routine interference with use and enjoyment of property had a profound effect upon the quality of young people's experiences of living in the PRS. They attempted to respond to the control and authority landlords exercised over them in a number of ways. However it was striking that the strategies adopted were generally of a cautious nature and were not formal attempts to exercise their rights to 'exclusive possession' and 'quiet enjoyment'. This inevitably reflected the lack of security of tenure, economic insecurity and the competitive nature of the rental market. Young people used social exchange in attempts to articulate their rights as this was considered to be a less contentious mechanism than, for example, asserting legal rights, which might result in unintended consequences, such as being asked to leave the property. However, the use of social exchange was less effective in achieving desirable outcomes, given that tenants actions were subtle rather than direct and there were no guarantees that landlords would respond in an appropriate way.

Many young people expressed the views that they did not know how to deal with landlords' 'inappropriate' behaviour, recognising that situations were 'awkward' and that they 'should say something' but finding themselves unable to do so. Instead, the strategies adopted included calling landlords by their forenames and no longer offering cups of tea when they visited repeatedly and unexpectedly (for further details see Lister, 2000). These behavioural subtleties attempted to readjust the delicate balance of the tenant–landlord relationships, but such actions do not fundamentally change their internal structure or their overall quality. Instead, these types of strategies generally only served to make tenants 'feel better' while avoiding confrontations with landlords in order to ensure that already problematic relationship did not deteriorate further.

Covert strategies to control young people's use of property were also adopted by landlords. A key feature of these strategies was close monitoring of the property combined with the exercise of direct control over tenants' activities if necessary. A surprising feature of tenancy relationships was that a number of landlords chose to live near their tenanted properties or had friends living close by, in addition to being on good terms with neighbours adjacent to tenanted properties. A common practice was to make "sure neighbours [of tenanted property] have my phone number" so that landlords were informed of any problems, such as noise or nuisance, caused by their tenants. It was apparent from the interviews with landlords that careful consideration had been given about the advantages of living in close proximity and in a number of cases landlords had purposely purchased or built property to let in the same street or opposite their own homes. Landlords felt that tenants' behaviour was likely to be inhibited by their close presence and as a consequence tenants were unlikely to assert their full use rights over the property. Furthermore, if tenants' behaviour was not compromised, landlords were close enough to exert direct control and take more extreme measures, as one landlord who lived opposite his tenants described: "I go around every night between 11 and 12 and if there's anything happening anywhere, like somebody playing music so loud that it's going to keep people awake, I go and tell them to turn it down".

These interactions revealed the difficulties young people had in achieving satisfactory relationships, allowed them to enjoy their rights of 'exclusive possession' and 'quiet enjoyment'. The social context of relationships distinguish them from formal contractual arrangements and give rise to a number of difficulties with control remaining an integral feature of landlords relationships with young people. The data also highlighted the differing priorities between the parties in that landlords regarded their social relationships with tenants as a way to exert control, rather than as a pre-requisite to conduct reciprocal relationships. Ultimately, although motives may differ between landlords, the close monitoring of property equates with regulation and restriction of tenants activities and interferes with tenants' rights to use property and feel comfortable in their own homes. In addition, landlords' volatile and idiosyncratic behaviour highlighted the vulnerability and insecurity of young people, who found it difficult to deal with unpredictable social situations.

Leaving the tenancy relationship

It is evident that throughout tenancy relationships the law is not the most important factor in regulating exchanges and interactions between landlords and young people. Instead, social exchange is a more prominent feature with economic arrangements providing a basis for relationships to take place but rarely playing a significant role. Furthermore, a key issue to emerge from the data is that, in spite of assumptions of equality, young people enter into relationships from an inequitable position and they, by and large, continue to occupy this position throughout the duration of relationships. This remains the case during the final stages where landlords exercise control over the circumstances in which young people leave relationships.

The encounters described above, such as repeated visits to the property, demonstrated how landlords' behaviour and management practices can have a profoundly negative impact on young people, the circumstances in which they live and their experiences of independent living. The enduring impact of landlords' actions and control, as well as the *lack* of control young people perceived they had over their environments and interactions with landlords, were often cited as reasons why they wanted to find alternative accommodation as soon as the fixed term of their tenancy expired. Although some young people voluntarily left relationships, their decisions to leave were as a result of feeling 'driven out' because they were unable to enforce their day-to-day rights effectively, rather than prompted by positive 'pull' factors to move. Regret was expressed by a number that "it could have been a really fabulous house but it was just totally marred by the attitude of the landlord" and that they were 'forced' to leave after exhausting all of their available resources to restructure relationships successfully. A student tenant evaluated her first experience of living in the PRS and described how she felt "driven out of a perfectly nice house" as "the landlord just grinds you down 'til you just give up and we thought 'We're leaving now and we'll never deal with him again and we've learnt from the experience', but you do kind of give up".

Although finding alternative accommodation was a rational response to difficulties perceived as too onerous to resolve, the true miseries of the situations endured were not conveyed to landlords. This was partly as a result of simply 'giving up' and also because of landlords' continuing authority over young people and a reluctance to make a problematic relationship deteriorate any further and run the risk of retaliatory actions, such as deposits being withheld. Furthermore, young people generally remained hopeful that they would find a 'better landlord' or 'somewhere nicer to live' and achieve a more satisfactory relationship. Moving appeared to be used as a 'last resort' and the high rates of mobility in the sector among under-25s – 75 per cent of such households in 1998/99 were resident in PRS accommodation for less than 12 months (McConaghy et al, 2000) – may be explained to some extent by the unsatisfactory nature of their relationships with landlords.

The circumstances in which young people were asked to leave tenancy relationships were closely controlled by landlords using a range of methods to regain possession of property that conflicted with tenants' legal rights. In contrast to the procedural simplicity of setting up relationships, ending them is complex, requiring compliance with specific and detailed legal procedures. Given the lack of knowledge of the legal framework displayed by landlords throughout the tenancy relationship, social practices dominated the way in which the leaving process was managed. The assumption that ownership of property bestowed upon landlords' certain rights to deal with tenancy relationships as they saw fit regardless of tenants' rights was a feature of this stage in the relationship. Once landlords experienced problems with young tenants, for example with rent arrears, they began to assert their perceived rights, often adopting a patriarchal approach towards and using their own age, status and authority in order to persuade and advise tenants to leave their accommodation. By adopting such subtle approaches landlords were able to mask the use of unlawful methods and unequal power to gain possession of property and legitimised their interventions on the grounds of preventing the situation worsening for tenants. One landlord described such an approach: "I got them over here and spoke to them [about rent arrears] and pointed them in the direction of alternatives. I didn't actually [end up with rent arrears] because I stopped it soon enough and asked them to leave [during the fixed term]".

Furthermore, a number of landlords did not regard the difficulties they experienced with tenants as legal issues, but instead "describe[d] legal problems in terms of social relations" (Conley and O'Barr, 1990, p 61). In these situations landlords perceived problems with tenants not as a conflict about rights over property but as a personal dispute where the law was inapplicable or did not coincide with their desired outcomes, and so they preferred to deal with them according to their own principles and ideas of justice. Landlords felt entitled to regain possession of property where tenants had not performed their obligations and they explained the simplicity of ending tenancies by 'just asking that this person didn't come back' or by 'throwing them out'. Although tenants' rights were infringed by landlords failing to use the correct legal procedures, it was practically possible to end tenancies in this way as young people were, as discussed above, often unaware of their legal rights. In addition, tenants generally assumed that landlords' practices were a true reflection of the law and so were unlikely to challenge landlords' requests for them to leave, particularly when they felt they were 'in the wrong' − if they had, for example, accumulated rent arrears.

Only a small number of landlords were aware of the legal procedures they should follow in order to take possession of property; however, they recognised that following these procedures placed constraints upon their control over property. Landlords were particularly concerned to avoid court proceedings because of the lengthy timescale involved and the financial costs. Negative perceptions and experiences of the law, as well as the unlikelihood of being challenged when using unlawful methods, influenced the approaches landlords adopted towards gaining possession of property. Knowledge of the legal framework and of the disadvantages associated with 'doing everything the right way' resulted in landlords becoming adept at assessing particular situations and choosing when to use and when to avoid the law As one landlord described: "If you need to invoke the law then you've got problems because of the time in getting people out. I use the law when it suits me and I override the law when it suits me".

The ease with which informal procedures can be adopted given the unlikelihood of prosecution for unlawful eviction inevitably contributed to misuse of the law in order to accelerate possession. Faced with a legal system which rarely penalises unlawful behaviour and which is considered to be inefficient and unresponsive by its 'users', landlords have little incentive, other than moral probity, to adopt formal legal procedures. Hence, inappropriate behaviour "in a quiet way behind the scenes" (Harvey, 1964, p 9) achieves landlords desired outcomes without the frustration, delays and costs. This final stage of tenancy relationships has highlighted the continuing tensions between the legal framework, the freedom of landlords to control their property and the limited ability of young people to assert their rights. At this stage in relationships the enduring impact of the levels of control exercised by landlords, during the whole relationship, has profound implications for young people. As a response to being unable to achieve a satisfactory relationship, young people chose mobility; where they remained past the fixed term, control over the circumstances in which they left their accommodation was easily exercised by landlords. The data also revealed the unregulated nature of property letting where a variety of illicit practices can be adopted and go unnoticed, making it difficult for young people to maintain relationships given landlords' unfettered claims over property.

Conclusion

This chapter has explored some of the everyday and mundane experiences of landlords and young people over the course of tenancy relationships and has shown how the parties rarely engaged with or understood the legal framework. The encounters and exchanges discussed do not reveal extreme behaviour but nevertheless are important as they have highlighted a range of uncomfortable and awkward situations faced by young people and the difficulties they have in enforcing their rights about day-to-day issues, given the unregulated nature of the sector. The discussion in this chapter has focused upon the dominance and control that landlords, during the three stages of the tenancy relationship, exercised over young people, who had little control or choice about the ways in which such relationships were conducted. A central feature of tenancy relationships was the way in which landlords' sentiments of ownership and possessiveness were expressed via control and regulation over tenants and property. These sentiments were demonstrated by the importance landlords attached to property rights over the rights of tenants, the use of social relations to achieve desired outcomes, and by overriding the law when it did not provide an acceptable or adequate remedy.

The chapter has also revealed the types of behaviour and relationships that are possible in a competitive rental market given the limitations of the legal framework and has also shown that current modes of redress and enforcement of rights are inadequate. The discussion has not been concerned explicitly with the policy implications of the relationships between landlords and young people, but they are important and the views of the landlords and young people expressed here are central to considerations about the law's effectiveness in dealing with problems between the parties and as a medium to enforce rights and protect interests. There is substantial evidence from the data that the parties are not equipped to negotiate and enter into legal arrangements on equal terms and it is apparent that landlords' actions fall outside of the scope of self-regulation, as they remain unaccountable to their tenants. The current legal framework in the PRS prescribes the nature of relationships between contracting parties, but fails to adequately provide for the realistic attainment of such ideal exchanges. As a consequence, there is scope for rethinking the current role of regulation in the sector in order to encompass the day-to-day activities of the parties. In addition, further implications relate to, for example, the structures and processes that need to be in place to enable both parties to exercise and enforce their rights, rather than placing the onus upon tenants to seek redress when landlords breach the terms of contracts.

EIGHT

Unlawful eviction and harassment

Jill Morgan

Introduction

The law protects residential occupiers against harassment and unlawful eviction by criminalising both activities, and by enabling a person who has been harassed or unlawfully evicted to claim damages or reinstatement through the civil courts. Harassment can take a wide variety of forms, and perceptions of what behaviour by a landlord constitutes harassment and what is reasonable may be interpreted quite differently by the other actors involved: tenants, local authority officers, the police and magistrates. Their understanding may not accord with what is covered by legislation, and they have "a considerable amount of discretion in interpreting landlords' behaviour, the severity of the case and how it should be dealt with" (Marsh et al, 2000, para 3.3).

The number of prosecutions for unlawful eviction and harassment is, and always has been, low given that they are "persistent problem[s] seemingly endemic within this residualised sector in which understanding of the consequences of letting is often poor and respect for the law limited" (Stewart, 1996, p 101). As a result, there appears to be a widespread assumption that the law on harassment and unlawful eviction is ineffective. The purpose of this chapter is to consider whether such criticism is justified, bearing in mind the rights and interests of the actors who operate within it, including the statutory security of tenure system to which they are subject.

Background

The most heavily regulated housing tenure has been the private rented sector. As demand for rented housing generally outstrips supply, the landlord is usually in the stronger bargaining position. It is this inequality which led to government intervention in the relationship, in particular to protect the tenant from rising rents and eviction. From 1915 until 1988, "the Rent Acts ... constituted an interference with contract and property rights for a specific purpose – the redress of the balance of advantage enjoyed in a world of housing shortage by the landlord over those who have to rent their homes" (per Scarman LJ in *Horford Investments Ltd v Lambert* [1976] Ch 39 at 52). In general, however, such

to carry out necessary repairs or starting but not finishing them, and sending abusive or threatening letters (Marsh et al, 2000, para 3.4). What in isolation may be comparatively minor actions can accumulate and cause the occupier considerable anxiety and distress.

The offence of harassment takes place where "any person with intent to cause the residential occupier of any premises to give up occupation of the premises or any part thereof; or (b) (a) to refrain from exercising any right or pursuing any remedy in respect of the premises or part thereof,

- does acts likely to interfere with the peace or comfort of the residential occupier or members of his household, or
- persistently withdraws or withholds services reasonably required for the occupation of the premises as a residence" (section 1(3), 1977 Protection from Eviction Act, as amended).

Two changes were made by the 1988 Housing Act that, theoretically, should have made prosecution more readily achievable. First, as regards the existing offence, the word '*likely*' was substituted for the word '*calculated*' by the 1988 Housing Act. The offence is now easier to establish, but still requires an intent to cause occupiers to give up their occupation or to refrain from exercising their rights. Second, for the purposes of establishing harassment, it had been difficult for the prosecution to prove that the landlord specifically intended to cause the occupier to leave, rather than just make life unpleasant in the hope that he or she might decide to go. To counter these problems the 1988 Act introduced s. 1(3A), creating an offence that can be committed only by certain individuals, that is, the landlord of the residential occupier concerned ('landlord' being defined as including any superior landlord (s.1(3C)), or an agent of the landlord. The *actus reus* is identical to s.1(3); the only difference being the mental state. Whether or not the landlord intended to cause the occupier to leave is not relevant; what matters is whether a reasonable man (having at his disposal the facts known to the landlord) would believe the occupier to be likely to give up possession as the result of the landlord's behaviour. This lowering of the evidential burden, however, has not led to any noticeable increase in the number of prosecutions

Before going on to consider the operation of the legislation, especially its enforcement through the criminal process, it is important to give an overview of both the place and perceptions of tenants and landlords in the private letting sphere.

Profile of the private rented sector

The private rented sector no longer caters for general housing needs in the way it once did. Most residents in the sector are under 25 and use it as 'easy access' accommodation, moving regularly (ONS, 2000), and thereby "[contributing] to a healthy economy by assisting labour mobility" (DoE, 1995, p 20). In the majority of cases, they will be assured shorthold tenants. The private rented sector is often a first stage for young people leaving home, and is commonly regarded as the first rung on a housing ladder up which households progress through a hierarchy of tenures to owner occupation (Kemp et al, 2001, p 22). Yet it also houses a significant, albeit shrinking, group of older householders. About 20 per cent of private sector tenants are aged 65 or older and 8 per cent have lived in the same house for 40 years or more (DoE, 1995, p 20), dating back to the time when private renting was a mainstream housing tenure. Such tenants are still likely to be covered by the Rent Acts and thus subject to a form of rent control and security of tenure.

What is particularly significant from the viewpoint of unlawful eviction and harassment, however, is the change that has taken place in the social composition of the sector. Particularly in areas where there is lower demand for rental accommodation from working households, it is increasingly the preserve of vulnerable households with complex social or behavioural problems who are in receipt of housing benefit. It is that part of the sector which local authority officers most closely associate with issues of harassment and unlawful eviction (Marsh et al, 2000, paras 2.5, 3.71). Around 756,000 occupants in the private rented sector rely on housing benefit to pay all or part of their rent (111,000 Rent Act tenants and 645,000 'deregulated' assured or assured shorthold tenants (Office for National Statistics, February 2001). It follows that 'the dynamics of the sector are intimately affected by changing the structure and generosity of the benefit system' (Marsh et al, 2000, 2.4). In the early 1990s, households who would be in priority need under the homeless persons' legislation accounted for around half of all harassment and unlawful eviction complaints made to local authorities. People from racial minorities were disproportionately affected, as were single parents and households with low incomes in receipt of housing benefit (Jew, 1994, p 9). Since then, the housing benefit system has been subject to a number of changes, which have imposed further strains on landlord and tenant relations. The level of rent payable through housing benefit has been limited with reference to circumstances within the local private rented sector; housing benefit payments to single people under the age of 25 have been restricted; pre-tenancy determinations have been introduced to ascertain, before a tenancy agreement is entered into, how much housing benefit is payable on the property (with the unlikely aim that tenants, armed with such information, can seek to renegotiate the asking rent); and, since October 1996, benefit is now paid four weeks in arrears for new tenants (see Chapter Three for detail on the impact of housing benefit). The most recent innovation has been the introduction of the verification framework (in an attempt to prevent benefit fraud), which requires claimants to prove their identities and provide detailed information – including the presentation of original documents – to support their claims. The average delay in payment is five months (National Housing Federation, news release, 15 June 2001). Not surprisingly, rent arrears, the housing benefit system and delays in possession proceedings are the most important specific triggers for unlawful action by landlords (Marsh et al, 2000, para 3.96).

Landlords become involved in the private rented sector for a variety of reasons and they will have different ways of operating in it. In the early part of the 20th century when private renting formed the principal source of housing, institutions such as insurance companies were major landlords. Between 1960 and 1980, spurred on by the shift towards owner occupation and the emergence of other types of investment which could be used as a hedge against inflation, most corporate and institutional investors broke up and disposed of their rental portfolios, selling either to private landlords or into owner occupation. Thus, while a minority of private landlords are property companies (which may also have interests in business and office accommodation and in property dealing and development), private letting is a small-scale industry which is dominated by private individuals. In this respect, therefore, it has changed very little and has not been subject to the trends towards concentration and centralisation witnessed in other areas of the economy (Kemp, 1992, p 17). More than half of all landlords in England rent out only seven homes or fewer. Over a quarter have only one letting, and many became landlords by, for example, inheriting a property, or having difficulty in selling one, or needing to move away temporarily for reasons associated with work. Others have entered the sector as an investment, but have done so only recently through 'buy to let' schemes (DETR, 2000, para 5.9).

When the 1965 Rent Act was passed, profiteering commercial landlords were thought to be the main culprits as regards unlawful eviction and harassment. However, the Milner Holland Committee on Housing in Greater London concluded that the type of landlord guilty of such conduct "... bears little resemblance to the big business stereotype" and that "... relatively few abuses can be attributed to companies" (Holland, 1965, pp 256, 260). As such, the law on harassment and unlawful eviction rarely affects the ways in which commercial landlords operate because harassment has never been a common business practice (Nelken, 1983, p 8). It is most relevant to small landlords who are often ignorant of their own obligations and of tenants' rights. Unless they employ the service of managing agents (and even then the "standards of competence and probity" of those agents vary greatly: DETR, 2000a, para 5.3), small landlords are less likely to vet tenants before they accept them and are more likely to conduct their arrangements on an informal basis (Nelken, 1983, p 12). Even where private landlords seek legal advice, the understanding of housing law possessed by many solicitors in private practice ranges from "inadequate to non-existent" (Burrows and Hunter, 1990, p 17).

There should usually be no need to recover possession from the tenant where rent is paid, the amount payable updated regularly, and the property maintained in a reasonable condition. Where, on the other hand, tenants fail to meet their obligations, the difficulty and/or expense of removing them may be a nuisance for commercial landlords yet, on the whole, they can either afford to tolerate them or to remove them – either via the legal process or by offering a financial incentive. For small landlords, however, far more is at stake and often, for them, "property ownership must include physical control if it is to mean anything, especially once they are in dispute with their tenants" (Nelken, 1983, p 19). This too has implications for what both tenants and landlords may perceive as acceptable behaviour on the landlord's part.

In the days before ASTs made such steps unnecessary, even business-oriented landlords, or their managing agents, often found it preferable and more profitable to try to circumvent the Rent Acts and thereby retain a greater degree of control of their properties (Nelken, 1983, p 19). One popular avoidance measure was to grant tenancies that were specifically exempted from protection, eg holiday lettings. As a result, landlords who could show that their tenants were 'holiday-makers' were given the opportunity "... to operate in the uncontrolled free market" (Lyons, 1984, p 286). Not surprisingly, this led to "... a remarkable boom in holiday lets in places not noted for the quality of their waters or the mildness of their sea breeze" (Widdison, 1982, p 29). By the early 1980s, Rent Act evasion and avoidance had become so commonplace that there was conjecture as to whether the Acts had any practical relevance at all (Doling, 1983). The main conclusion of Nelken's classic study of unlawful eviction and harassment was the success with which the response to Rachmanism – including the 1965 Rent Act – "reflected and reinforced established boundaries of propriety and impropriety in the use and abuse of property rights" (Nelken, 1983, p 27). Thus, harassment – which was generally associated with small landlords – was "the only malpractice to emerge from the Rachman scandal which deserved to be treated as a crime" while others, such as the use of, for example, 'holiday' lettings to evading security of tenure remained legal.

Enforcement and compliance

The police do not normally intervene in cases involving allegations of unlawful eviction and harassment unless physical violence is involved. Even then they prefer to rely upon 'ordinary' criminal offences such as assault, obstructing a police officer, conduct likely to provoke a breach of the peace or criminal damage (Ashworth, 1978, p 77). It has even been suggested that a lack of awareness and understanding of the law on unlawful eviction and harassment has led to police officers sometimes actually assisting landlords in evicting tenants illegally (Jew, 1994, p 11).

Following the criminalisation of harassment and unlawful eviction, the Francis Committee recommended the establishment within local authorities of tenancy relations officers (TROs) to implement the unlawful eviction and harassment provisions of the 1965 Rent Act and to police the private rented sector, investigating complaints and either settling disputes or collecting the necessary evidence to support a prosecution (Francis, 1971, p 111). However, local authorities were never placed under a statutory duty to employ TROs nor to investigate complaints of harassment or unlawful eviction. Consequently, tenancy relations services have developed sporadically, and some authorities have failed to provide any service at all (Strudwick, 1991, p 9). It is worth noting, however, that failure by a local authority to introduce policies, procedures and services to deal with harassment and unlawful eviction may result in a finding of maladministration by the Local Government Ombudsman (Commission for Local Administration) (see complaint numbers 86/B/852, 89/A/1230, 89/A/1581, 90/A/1356 and 94/A/3711). Very often the task of dealing with harassment and unlawful eviction complaints is given to other officers within local authorities, including environmental health officers, homeless persons officers and members of the legal department. Some authorities have contracted out the tenancy relations role to independent agencies such as local LSVT (large-scale voluntary transfer) housing associations or housing advice centres (Marsh et al, 2000, para 4.11). Wherever the precise location of the tenancy relations role, however, local authorities rather than the police may be regarded as the regulatory agencies charged with the responsibility of enforcing the law on unlawful eviction and harassment.

The low number of prosecutions for unlawful eviction and harassment, already referred to, is sometimes seen as proof that the law in this area is ineffectual, but such a view fails to take into account that, especially in the regulatory sphere, the nature of 'enforcement' encompasses far more than prosecutions brought. Two essential strategies or systems of enforcement may be identified: sanctioning and compliance (Hawkins, 1983). The former relies upon formal action and the imposition of sanctions, while the latter (which appears to be the primary system of enforcement used by regulatory agencies involved in, for example, consumer and environmental protection, housing and industrial health and safety) takes a more holistic approach, relying upon negotiation, education, advice and – as a last resort – prosecution as ways of securing compliance.

One feature of regulatory offences is their continuing nature which, together with the method of detection used, leads to enforcement officers and their 'client group' developing bilateral relationships. By contrast, 'conventional' crimes (such as assault or theft), tend to be discrete events, and the relationship between police officers and offenders is equally limited to detection and arrest (Rowan-Robinson et al, 1990, p 231). Harassment may be of a continuing nature but there is not the same ongoing scrutiny by TROs of landlords' activities as there may be by, for instance, health and safety inspectors of factories. Nonetheless, TROs may incline to mediation rather than prosecution because of the increasingly important role played by private landlords in providing housing for homeless applicants and the consequent development of a mutually reliant (and potentially beneficial) relationship between private landlords and local authorities (particularly where tenants are in receipt of housing benefit). Indeed, the Code of Guidance issued by DETR to local authorities on the Allocation of Housing Accommodation and Homelessness (currently under review) points out that "an authority will benefit from building up contacts with reputable private landlords to provide a readily accessible service" and highlights the powers that authorities have to incur expenditure on rent deposits and guarantees to private landlords to help people secure accommodation in the private sector (para 21.24(b)). The change of emphasis from prosecution to preventative work – through conciliation and mediation – may be evidenced by the practice in some local authorities of locating tenancy relations functions in the homelessness section. However, homelessness is not always the driving force behind a local authority's private rented sector strategy. It may also be concerned to improve the condition of accommodation in this sector, to bring empty properties back into use, and to instigate area regeneration (DETR, 1998b), all of which will be facilitated by the development and maintenance of a workable relationship between the two sectors.

Another feature of the compliance model is the emphasis placed upon the educative function of the regulator. Advising a tenant can help that individual but education of landlords in their responsibilities and the correct procedures they should follow in, for instance, evicting a tenant, can have a greater potential impact because it may affect the experiences of several tenants. (Marsh et al, 2000, para 4.24). From the viewpoint of enforcement, regulators may regard offences as stemming from ignorance rather than intentionality. Given a perceived role as the instruction of those regulated on the nature of their statutory responsibilities, it is hardly surprising to find a reluctance to prosecute (Rowan-Robinson et al, 1990, p 208). As Hutter (1988, p 179) explains:

> It is only when offenders are perceived to align themselves with more 'traditional' criminal behaviour – such as a blatant or intentional disregard of the law, or violent or hostile actions – that it is felt appropriate to redefine them as 'criminal'.

Obstacles to identification of breaches

In spite of the tarnished reputation that private landlords have historically endured (and not infrequently deserved), the 'official' view tends to be that despite their "ordinary human instincts of kindliness and courtesy, [they] may often be afraid to allow to a tenant the benefit of those natural instincts in case it may afterwards turn out that the tenant has thereby acquired a position from which he cannot subsequently be dislodged" (per Sir Raymond Evershed MR in *Marcroft Wagons v Smith* [1951] 2 KB 496 at 501). The recent Green Paper sees most private landlords as "... basically well-intentioned and anxious to do a good and responsible job" and, mindful of the "... great mass of legislation" with which they have to come to terms, sees their lapses from the law as stemming from inadvertence rather than intentionality. It also points out that they may "... fall victim to irresponsible or unscrupulous tenants. In short, to raise standards and prosper, they need encouragement, support and education rather than further heavy regulation" (DETR, 2000a, p 45).

Regulatory agencies in areas other than housing are often faced with rule-breaking which consists of morally problematic states of affairs, and this is another reason why they may adopt a compliance rather than a sanctioning strategy. According to Hawkins (1983, p 67), the latter is appropriate "... only when the officer is confronted by behaviour possessing moral features aligning it with forms of traditional criminal conduct". Although some acts of harassment may accord with traditional notions of criminal activity (eg physical violence), others, given the ambivalent feelings generated by the surrender of control over the property which has been let, may not have the taint of criminality at all, such as serving invalid notices to quit. During the past decade unprecedented political and media attention has been focused on anti-social tenants in the social rented sector. As a result, perhaps, there has been an increasing awareness that landlords do not have a monopoly on unacceptable behaviour. Moreover, the changing nature of the tenant population in the private rented sector – in which "increased poverty, hard drugs and deinstitutionalisation" (Marsh et al, 2000, para 3.71) all play a part – means that infringements of 'normal' tenant behaviour are more likely to occur. Acts of harassment may be 'legitimated', therefore, by transgressions on the part of the tenant – for example, nuisance and annoyance, especially in houses in multiple occupation, which provokes complaints by other tenants or neighbours to the landlord, requiring him or her to take action – or non-payment of rent.

Of course, the problems and pressures of private renting are writ large in the context of resident landlords, for whom control over what is, after all, their own home is particularly important. The resident landlord exemption – which removes tenants of resident landlords from the full protection of the Rent Acts and denies them any protection at all under the 1988 Housing Act – was introduced to encourage owners to let spare rooms in their homes confident that "… they will be able to recover possession at the end of the contractual tenancy (as they may very understandably wish to do so should the tenant prove incompatible)…" (*Barnett v O'Sullivan* [1995] 04 EG 141,143 per Hirst LJ). It was also intended to avoid "… that sort of social embarrassment arising out of close proximity which the landlord had accepted in the belief that he could bring it to an end at any time allowed by the contract of the tenancy" (*Bardrick v Haycock* [1976] 31 P&CR 420, per Scarman LJ). Occupiers who share any accommodation with their landlord or with or a member of the landlord's family have no security of tenure and are not even entitled to the limited protection afforded by ss.3 and 5 of the 1977 Protection from Eviction Act (see above). About 1 household in every 100 has lodgers (DoE, 1995, p 204) but, in a recent DETR study, most local authority officers admitted to having only the vaguest idea of what was going on in this part of the sector:

> Most authorities felt that tenants of resident landlords considered themselves to have so few rights that they did not seek help when they encountered problems. Where local authorities had experience of cases involving a resident landlord there was often a personal element to the dispute – the fact that the parties were not getting along was a key issue – and the local authority became involved when it was clear that landlords were not following the correct process for removing a tenant. (Marsh et al, 2000, para 3.78).

Indeed there are other circumstances restricting the chance of identification. Whereas most regulatory agencies are made aware of transgressions by carrying out routine inspections, harassment and unlawful eviction are generally only brought to the attention of TROs by the victims themselves. However, victims may not be aware that any offence has been committed or that there is legislation and an enforcement mechanism to afford them redress. Even if they are, they may be reluctant to come forward.

Many unlawful eviction cases arise from informal, verbal tenancy agreements (Carter and Dymond, 1998, p 49). Before the changes effected by the 1996 Housing Act, a landlord wishing to grant an assured shorthold tenancy had to serve notice on the prospective tenant, and nearly all AST agreements were in writing. Since the relevant part of the 1996 Act came into effect, no prior notice needs be served and an AST can be created verbally. The then government resisted attempts by the Opposition to require landlords to provide a written tenancy agreement for all shortholds but did concede the right to a written statement of certain terms of the tenancy when demanded by the tenant. This, of course, puts the onus on tenants, many of whom are unlikely to be aware of their entitlement to a written statement. As Cowan neatly puts it, "Paper has a particular currency for tenants" (Cowan, 2001, p 254), and it may well appear to many tenants that an arrangement so easily entered into can be terminated with equal ease and lack of formality (see Chapter Seven).

Indeed, recent research on behalf of the DETR revealed a basic belief by many landlords that they have complete control over the property they let and are able to exercise rights of entry and possession regardless of the tenant. The climate of deregulation and the various changes in the law regarding possession and security of tenure has, if anything, encouraged this belief. It showed that many tenants are unclear as to the kind of tenancy they have and do not understand the implications of this for their security of tenure, the grounds on which landlords can ask them to leave, or the required procedure for doing so. Many are aware that a court order is necessary to evict legally but others assume that the landlord's word would suffice (Marsh et al, 2000, paras 2.15, 3.39, 3.65). As Cowan (2001, p 254) points out, the knowledge which tenants have of their rights will clearly affect their perception of what amounts to an "injurious experience". Moreover, actual physical violence appears to be rare (Jew, 1994, p 15), and with tenants seeming to associate harassment with 'strong arm tactics', they may not therefore identify lesser acts of harassment as criminal. Further, even where tenants are aware that they have been the victims of an offence and are willing to make a complaint to the local authority, they may be reluctant to give evidence and there may be no other witnesses, credible or otherwise, to corroborate their version of events.

Also important is the reason why tenants come forward in the first place. Often they simply wish to be rehoused by the local authority. If this occurs, there is no obvious reason for their continuing to be involved in a prosecution. If they are not rehoused, because perhaps no other alternative accommodation is available, they remain vulnerable to reprisals by the landlord. Assured shorthold tenants may feel that it is not worth their while to take matters further. If it is only a short time before the tenancy ends anyway, many tenants will silently endure their landlord's criminal actions in the hope that the tenancy will be renewed. As a result and, not least, because harassment often results in the tenant being in a constant state of fear, the majority of incidents and offences remain hidden, unreported to statutory authorities (Jew, 1994, pp 21-2).

Difficulties of bringing a prosecution

Local authorities generally prosecute wherever there is any real chance of success but the prosecution process is hedged about with problems. Authorities sometimes have difficulty in discovering the landlord's true identity or address. Other constraints include the difficulty of proving the case, the delay between the initial complaint and the court hearing, the time spent by hard-pressed local authority officers in preparing the case and in court, and what is widely regarded as the inadequacy of the sanctions the courts impose.

Unlawful eviction is relatively easy to prove but harassment is more problematic. First, the examples of harassment given above may be "... acts likely to interfere with [the residential occupier's] peace and comfort" or the withdrawal or witholding of services, but it is often difficult to prove that the perpetrator of those acts has the requisite of state of mind, that is, the intent to cause the residential occupier to give up occupation as a result. Second, the harassment may consist of a series of incidents which, if viewed separately may be relatively minor; but only when taken together does the severity of the situation become apparent. The criminal law, however, is generally organised to deal with specific incidents and is often less effective where the totality of what is happening is more than the sum of its parts. Third, prosecutions may fail because the charges as framed did not convey to the court the real nature of the alleged offence. This will be a particular problem where there is no corroborative evidence – and that in itself will often be difficult to obtain where there is a long delay between the commission of the alleged offence and the court hearing (Burrows and Hunter, 1990, p 59). In a minority of authorities the decision to prosecute is made by a council committee, which causes further delays in processing complaints (Jew, 1994, p 11).

Each of the offences under the 1977 Act is triable either in the magistrates' or Crown Court. On conviction in the magistrates' court they are punishable by a fine up to level 5 on the standard scale and/or to imprisonment for up to six months. Conviction in the Crown Court carries an unlimited fine and/or a maximum of two years' imprisonment. In *R v Brennan and Brennan* (1979) Crim LR 603 (in which the landlord accompanied by a "... very large man and an Alsatian dog" evicted a group of students from their rented premises), it was said that "loss of liberty should be the usual penalty where landlords use threats or force, in the absence of unusual mitigation". It appears, however, that "... many judges and magistrates fail to take harassment and unlawful eviction seriously and to punish it to the degree it warrants" (Marsh et al, 2000, para 5.45). It has been suggested that, although heavier fines may well be imposed where there is evidence of financial motivation, the low level of fines generally imposed may discourage authorities from instituting criminal proceedings (Nelken, 1983, p 9).

Limited impact of the civil remedy

Given that "the criminal system is hardly employed" (albeit for understandable reasons), it might be expected that the occupier might be "effectively compensated through the statutory tort" (Cowan, 1999, p 444). This, created under the 1988 Housing Act, was heralded as "an important additional deterrent to harassment" (DoE, 1987, p 3.17). It gives the residential occupier a right to sue the landlord, or any person acting on the landlord's behalf, for committing an act which amounts to one of the criminal offences of unlawful eviction or harassment, and which has caused the occupier to give up occupation of the premises as a residence. The remedy, under section 27, does not replace the traditional causes of action in tort and contract which can still be used where, for instance, the occupier did not give up occupation or has been reinstated, or had little or no security of tenure so that the damages recoverable would be low. Although local authorities may encourage tenants to pursue the civil law route, because of its relative speed and effectiveness (including the lower standard of proof), many tenants cannot afford to do so and may experience difficulties in obtaining legal aid.

Another area of concern regarding the civil law is the level of damages awarded. By section 28 the measure of damages is the difference in value, as at the date when the residential occupier left the premises, between the property with the occupier in it and the property with vacant possession. In other words, it is the profit that the landlord stood to make by acting unlawfully, whether or not in fact he or she makes that profit. Stewart (1996, p 102) describes this as a "private law approach, which attaches monetary value to the tenants occupancy" and it seemed initially to have added an effective new weapon to the occupier's armoury, the courts awarding relatively high sums in some early cases (eg £31,000 in *Tagro v Carfane and Patel* [1991] HLR 250). However, as it is the right of occupation which is to be valued, the eviction of someone with a lesser right, such as an assured shorthold tenancy, or a tenant who has only a few days of the tenancy remaining, will produce a lower amount of damages than an assured or protected tenant with full security of tenure. In *Melville v Bruton* [1996] EGCS 57, the Court of Appeal made it clear that the purpose of the 1988 Act was not so comprehensive as to provide damages for evicted tenants in all circumstances but only where the eviction has materially increased the value of the landlord's interest.

Conclusion

Private renting is seen as a central plank in the housing policy of 'New' Labour, which has made it clear that it will not reintroduce rent control, nor change the present structure of assured and assured shorthold tenancies, which has made it easier for landlords to gain possession. The government sees it as "working well" (DETR, 2000a, Green Paper). For many people the private rented sector represents a temporary stage on the route to home ownership, and more positive images, both of private landlords and of private renting, are now more commonplace than they were a decade ago (Kemp and Keoghan, 2001, p 34). Nevertheless, it still houses many disadvantaged members of the community, a large proportion of whom are non-nuclear households on low incomes and dependent on housing benefit, who will never be in a position to achieve owner occupation. It is not now, as it was once and remains elsewhere in Europe, a source of accommodation for large numbers of middle income, middle class people who can afford to look after their own interests.

Before the 1988 Housing Act, many landlords sought to avoid or evade the Rent Acts but the devices they employed made it difficult to be sure exactly of the legal status of the arrangements and whether the legislation had effectively been side-stepped. The 1988 Act undoubtedly introduced a greater element of certainty but whether it has made any difference to unlawful eviction and harassment is open to question. As Cowan (1999, p 424) points out, it might be expected that "... in these post-Housing Act 1988 days of assured shorthold tenancies with their limited security and within the broader context of a move towards the 'casualization of housing' (Morgan, 1996)", incidences of unlawful eviction and harassment might have declined. What the 1988 Act has achieved, of course, is the replacement of insecurity via extra-legal means with legally sanctioned insecurity and, as history shows, it has been those with the least security who have been most affected by unlawful eviction and harassment. As Kemp (1990, p 152) maintains, "Rachmanism will not return because it never really went away".

Prosecution is central to a sanctioning strategy and "... as such it may well be used as an indicator of work undertaken and a sign of success" (Hutter, 1988, p 7). The number of prosecutions and convictions should not, however, be seen as the only indicator of how well the law is working. A rigorous prosecution strategy, together with the imposition of tough criminal penalties, might be a deterrent to some landlords who would otherwise be inclined to take the law into their own hands. However, many landlords are unaware that their conduct is criminal and it is hardly surprising, therefore, that mediation and education have become more important components of tenancy relations work with a strong focus upon the value of compliance.

NINE

Changing Rooms: the legal and policy implications of a burgeoning student housing market in Leicester

Martin Davis and David Hughes

Why Leicester?

Leicester is in many ways typical of current United Kingdom cities: culturally and ethnically diverse, yet retaining much of its traditional role as a market centre, and also supporting major sports teams. It has undergone considerable economic change during the last 40 years moving to a diverse pattern of activity now encompassing service and leisure provision, distributive trades, plastics, food manufacture – and higher education. Leicester has become a 'student city'. The city's population is almost 300,000. Leicester University has some 8,440 of its 16,929 students resident in the city or the immediately surrounding districts (1999 figures). De Montfort University had some 30,550 students in 1998/99, and over half of these were Leicester based. About one in ten of Leicester's population is a higher education student – and that figure is certainly met if the numbers of those in further education are added in. The considerable numbers of students in Leicester make a marked impact on the economic life and functioning of the city; they also generate a demand for accommodation. This has, to a high degree, been largely met by a rapidly reviving rented sector in housing – though it is clear that this revival is a developing phenomenon not simply dependent on the student market.

A little legal and policy history

Even before the expansion of the higher education sector in the 1960s, (Robbins, 1963) universities were generally unable to accommodate all their students domestically. There was a clearly established role for the private rented sector in providing undergraduate student accommodation either in the form of 'digs' or via the renting of flats and houses. The creation of a 'new wave' of universities in the 1960s and 1970s alongside that of the polytechnics, created increased demands for rented accommodation in university and college towns, a phenomenon noted in House of Commons debates where it was pointed out that at the University of Sussex half the students had to find accommodation off campus (*Hansard*, 1974(a)).

This chapter will consider student housing as it has since developed, with particular regard to Leicester, under two headings: 'provision' and 'governance'.

Provision

Institutional accommodation

Students occupying institutional accommodation have generally occupied either traditional 'catered hall' accommodation or 'self-catering' blocks of study bedrooms with associated kitchens. This has been the pattern in Leicester. From 1948 the then Leicester University College pursued a policy of building catered halls with resident wardens and senior common rooms. This pattern (repeated in many other university towns, and paralleled to a degree by accommodation provided by the constituent elements of the former Leicester Polytechnic) continued until 1970. Thereafter, institutional provision of accommodation in Leicester increasingly took the form of self-catering developments. Arguably, irrespective of whether meals, a warden and senior common room were provided, the accommodation remained an academic community where all residents were pursuing a common purpose and thus had a common interest in maintaining that order and freedom from noise and disruption which is of such importance for academic study (and to which we shall return when considering the issue of governance).

In *Groveside Ltd v Westminster Medical School* (1984) 47 P&CR 507, accommodation managed by the medical school (although owned by another) was expressly acknowledged by the Court of Appeal as representing part of the 'academic community' and as being distinct from 'normal' residential accommodation. Lord Justice Stephenson (at p 514) cited (seemingly with approval) the words of Judge McDonnell at Westminster County Court, to the effect that: "[The medical school]... provided the accommodation for the purpose of the education of students...[and]...for the benefit of the...school as a whole and the advancement of the general object of the education of the medical students." He also cited (again with seeming approval) evidence from the secretary of the medical school that the accommodation was provided "... to get better educated students by discussion amongst the school and by the development of [a] corporate spirit".

The private rented sector

Students have occupied – and continue to occupy – inner urban terraced, or immediate suburban semi-detached dwellings. The anecdotal evidence available to the present authors suggests that problems arising between landlords and student tenants have been generally classifiable as those stemming from fundamental misconceptions about the binding contractual nature and legal implications of the arrangement entered into; those concerning disputes over repairs and/or the provision of furnishing items; and arguments over liability for breakages and so on and the return of deposits. But law has played but little part in the day-to-day relationships of students and private landlords. The latter have been happy to let to the former knowing they would only be in occupation for a year or so, while students have been willing to put up with less than optimal conditions, or unwilling to complain about defects, sometimes because of fear of the landlord, sometimes because: "the landlord is a nice man really, and we don't want to bother him". The general impression has been that, from a *legal* point of view, the pattern of relationships, and any difficulties arising therefrom, was not markedly dissimilar to that prevailing in the non-student lettings sector. This impression is supported by the limited amount of empirical research that has been undertaken in relation to the private rented sector (Thomas et al, 1995; Crook and Kemp, 1996a; see also Harloe 1985).

A changing national pattern of housing provision for students?

Observable changes in the pattern of students' lettings have occurred over the last seven to eight years. These have related both to the identity of landlords (where there has been an increasing corporate involvement and, in the case of private individuals, use of letting agents) and to the character of properties let. We shall examine this issue in the context of Leicester, but first the factors driving change at a national level have to be examined.

The first and most obvious reason for change is the massive increase in student numbers. Between 1979 and 1995/96, the total number of higher education students almost doubled to reach 1.5 million. Growth has been particularly marked since 1988. Between 1988/89 and 1995/96 full-time student numbers grew by 77 per cent; the numbers studying in the post-1992 'new' universities rose by 192 per cent. (Dearing, 1997). The new universities were, however, historically, the least well off in terms of their own student accommodation; though many are situated in inner urban areas, near to factories, mills, warehouses and office spaces made redundant by industrial change and relocation in the 1980s and 1990s. Both central and local government, in the pursuit of urban regeneration and sustainable development, have desired those redundant buildings brought back into use. In March 2000 the Department of the Environment Transport and the Regions (DETR) released *Conversion and redevelopment: Process and potential* (Llewelyn-Davies and The University of Westminster, 2000) which argued that some 18,000 to 26,500 additional dwellings could be provided each year in England by converting buildings and redeveloping existing housing. This particularly mentioned such development in university towns, and identified the potential for conversion of industrial and commercial buildings, particularly in larger towns and cities where the housing market is already strong, though it appears that the former DETR did not count student units of accommodation as contributing to the overall policy target of having 70 per cent of all new housing provided on brownfield sites. There has also been desire by local planning authorities to revive central urban areas by promoting what is somewhat euphemistically termed 'café society'.

The outcome in many places has been the growth, frequently by conversion of existing premises, of considerable numbers of large public houses and clubs. The growth of this 'night life' portion of the leisure trade has a synergistic relationship with higher education: academics involved in admissions know that a frequent question asked by university applicants is, "what are the pubs and clubs like?" The survey evidence also shows that 'night life' provision is largely aimed at meeting the perceived needs and wants of 18 to 25 year olds. (*The Independent,* 2000; Rugg et al, 2000; Benjamin, 2001).

To provide for the rather more domestic needs of students there has been an increase in the amount of purpose built and, more commonly, purpose converted accommodation created by the private sector.

Changes in Leicester

Through the cooperation of Leicester City Council the authors surveyed applications for planning permission to develop residential accommodation made between March 1992 and February 2001 within the five innermost wards of the city: Abbey, Castle, St Augustines, Westcotes and Wycliffe. Of 554 applications most fall into the category of small developments, for example applications to create one residential unit out of two or vice versa. However, 171 were for larger scale developments, though many of these were still comparatively modest. It also has to be remembered that applications made do not always result in developments being carried out, while it was also clear that many schemes figured in a number of revised forms.

Most applications were consented, albeit conditionally, 11 were withdrawn between 1992 and 2000, though some were later resubmitted as were several of the four that were refused. Of the 171 applications identified by us as for more substantial developments the majority, 94, were in Castle Ward – significantly the area closest to De Montfort University. Wycliffe ward which lies to the north east and east of the historic city core features next most prominently in proposals, and some residential provision may have been encouraged by proximity to Leicester University. The most obvious signs of major urban regeneration to date are to be found in Castle ward. This ward has also seen the investment of considerable sums of public finance, inter alia, to clean up derelict and contaminated inner urban sites such as the former scrapyards and railway land known as Bede Island North. This investment has 'levered in' private finance for a range of residential developments from student accommodation to family housing.

Of the 171 applications considered in detail a sizeable minority (44) were classified by the City of Leicester as 'DEV', that is, full permission, normally involving new building. The majority of applications were for a 'change of use', usually from offices or factories to flats. Applications in respect of former office buildings often related to permission sought for change of use of upper storeys only – the ground floors remaining in use as shops. Most applicants appear to be small-scale or independent developers. There has been little involvement by 'volume' house builders save, historically, for the large regeneration sites, though – particularly in more recent years – there is evidence that some larger scale developers are becoming involved in residential development in the area. Some applications may be received from developers using a number of company names, so that the actual number of applicants may be less than it appears to be. There are certainly a number of 'repeat players' among applicants.

Most requests for planning permission in the 171 considered in detail were for flat development. In some cases the application either specifically stated student accommodation was envisaged or 'cluster flats' were mentioned. These are found within the envelope of a larger building and consist of a number of bed-sitting rooms with shared toilet and kitchen facilities: they are appropriate to student accommodation. But clearly not all applications envisaged provision for students. 'C3 Flats' were mentioned in many applications. This means, in planning terms, that the flats are intended for use either by a single person or by people living together as a family, or by up to six residents living together as a single household; but clearly some such properties could be occupied by students.

Supplementing the survey of planning applications by a tour on foot of developments completed, particularly in Castle ward, enabled certain conclusions to be made. Development of flats has followed a diverse pattern; a considerable amount has taken place specifically for students. Equally, however, there has been a noticeable amount of general development of small units of accommodation; in the last years of the century this was complemented by developments of flats for sale on a long leasehold basis.

Leicester's housing has, during the 20th century, grown peripherally with, apart from minor developments in the decades of the 1970s and 1980s, no residential development in the historic core area (Nash and Reeder, 1993). That pattern has been substantially altered in the decade from 1990 onwards. Hundreds of bedroom spaces have been developed, primarily by the private rented sector. While these have not been exclusively student focused, they have been student led. The growth of the city's universities has had a catalytic effect, but in parallel to units for students there has also been provision made for single persons. The long leasehold portion of the market appears to be aimed at younger single persons or childless couples who desire to utilise central area amenities. The prices of long leasehold flats coming 'on stream' at the time of writing (summer 2001), ranging from £69,500 to £120,000, seem to indicate a desire to attract those ready to 'trade up' from renting, but who do not wish to move out to terraced or inter-war housing – in short the better paid young professional group. Clearly demand, in conjunction with appropriate planning policies and the limited security of tenure now enjoyed as a general rule by private rental sector tenants (see further below), has encouraged a major reversal of some residential trends in Leicester.

Governance

Throughout the 1950s and 1960s from a legal point of view most students were either licensees (people having a purely personal right to live in a property, for example as a 'paying guest' of the resident landlord), or tenants having no real security of tenure because of the furnished nature of their accommodation. Section 2(1)(b) of the 1968 Rent Act expressly excluded from protection tenancies under which a dwelling house was let at a rent including payment in respect of board, attendance or the use of furniture.

The position following the 1974 Rent Act

In 1974 a major revision of the Rent Acts was made which brought furnished dwellings into protection, and new rules had to be made for student lettings. The 1974 Act laid down that a tenancy should be excluded from security of tenure where it was granted to a person who was pursuing or intended to pursue a course of study provided by a specified educational institution, as long as the tenancy was granted either by that institution or by another specified institution or body of persons. That rule became Section 8 of the 1977 Rent Act, which empowered the Secretary of State to make regulations laying down who should be 'specified' institutions and bodies.

The power to create such 'exempt landlords' had not found its way into law, however, without controversy. While the changes made in 1974 were being considered by Parliament, attempts were made by the Conservative Party to exclude from security of tenure virtually all those pursuing courses of study or vocational training. These were resisted by the government, which was considering a system of registration of private lettings approved by specified educational establishments for student occupation; any such dwellings were to be exempt from Rent Act security of tenure. The government reiterated its commitment to its registration proposals, which were to be the subject of other legislation. (*Hansard*, 1974 (b)-(g)).

In April 1975 the Department of Education and Science (DES) and the Department of the Environment (DoE) jointly issued consultative proposals for a registration scheme. This was, however, resisted by the National Union of Students who apparently considered it discriminatory in favour of students. No further progress was made with the scheme proposal: instead a very limited range of institutions were granted exempted status as 'specified bodies' within the first regulations made under the 1974 Act. The Protected Tenancies (Exceptions) Regulations, SI 1974/1366, listed only universities, university colleges, constituent colleges, schools or halls of any university, certain colleges of education, certain further education institutions and designated polytechnics which fell within Section 42 of the 1944 Education Act.

The Protected Tenancies (Further Exceptions) Regulations, SI 1976/905, then began a process that has continued down to the present day, namely that of listing further bodies granting tenancies exempt from protection. These have been added on an apparently ad hoc basis, but they have had certain common characteristics being apparently either of a charitable or religious nature or being housing associations or housing societies.

The regulations were consolidated and were applied to the relevant exclusionary provisions of the 1988 Housing Act (Section 1 and Schedule 1, para 8) in respect of assured tenancies by the Assured and Protected Tenancies (Lettings to Students) Regulations, SI 1988 2236. The list then contained 20 names. The 1988 list was further amended by The Assured & Protected Tenancies (Lettings to Students) (Amendment) Regulations, 1989/1628. These provided that certain bodies or persons – whether incorporated or not – could be 'specified'. However, *nothing* suggested that commercial organisations were to be specified, and none apparently were.

The Assured & Protected Tenancies (Lettings to Students) (Amendment) Regulations, SI 1990/1825, introduced a measure of logic by inserting further new regulations under which *all registered* housing associations were stated to be exempt landlords with regard to student lettings, though it also continued the specific designation of particular bodies and organisations. Further minor changes and additions were made in 1991, 1992 and 1993; however, once again, there was *nothing* to suggest the inclusion of commercial landlords.

It is always tempting for students of housing policy to envisage a broad development of policy and its inevitable reflection in legal forms – that is, to see the law as 'the child of policy'. But it is arguable that, at least on occasions, matters are the other way round, and sporadic changes in the form and content of legal regulation may lead to policy changes in a less than well ordered fashion.

The authors' thesis is that since 1974, rather than pursue the notion of a list of registered exempt landlords drawn up in consultation with, inter alia, universities and colleges, the approach of government has been to add bodies in a piecemeal fashion to the list of 'specified bodies', the only major exception to this being the addition of all registered housing associations in 1990. Nevertheless those bodies have all been reasonably homogeneous in that they have generally either been educational, charitable, philanthropic or religious institutions, or subject to regulation by the Housing Corporation, or both. It may be that a number of bodies had to argue their cases for exempt status, and had to be approved as such by the relevant department of state. This, it appears from communications from central government to the authors, was the DES – as it then was. The ability for both law and policy to develop sporadically is a matter we shall return to below.

The current regulations

The Assured & Protected Tenancies (Lettings to Students) Regulations, SI 1998/1967, continue the pattern of their predecessors and grant blanket exemption to universities and colleges, registered housing associations and a number of specific organisations – some 23 in all. The most recent amendment to these regulations (SI 2000/2706) continued the previously well established trend of adding educational landlords to the list of those enjoying exempt status by designating SOAS Homes Limited, which, of course, refers to London University's School of Oriental and African Studies.

To sum up so far

Students living in the 'exempt' sector have no security of tenure; those who rent from private landlords historically enjoyed 'protected tenant' status while the 1977 Rent Act applied, but since the changes wrought by the 1988 and 1996 Housing Acts they have normally had the rather more limited form of security known as 'assured shorthold'. Even so from a legal point of view the distinction between the two groups has been an important one, and it has reflected what has apparently been policy that 'exempt' status should apply only to educational institutional landlords or those who are otherwise, to a degree at least, publicly funded and socially regulated, that is,. housing associations. However, in Leicester that long-established pattern once more has been challenged.

The new exemptions

In 1999 two further organisations were added to the list of 'specified bodies' in Schedule 2 of the 1998 Regulations, by SI 1999/1803 and by SI 1999/2268. In itself this might seem of little interest. The history of the regulations since 1974 is one of new organisations dedicated to student housing being periodically added to the list of 'exempt' landlords. However, closer scrutiny reveals much more interesting issues. Previously, as already stated, all organisations specifically exempted on the basis of being student landlords have been either educational, charitable, philanthropic or religious institutions, or subject to regulation by the Housing Corporation, or both. The policy underpinning the exemption is that it assists non-profit making organisations providing accommodation for students. Both new bodies are commercial private landlords, albeit ones who operate student-orientated accommodation with significant structural similarities to traditional university owned or operated halls and flats.

The authors' attention was drawn to this departure because both companies operate in Leicester, and a number of the authors' students live in one or other of the units operated by the companies. Both are situated in central Leicester, adjacent to the campus of De Montfort University; one is purpose built and stands on the site of the original home of Fox's Glacier Mints, the other is an enlargement of a former hosiery factory consisting of the renovated original building and a substantial new block.

There is, however, some history behind the development of both sites going back to 1997/98, and for the details of this the authors are indebted to Mr Harry Perry, Chief Executive of Leicester Newarke Housing Association (LNHA), which was at one time interested in the development of the sites. In the case of the purpose built block the owners made an initial overture to LNHA to explore the possibility of joint ventures for the residential redevelopment of a number of sites owned by that company in the central area of Leicester. LNHA was at that time in the course of redeveloping as a site for student dwellings land on Oxford Street in Leicester lying adjacent to the site owned by the company in question. A contractor had initially acquired the site in which LNHA were interested and was able to involve English Partnerships, the government's urban regeneration agency, in providing grant aid for its redevelopment. LNHA subsequently acquired the development using private finance, not monies from the Housing Corporation. This development led to discussions between LNHA and the neighbouring site-owning company. LNHA drew up a specification of a desirable development of that site. At this point, it appears, problems arose. The amount of grant aid offered by English Partnerships was limited, which led LNHA to fear a gap between the funding available and the development costs, with a liability to unspecified costs on LNHA's part. Those acting on behalf of the company were, however, able to rework the initial specification, which made the project financially viable within the grant aid available, and a planning application in those revised terms was made. The relationship between the two organisations ended at this point, and it appears the company then determined to manage the property themselves rather than 'build and sell on' as originally envisaged.

LNHA was also tangentially involved in the development of the former hosiery factory site. For a while the association employed a development manager who had considerable previous experience of student housing at The University of Central England in Birmingham and at Nottingham Trent University. The officer in question formulated development proposals for a number of former factory sites in Leicester, including the site currently under consideration. LNHA, however, at that point concluded that the proposed scheme for this site was too large, involving the refurbishment of a huge existing building, even without the erection of major new additions. It decided not to proceed with the development proposals. The officer in question not long afterwards left LNHA at the end of his contract. It appears, however, that the full scheme in respect of the site was kept alive, and that the owner as a commercial company was able to proceed with the scheme on a basis considered financially viable, with a significant injection of funding from English Partnerships.

In these developments students occupy 'study bedrooms' organised into flats of five or six rooms with shared kitchens, toilets and communal facilities: an arrangement nearly identical to that of accommodation built by De Montfort University recently. The university's administrative arrangements for accommodating new students appear to have incorporated the developments. This semi-institutionalises their position. No doubt such developments are taking place elsewhere, either by universities formally 'outsourcing' their accommodation (Mulholland, 2000, Crace, 2000) or simply informally incorporating privately run halls and flats into their accommodation literature.

The addition of these two private landlords to the list of 'exempt' landlords may seem to some unsurprising: are they not in much the same position as many other exempt organisations? However, that ignores the fact that, as a commercial companies, they are quite distinct from the other organisations which are charitable or philanthropic housing providers.

The consequent concerns

Once a body acquires 'exempt' status it is free from the constraints of the 1988 Housing Act with regard to security of tenure and rent control. Now nearly all 'normal' private sector lets to students are assured shorthold tenancies, so that true long-term security of tenure is rarely present, but even an assured shorthold tenancy guarantees at least six months initial security (1988 Housing Act, section 21(5), as amended by the 1996 Housing Act), and a limited challenge to rents in the first six months of the tenancy can be made. (1988 Housing Act, section 22(2), as amended by the 1996 Housing Act). Moreover, assured shorthold tenants have a legal right to a written statement of specified 'core' tenancy terms. (1988 Housing Act, section 20A, as amended by the 1996 Housing Act).

None of these rights apply to an 'exempt' tenancy, which is governed by the common law, as modified by the 1977 Protection from Eviction Act. Admittedly, even an 'exempt' landlord needs to serve a valid notice to quit (one in writing and giving four weeks notice) to commence valid possession proceedings (section 5) and needs to obtain a court order before evicting a tenant who ignores the notice (section 3). Oddly, however, the standard agreements of both the companies in question state prominently that: 'no court order is required to end [your tenancy]'. The companies appear to have overestimated the width of the exemptions that they have acquired.

However, overall, the legal position of a student occupying a property owed by an exempt landlord is precarious. A valid notice to quit has to be served, and a court order obtained, but there is no effective defence to a landlord's wish to repossess at any time.

Perhaps the position of universities and other bodies traditionally given exempt status justifies their strong legal hold over the accommodation that they operate. Arguably they need to have flexible powers over admission to, and removal from, their properties, for example to remove disruptive students and to preserve the 'academic community'. But is this justifiable in the case of private landlords? The authors do not ask this to question in any way the integrity of the two companies who are both entirely reputable and who certainly provide a much-needed service for students. The authors' concern, rather, is with the legal and policy making processes.

Nationally there may be other landlords in position analogous to that of these two companies in Leicester who now have exempt status. The DETR suggested to us that the extension can, perhaps, be justified on the basis that '[the organisations] are providing student accommodation on behalf of educational establishments'. But does not this explanation imply some kind of formal, near-agency, arrangement between De Montfort University and the companies? Currently none such is in force.

More worrying from a legal point of view is the fact that exempting private landlords via statutory instruments is achieving, by means of regulations, an exemption for student landlords which was rejected in Parliament in 1974, and which has never been raised since in parliamentary debate.

A wider policy issue

The authors wrote to the then Parliamentary Under Secretary of State for Lifelong Learning, Mr Malcolm Wicks, at the Department for Education and Employment (DfEE), whose responsibilities included higher education and who signed the statutory instruments in question on 31st October 2000. The authors asked whether the designation of the companies "represents any change of policy with regard to lettings to students towards a policy of greater exemption from control for specialist providers of student housing".

The ministerial response

This was dated 29 November 2000 and stated, inter alia:

> The decision last year to grant specified body status to [the companies] does not constitute a change in our policy towards student lettings. As you may know, these Regulations are designed to maintain and encourage reasonable turnover of student accommodation by allowing certain bodies and higher education institutions, registered social landlords and other specified bodies exemption from the provisions relating to assured tenancies. We included these two commercial organisations in the regulations, after consultation with the DETR, simply because they provide student accommodation on behalf of higher education institutions.

A number of points follow from this response:

- It was accepted that the companies in question are commercial organisations. The authors therefore reiterate that they are, to a clear degree, different from other exempted landlords as their motivation in providing accommodation is profit led, though it is again stressed that this does *not* question the integrity, honesty or management standards of the companies, nor the quality of the accommodation they offer.
- No general change in policy was intended. This was confirmed to the authors in a further letter from the DfEE on 25th July 2001. However, the authors ask whether a model has been established to which recourse could be had for future policy change on either a wholesale or piecemeal basis.

- The statutory instruments relating to the companies were made only after internal consultations between the DETR and the DfEE, the justification being that there was in the circumstances of these two companies a sufficient similarity to other exempt landlords because of their provision of student accommodation on behalf of higher education landlords.

Arguably both of the companies have a strong 'local connection' with Leicester and Leicestershire in terms of their foundation and incorporation, and certainly both meet very real student accommodation needs. However, there appear to be no formal links between either company and De Montfort University, nor any formal nomination scheme. In the summer of 2001 the university was, however, pursuing nomination arrangements with a number of landlords.

Earlier in this chapter the authors examined the history of the exempting regulations. The list of exempted bodies grew sporadically and only over a period of time did a general policy emerge in a regulative form that exempt status was appropriate not just for the universities and colleges, but also for non-profit making landlords such as housing associations. On a 'me too' basis could other commercial bodies argue an analogy with the two companies here in Leicester in that they also are primarily providers of student accommodation? Second, if that analogy can be made will there be an incremental development of policy under the form of law?

The policy questions for the future

Provision

It is clear that in Leicester favourable planning policies, aided by the liberal (so far as landlords are concerned) regime on security of tenure following the 1988 and 1996 Housing Acts, coupled with market demand for city centre residential accommodation – in which student demand has a catalytic effect – have led to a major turnaround in the fortunes of the private rented sector. Considerable provision is being made for the student-age and immediate post-student-age groups, the 18- to 25-year-olds, and even beyond that in terms of the new long leasehold schemes coming on stream. The long-term issue that Leicester (along with other cities) has to face is whether other age groups should be encouraged to move back into the city centre to ensure the creation of a balanced and sustainable community. To do that needs more than just the creation of units of accommodation, bars, restaurants and sports clubs: it needs, for example, the provision of schools, healthcare and dental facilities.

Governance

Within the private rented sector two legal regimes are found, often existing almost side by side in rather similar types of development. Students renting from exempt landlords are effectively without any form of security of tenure or rent control: something enjoyed, albeit to a limited degree, by those (irrespective of educational status) who rent from private landlords. The policy justification for this is arguably the need to ensure 'educational landlords' have flexibility of management to remove disruptive occupants and to protect public investment in student accommodation provision. However, it is clear that this policy emerged over a period of years and was extended only incrementally to registered social landlords. Furthermore private landlords, it can be argued, may have just as great a need to expel any disruptive tenants. Meanwhile in Leicester the granting of exempt status to two private landlords calls in question the 'public investment' basis for the policy.

If students are to continue to be treated as a special group for security of tenure purposes, there is a strong argument for going back to the proposals last debated in Parliament in 1974. It is not acceptable, without public debate, for policy in this area to be made incrementally as a consequence of the drawing up of individual items of statutory regulation by ministers. We need new legislation to enable the creation of a locally arrived at and properly regulated system of exempt landlords.

TEN

The Scottish system of licensing houses in multiple occupation

Hector Currie

Introduction

A common concern in Scotland, England and Wales has been the inadequacy of existing statutory powers to regulate and improve standards and safety in houses in multiple occupation (HMOs). Over many years, argument and debate have been engaged about the need for stronger legislation, particularly the licensing of HMOs, to deal more effectively and consistently with the diverse problems posed by badly managed and maintained HMOs.

Throughout the 1980s, demands for more interventionist action were made by housing pressure groups, academics, professional housing and environmental health institutes and numerous local authorities across the United Kingdom. This shared advocacy for HMO licensing made no impression on government policy either in Scotland or in England and Wales until the early 1990s when the policy framework in Scotland diverged from elsewhere in the U.K. As Murie (1996, p 212) noted in a review of the similarities and differences in housing policy between Scotland and the rest of the UK: "common pressures acting on different landscapes do not produce the same outcomes".

A *discretionary* power to allow local authorities to license certain HMOs was introduced in Scotland in 1991 and since October 2000 their regulation has become a *mandatory* duty covering all local authorities and most HMOs in the private, public and voluntary sectors. Meanwhile, in England and Wales, the status quo essentially persisted through the 1990s with the same arguments for licensing continuing to be made, to little effect. With the arrival of a Labour government in Westminster in 1997, with a manifesto commitment to license HMOs, a more sympathetic attitude emerged. However, progress has been painfully slow and at the time of writing there is only a ministerial promise that new legislation to introduce mandatory HMO licensing in England and Wales would "be launched in the autumn" (Inside Housing, 2001, p 3).

This aim of this chapter is to chart the divergent policy direction taken in Scotland from the rest of the UK in responding to the problems posed by HMOs. After setting the context, the chapter describes the pressures that led to local authorities gaining the discretionary power to introduce local licensing schemes when the wider political environment emphasised market deregulation. The discretionary licensing framework is summarised and its effectiveness reviewed as it helped to shape the current mandatory scheme. The key features of the mandatory framework are detailed and some of its potential benefits and drawbacks are discussed. The chapter concludes with an agenda for future research to investigate the scheme's success and its impact on the private HMO sector and the non-profit, shared accommodation sector. It is argued that such an agenda needs to be addressed before decisions are taken to extend licensing powers to the wider private rented sector in Scotland, or in England and Wales, as the effectiveness and impact of the Scottish mandatory scheme are, as yet, unproven.

The HMO context in Scotland

As a result of the introduction of licensing there are now two principal legislative definitions of an HMO in Scotland. The definition for licensing purposes is discussed in a later section but to set the context about the nature, scale and diversity of multiple occupancy it is more appropriate to draw on the broad interpretation provided by the 1987 Housing (Scotland) Act, section 152, which refers to HMOs as "... houses which, or a part of which, are let in lodgings or which are occupied by more than one family ...". While commonly interpreted as a shared living arrangement found in the private rented sector, HMOs are also a small but important feature of public and voluntary housing provision. As in England and Wales, various problems have arisen in trying to gauge the number of HMOs. Legislative definitions have been difficult to apply to some building and living arrangements, the definitions used by the census and in housing legislation have not coincided, the 1996 Scottish House Condition Survey (Scottish Homes, 1997) could not produce statistics for HMOs because of the very small numbers involved, while local authority surveys have tended to sample-survey private rented sector HMOs and thus lacked comprehensive coverage.

The scale of multiple occupancy in Scotland is known to be very small relative to the national stock of over 2.2 million dwellings but its precise size is elusive (Currie et al, 1998). The overall private rented sector accounts for only 8 per cent (around 176,000 dwellings) of the housing stock. From local authority estimates it is possible that there are over 5,000 HMOs in the traditional private rented sector but additionally there are a smaller number of shared living arrangements in the non-profit sector.

HMOs in the private rented sector – bed-sits, shared flats, hostels and bed and breakfast hotels (B&Bs) – have been the focus of recurring political concern over many years. The development of HMO legislation and policy has been designed, not very successfully, to eliminate the substandard conditions and exploitation of residents in private HMOs. While HMOs do accommodate many for whom access to other tenures is denied by allocation rules or lack of finance, it is important to recognise that not everyone living in privately rented HMOs is there out of necessity and lack of an alternative. HMOs can also be the preferred choice of a minority of people for a variety of personal or lifestyle reasons such as location (in relation to local amenities or employment opportunities) anonymity, privacy, freedom or avoidance of complicated renting obligations (Currie and Miller, 1987).

The B&B sector has gradually declined over recent years but one potentially significant aspect of post-devolution housing policy in Scotland – the 2001 Housing (Scotland) Act – could, ironically, boost the B&B market. This legislation augments previous homelessness legislation by placing additional homelessness duties on local authorities to provide temporary accommodation and advice and assistance to anyone they believe to be homeless, *regardless* of whether they have priority need or are intentionally homeless. Although local authorities had made great strides under previous legislation to reduce their dependency on B&Bs to meet their obligation to provide temporary accommodation to those in priority need and not intentionally homeless, B&Bs had still been used by authorities. With a far wider responsibility now falling on them, particularly for single persons, the issue that will arise is where the additional provision will come from? Developments of new non-profit sector temporary accommodation provision will take place but will take time to materialise and in response to immediate needs and duties, there is a real possibility that the numbers and resort to the use of B&Bs will increase.

Multiple occupancy is also to be found, though not always to the standards expected, in the non-profit sector encompassing local authorities, registered social landlords, voluntary care agencies universities and colleges. Mainstream and specialist hostels, cluster flats, shared accommodation projects, community homes, halls of residence and other forms of shared accommodation for many client groups have emerged in the last 20 years to meet public policy objectives, particularly care in the community policy. There was a growth in local authority homeless hostels in the 1990s. Over the period 1991 to 1994, the Scottish Office provided authorities with £29 million of additional capital borrowing consents to provide more temporary and permanent accommodation in response to the growing pressures of rising numbers of homeless applicants. Criteria for this challenge funding included projects to provide supported accommodation and hostels for housing young single homeless people (Dyer, 1996). Under licensing, such schemes, unless exempted, are assessed in exactly the same way as privately rented HMOs.

The evolution of licensing in Scotland

The origins of the introduction of licensing in Scotland can be traced to the mid-1980s and the influence of research and campaigning about HMOs on political debate about homelessness and vulnerability. The major city authorities of Glasgow and Edinburgh and pressure groups such as Shelter Scotland and the Scottish Council for Single Homeless (SCSH) had voiced increasing concern about the problems posed by HMOs, particularly the rising number of poor standard B&Bs. A national HMO group involving local authorities and voluntary agencies campaigned on a range of HMO problems in the traditional private rented sector, including the lack of statutory, national, minimum physical standards to reinforce locally determined policies, high rent charges for poor quality accommodation, the inefficient bureaucratic regulatory procedures of the 1987 Housing (Scotland) Act and the failure of Housing Act powers to address the unsatisfactory management by some HMO landlords.

A research survey of HMOs by SCSH concluded that a key obstacle to improving standards and protecting residents was the standard of tenancy and property management by landlords. Until the issue of whether the landlord was a 'fit and proper person' to operate an HMO was answered, no comprehensive or lasting solution would be achieved. The study advocated new primary HMO legislation but recognising the timescale such an enactment would involve, "The Scottish Office should require commercial forms of multiple occupancy, particularly boarding houses, to be licensed under the terms of the Civic Government (Scotland) Act 1982" (Currie and Miller, 1987, p 84). To a degree, this was an opportunistic proposal as the normal application of this legislation's licensing powers was for commercial activities such as operating taxis, dealing in scrap metal, boat hiring, street trading and window cleaning, not activities that involved something as critical as peoples' homes.

This argument for more powers to be given to local authorities challenged the prevailing deregulatory ethos of the Conservative government. The late 1980s witnessed the passage of the 1988 Housing (Scotland) Act, which incorporated a raft of market liberalisation measures including deregulated tenancies, easier grounds for property repossession and a market basis for rent setting in the private sector. During the committee stage of the preceding Bill, the Housing Minister rejected opposition amendments to address the specific problems in HMOs particularly poor conditions, rent exploitation, inadequate tenancy rights for residents of shared bedrooms and the lack of protection for lodgers in private owners' homes. However, the government accepted that there were problems with some HMOs and subsequently the Scottish Office issued a Consultation Paper (Scottish Office, 1988) seeking views on whether there was a need for change in HMO legislation. The paper surprised many of the government's critics as it represented a positive analysis of the problems in the HMO sector: the imbalance between supply and demand, the inefficiency and bureaucracy surrounding the current enforcement powers, the vulnerability of some HMO residents, and possible gaps in the existing range of powers. Nevertheless, the paper rejected the idea of a new unitary HMO Act drawing together the different public health, planning, fire safety and housing legislation on HMOs but offered two alternative proposals for consideration.

First, it proposed the maintenance of the legislative status quo but with local authorities given new good practice guidance about how they could more effectively operate their existing powers. Its second and quite unexpected proposal was the more radical option to consider the introduction of a licensing scheme for HMOs. In a climate where the powers of local authorities were being reduced, this latter option was cautiously presented: "... the Government are not yet convinced that a licensing scheme is necessary. However, in the interests of debate the following outline proposals are put forward to suggest features a scheme would need to have to be more effective than the existing powers" (Scottish Office, 1988, p 8). The paper was a turning point in government policy in Scotland although local authorities were sceptical that a Conservative administration, ideologically committed to promoting deregulatory, free market values would agree to introduce measures that limited individual freedom, reintroduced controls on the rented housing market and reinvested local authorities with more interventionist powers.

The 1991 discretionary HMO licensing scheme

Contrary to all expectations, in 1991 the Scottish Housing Minister introduced an Order (Statutory Instrument SI 1991 No. 1253 (S.123)) approved by resolution of Parliament, allowing local authorities to establish, *if they wished*, a licensing scheme for particular houses in multiple occupation. Up to that point, the statutory framework for the regulation of HMOs in Scotland and England, while not identical, had not diverged in such a major way. This political decision in Scotland, eight years before devolution, was not mirrored in England due to the rejection by successive Secretaries of State for the Environment of the need for licensing, a position that persisted until 1997.

This discretionary Scottish licensing framework was based on the 1982 Civic Government (Scotland) Act, section 44, which allowed the designation by the Secretary of State of any activity as one that would require a licence to operate. As no primary legislation was required, it offered a quick, straightforward parliamentary procedure. The central statement of the approved Order was that, "Use of premises as a house in multiple occupation is hereby designated as an activity for which, subject to a resolution of the licensing authority in relation to it, in accordance with section 9 of the Act, a licence shall be required" (Scottish Office Environment Department, 1991).

An important feature of the Order was its definition of a licensable HMO. It differed significantly from the generic definition in the 1987 Housing (Scotland) Act, which had no licensing powers. It set *a minimum numerical threshold of five persons from more than two families* for defining an HMO and requiring it to obtain a licence (Table 10.1). Note that this numerical threshold was not adopted by the subsequent mandatory scheme (see later section).

A Scottish Office circular (Scottish Office Environment Department, 1991) provided guidance to authorities on good practice and their available powers across different legislation, including their licensing power. The guidance was not mandatory but the Scottish Office was still concerned about this new regulatory power and wished authorities "wherever it is possible, to resolve any problems by negotiation and persuasion in the first instance before resorting to the use of statutory powers" (Scottish Office Environment Department, 1991).

Table 10.1: Housing and civic government definitions of a house in multiple occupation

Statutory basis	Definition of an HMO
Discretionary licensing under the 1982 Civic Government (Scotland) Act (Licensing of HMOs) Order 1991	An HMO is a house which is the only or principle residence of more than four persons being persons who are not all members of either the same family or of one or other of two families
The 1987 Housing (Scotland) Act s.152	An HMO is a house which, or a part of which, is let in lodgings, or which is occupied by members of more than one family

The Order giving authorities discretion not only to introduce a scheme but to decide the threshold level of occupancy for eligibility for licensing led to widely differing thresholds. Glasgow's original minimum level was HMOs with ten or more residents at least two of whom had to be on housing benefit, Edinburgh's threshold was originally 11 or more residents and Aberdeen's was five or more residents (from more than two families). In each case, the property had to be the only or principal home of the persons resident in it to avoid schemes encompassing tourist hotels and youth hostels but ensuring student term-time accommodation in shared flats and halls of residence was covered.

A central feature of each scheme was its focus on the licence applicant. In considering an application, local authorities could take into account not only the conditions of the HMO but whether the applicant was a "fit and proper person to be holder of a licence" (Schedule 1 of the 1982 Civic (Government) Scotland Act). This sought to address one of the long-standing weaknesses of the powers in the 1987 Act that only addressed the physical and fire safety standards of the property, not the honesty, competence or past criminal record of the owner or manager.

The Order allowed authorities to apply "such reasonable conditions", but not rent controls, to the requirements for licence approval and to charge a fee to cover their administration costs in processing applications (including inspection work). Licences could be approved conditionally to allow a licensee time to meet all the licence conditions. Licences could be refused and, if awarded, could subsequently be revoked. No specific duty was placed on local authorities or HMO owners to rehouse any residents displaced by refusal or revocation. Failure to apply for a licence when one was required, and breach of licence conditions, were a criminal offence that on conviction could result in a fine of up to £5,000 maximum.

The failings of the discretionary framework

The election of a Labour government in 1997 with a manifesto commitment in Scotland (and the rest of the UK) to require all local authorities to introduce "a full system of licensing" (Scottish Labour Party, 1997) to protect HMO tenants led to Scottish Office commissioned research to assess the effectiveness of the discretionary licensing schemes and identify good practice for the forthcoming mandatory scheme (Currie et al, 1998).

The study found that only seven of Scotland's 32 unitary local authorities, including the four main cities – Glasgow, Edinburgh, Dundee and Aberdeen – had taken advantage of the powers. These tended to be the authorities that had a traditional enforcement role with HMOs. Most other authorities had never developed any role in relation to multiple occupancy either because of its low policy priority or its incidence was considered too low to merit action. The seven authorities had no clear view of the future role and contribution of HMOs to meeting need or market demand and no authority had developed a wider strategy for the private rented sector within which a housing policy for HMOs could be developed. Monitoring of the impact of licensing on the private HMO market was generally absent, with no authority having calculated the likely impact of licensing on the growth or decline of the sector. A crucial finding was that the schemes had very limited effectiveness and that very few properties had been licensed. Some progress had been achieved by the City of Edinburgh Council but a number of factors limited the success of all the schemes:

• Lack of staff dedicated to HMO licensing work and inadequate financial resources to support implementation.
• Low political and managerial priority for HMO work within authorities.
• Procedural constraints imposed by civic government licensing rules, especially the limited timescale to decide on applications.
• Limited powers to enforce licensing requirements on HMO owners who failed to submit applications.
• Failure of effective corporate working across departments and agencies.
• Inconsistencies between licensing powers and other statutory powers such as building control regulations and local policies such as residential planning controls on HMOs.

The study surveyed residents and owners of licensed HMOs and found residents were generally satisfied with the quality of their accommodation and their landlord's management but, other than improved fire safety features, were unaware of specific benefits from licensing. Almost all thought licensing was a good idea and would make landlords more accountable. Licensed owners were very dissatisfied and voiced numerous criticisms of the implementation procedures particularly:

• poor communication of licensing requirements and information about procedures and standards;
• too many inspection visits and inconsistencies between, and even within, departments about standard-setting;
• too much discretion to individual officers;
• the high cost of fire safety work but the lack of any grant aid;

• high fees, particularly for renewals in the two main cities, Edinburgh and Glasgow.

Licensed owners believed that schemes were failing because the worst HMO owners were avoiding licensing, but they could come to terms with the principle of licensing and could cooperate with schemes "as long as they [the schemes] were perceived to be reasonable in their requirements, not expensive, workable in their implementation and were enforced on all those eligible" (Currie et al, 1998, p 67).

The mandatory HMO licensing scheme

This critical evaluation of the effectiveness of the discretionary system helped to shape the detail of the mandatory licensing proposals although the overall framework of civic government licensing procedures placed constraints on the extent to which the national framework could be modified, as the 1982 Act had never been drafted to deal with such a complex activity as peoples' homes. The mandatory scheme was introduced, with some haste, by statutory instrument (Scottish Executive 2000a). In September 1999, the Minister for Communities announced that a mandatory licensing scheme under the 1982 Civic Government (Scotland) Act would be established by all Scottish local authorities by April 2000 (Scottish Executive, 1999). However, the guidance to local authorities on how to implement local schemes (Scottish Executive, 2000b) could not be finalised in time because of the need for consultation. Introduction of the Order was delayed until 1 October 2000. Discretionary licensing schemes were to cease after October 2001.

Mandatory licensing was designed "to give local authorities the duty to inspect and monitor shared accommodation so that all those tenants can have safe, quality accommodation" (Scottish Executive, 1999, p 2) but for equity of treatment, the scheme had to encompass shared accommodation in the non-profit sector of local authorities, registered social landlords, voluntary care agencies, and universities and colleges. In other words, as well as traditional private sector multiple occupancy, local authority hostels, housing association cluster flats and group homes, Woman's Aid refuges and halls of residence for full-time students during term-time, all had to be licensed within the relevant time period. To prevent the exposure of the location of Woman's Aid refuges, the Order exempted refuges from having to display their licence application notice at their premises and from having their applications publicly advertised in newspapers, although the responsibility to give letters to neighbours about the application was retained, as it was assumed neighbours already knew a refuge was 'next door'.

The only exclusions from licensing were properties covered by alternative regulatory regimes and certain unusual types of shared occupancy. This meant exemption for residential establishments registered under the 1968 Social Work (Scotland) Act, nursing homes registered under the 1938 Nursing Homes

Registration (Scotland) Act and private hospitals covered by the 1984 Mental Health (Scotland) Act. Also excluded were school boarding accommodation, accommodation associated with religious communities (for example monasteries and convents), property occupied only by those who each had a title to ownership of the property (and members of their family) and any HMO already covered by a Control Order under the 1987 Housing (Scotland) Act.

The scheme maintained the requirement of the discretionary scheme that those resident must be living there as their only or principal home but a major divergence from the discretionary system (not recommended in the discretionary scheme research) was the adoption of a lower minimum occupancy level for which a licence was required. A phased reduction over three years to a final threshold of *three* persons, not all from one family, or from one or other of only two families, was now the obligation (Table 10.2).

As it was accepted that in almost all areas there would be more smaller HMOs than larger HMOs, the phasing was designed to spread the workload and allow authorities more time to inspect and process applications. It was also designed to help alleviate the financial impact of licensing as no additional funding for planning and implementing local schemes was provided by the Scottish Executive. For the city authorities such as Glasgow and Edinburgh it is a moot point whether they will be able to achieve full licensing of all three and above HMOs, including renewal application processing, between 2003 and 2004.

The rationale for reducing the minimum threshold from the discretionary scheme level of five to the ultimate level of three was not set out by the Executive but there are two possible reasons. First, small HMOs were not necessarily better managed or of better quality than larger HMOs so should not be exempted. Second, there was strong public and political reaction to the deaths of two students trapped in a fire in a small three-person basement flat in Glasgow in 1999. Fire fatalities in HMOs are very rare in Scotland. Even though the flat was too small to be licensable under the previous discretionary scheme, the Executive could not be seen to introduce a mandatory scheme that *ex*cluded small flats or houses that could accommodate three single persons.

The recurring tension between central direction and local discretion was evident in the guidance accompanying the Order on conditions for the approval of licences and on adoption of detailed 'benchmark' standards. The guidance was not mandatory so local authorities could set their own standards to meet

Table 10.2: Phased reduction in minimum occupancy threshold for mandatory licensing

Time period	Minimum occupancy threshold for licensing	
1 October 2000-30 September 2001	more than	5
1 October 2001-30 September 2002	more than	4
1 October 2002-30 September 2003	more than	3
After 1 October 2003		3

local circumstances but the Executive expected them to take cognisance of its advisory conditions in order to achieve comparability and 'reasonable' standards across the country: "There should be similar arrangements for similar sorts of properties, with some flexibility across different types of HMO" (Scottish Executive, 2000b, p 19). However, one issue that was deemed as an essential prerequisite of licence approval was planning permission. The guidance, though not the statutory Order, stated that "... where an application for planning permission is required, a licence should not be granted unless it has been established that the HMO has received planning permission" (Scottish Executive, 2000b, p 20).

Standards were divided into two categories: those covering physical conditions and safety and, for the first time in the statutory regulation of HMOs, standards dealing with tenancy management. Minimum physical and safety benchmark standards included those dealing with bedroom space, kitchen sinks, cookers, work surfaces, food storage, wcs, showers, baths, hand basins, space heating, lighting, ventilation and fire and electrical safety. The standards combined well established values and ratios familiar to those local authorities with discretionary licensing schemes or registration schemes, with standards drawn from the Technical Standards required for new build properties. The logic of the guidance setting out detailed new building standards as licence benchmarks yet allowing local authorities a fair amount of discretion to modify or ignore them, has proved debatable. While Technical Standards offer the highest standards possible, they are demanding to apply to existing HMOs, particularly those in older properties with limited structural flexibility.

The incorporation of tenancy management standards into licence conditions was a major innovation and recommended by the discretionary licensing scheme research. Tenancy management was defined as "... the owner's responsibilities to respect the legal rights of his or her tenants, to operate lawfully at all times and to manage the property with due care for the welfare of the tenants" (Currie et al, 1998, p 47). Based on this definition, the guidance identified three tenancy management categories for local authorities to consider in developing criteria for assessing a licence and licensee:

- *Tenants' legal rights* Authorities were advised to check that occupants have peaceful enjoyment of their accommodation, lawful tenancy agreements were employed, rent deposits were not unfairly retained, 24 hours notice was given prior to an intention by the owner to enter occupants' personal accommodation (for example for survey or maintenance) and that repossession procedures were lawful. The guidance emphasised the importance of tenants also having some form of written tenancy or occupancy agreement setting out the landlord's and tenant's mutual rights and responsibilities.
- *The owner is a fit person to operate the HMO* The requirement for the owner, or the manager, to be a 'fit person' derived from a general obligation on local authorities in assessing all licence applications under 1982 Civic Government (Scotland) Act procedures. It allows authorities to take account of the character

of the applicant and relevant former criminal convictions. Significantly, it allows the police to comment on the applicant and lodge objections to the approval of an application.

• *The owner's responsibilities in relation to tenant anti-social behaviour* The guidance placed a responsibility on owners to ensure that tenants did not cause a nuisance to other residents or to neighbours. Neighbour problems had been a long-standing issue with HMOs in tenement flats where communal stairs and close proximity placed a premium on showing respect for the right to peaceful enjoyment of one's home. As part of effective tenancy management, owners would be expected to take steps to resolve problems of anti-social behaviour and authorities would be expected to monitor such situations and to respond to complaints made to them.

Relationships with HMO owners

Despite the scope of the national mandatory scheme, the main motivation within the Scottish Executive, politically and professionally, for the introduction of mandatory licensing reflected traditional concerns about unsatisfactory health, safety and management standards in privately rented HMOs. The prime emphasis of the mandatory scheme was on powers of intervention, regulation and enforcement which the accompanying guidance underlined with its focus on implementation procedures and the appropriate standards and conditions for licence approval.

While very much a secondary feature of the national framework, the Executive did recognise the importance of licensing being promoted in a positive manner that could appeal to owners of privately rented HMOs. There was no duty placed on authorities to promote and implement licensing in a positive 'owner-friendly' way as the civic government legislation constrained the terms of the Order setting out the scheme to matters directly relevant to the licensing process. One helpful procedural change that the Order was able to make was to allow licence applicants up to 12 months, rather than the previous 6 months under the discretionary scheme, to have their application approved. This was intended to give owners a more realistic length of time to obtain necessary consents (for example building warrant) and carry out possibly substantial works to meet licensing standards. Generally, however, ideas about promotion and partnership between authorities and owners had to be addressed by the advisory guidance. It recognised that owners could need incentives to licence and to believe that licensing would 'add value' to their business. By this means, the Executive hoped that mandatory licensing could be promoted in a non-hostile manner, creating partnerships between authorities and owners while also enhancing the public perception of the private rented sector generally.

Proposals included providing owners with an information and advice service, offering model leases to adopt, explaining how sanctions worked (and could be avoided), arranging seminars (for example on housing benefit administration) and developing landlord forums. Accreditation as an accompaniment to licensing approval was also suggested, based on owners meeting additional standards (as recommended in the research review of discretionary licensing). Not all these ideas were new. Prior to mandatory licensing, the City of Edinburgh Council had developed a housing benefit/private landlord forum and a model lease for landlords to use, and Fife Council had published a landlord's newsletter and established a landlord's forum to stimulate dialogue between the authority and owners. However, arising from the new guidance, Glasgow City Council planned to set up a customer services group that included four private landlords, voluntary agencies, university and student representatives and letting agents.

Benefits and drawbacks of mandatory HMO licensing

There are arguments for and against the adoption of compulsory licensing of all HMOs down to an occupancy level of only three, non-related person households. King (2000) believes that it will force local authorities to use their powers, ensure national consistency, achieve good internal coordination in authorities, bring clarity to licence conditions – reducing the likelihood of a legal challenge – and allow a fee to be charged that recoups costs. However, she notes that it will be bureaucratic to administer as it is not tailor made for HMOs and that it fails to incorporate a risk assessment procedure, relying instead on the more time-consuming and costly inspection approach.

While the mandatory licensing system will provide a consistent legislative approach to multiple occupancy across Scotland, there is still room for considerable policy and practice variation at local level. The guidance allows flexibility in implementation, for example in the number of years a licence can run (up to three), on fee levels, on incorporation of a degree of self-certification by licensees after their first licence and, as noted previously, in variations to the national benchmark standards. Overall, such local discretion is beneficial as it allows local schemes to be shaped to local HMO markets, landlord and property types and, not least, to residents' needs. However, national consistency will be obligatory on authorities in relation to the categories and tenures of HMOs that licence schemes must cover. Exemptions from licensing are very limited and set by statute. This is a positive feature of the national scheme as it will minimise anomalies in treatment at a local level and eliminate variations in approach to similar types of HMOs across local authority administrative boundaries. Such variations had been a cause of grievance by landlords under the discretionary scheme.

The introduction of tenancy management criteria is a positive policy breakthrough. Now, the way in which landlords manage their tenancies is an obligatory factor in the determination of standards and in licence approval. Allied to this is the requirement that authorities take account of the character and any criminal convictions of HMO applicants in determining licences. These factors enhance mandatory licensing as they extend the scope of state interest in multiple occupancy beyond its traditional preoccupation with sanitation, overcrowding, cleanliness and fire safety. They also offer the opportunity to protect vulnerable HMO residents from exploitative or abusive landlords. However, a question mark hangs over where the skills will come from within local authorities to deal with assessing tenancy criteria. Environmental heath officers often lead their authority's HMO enforcement work (with exceptions such as in Edinburgh and Dundee) but have no background in landlord/tenancy matters. Local authority solicitors and housing staff are often no more knowledgeable or skilled in this specialist area of work. Training programmes, possibly using outside agencies, may prove necessary to ensure this crucial dimension of licensing assessment is carried out correctly.

The mandatory scheme has also removed an obstacle to efficient enforcement as local authorities no longer have to rely on the vagaries of the operational priorities of the police in order to gain entry to unlicensed HMOs to determine occupancy levels and collect evidence for possible prosecution by the Procurator Fiscal's office. However, this efficiency gain will only be realised if the Crown Prosecution Service acts on a local authority's submission.

The scheme does not incorporate a risk assessment procedure, which is a major weakness as inspections are administratively demanding and where not well coordinated, often cause much grievance among owners. The Scottish Executive has commissioned research into a risk assessment methodology for HMOs which, if successful, may be able to streamline the licensing system and allow a more efficient use of the limited staff resources that tend to be devoted to HMO activity.

The requirement for prior planning consent, if required, before the award of a licence is a questionable prior condition to have incorporated into the national framework. If planning permission is refused, the HMO must cease operating. However, the residents still have their tenancy rights, which cannot be eliminated by the refusal of a civic government licence. The property will continue to operate without planning permission or a licence, as long as residents abide by their occupancy or tenancy rights and obligations including the duration of their agreement. Over many years, the planning system has never proved a very efficient and effective vehicle for dealing with HMO problems related to amenity, neighbour disputes and the 'not in my backyard' syndrome. Planning consent as a precondition of award of a licence may well cause the same protracted delays in decisions and action as arose with discretionary licensing. It may also put out of business some HMOs that, other than for a failure to gain planning consent, fulfilled all other licensing standards and conditions.

While the Executive's proposals on creating landlord incentives and developing accreditation schemes have merit in principle, whether they will achieve their objective of cultivating a positive environment for licensing is a moot point. Accreditation schemes will have little value in the cities where demand for private renting exceeds HMO supply. More fundamentally, there is a clear lack of tangible financial incentives on offer to owners and a failure by the Executive to recognise and respond effectively to the central importance to owners of the potential costs of licensing. Although the Executive notes that there is a possibility of some grant aid to owners, this is unlikely to materialise. Local authority budgets for all types of grants to private owners have been greatly reduced since 1996 when the ring-fencing of the Non Housing Revenue Account (a spending head for private housing purposes) was removed and such expenditure was absorbed into each authority's general fund, requiring private sector managers to compete against education, social work and other services with much higher political priority.

For the first licence application in particular, HMO owners' costs of meeting standards and conditions could be considerable and lead to a decision to exit from the market as soon as possible. Other than a possible 20 per cent grant towards eligible costs of no more than £20,000, for providing a satisfactory means of escape from fire (only if a fire safety notice has been served), there is little chance of grant subsidy. Other property upgrade costs are very unlikely to be grant aided. As well as the licence fee there could be a planning application fee and a building warrant fee together with a professional consultant's fee, possibly a separate inspection and report fee to the fire brigade and potentially solicitor's fees in relation to leases and attendance at the licensing committee. It is not only for small HMO landlords for whom such costs could prove prohibitive. Their impact on large institutions could be significant. Edinburgh University estimated that over the three years to 2003, initial and renewal licence application fees (excluding any upgrade costs) could cost it £115,000 at current prices. The City of Edinburgh's fee scales were £480 for first application for a one-year licence and £360 for a renewal fee. In its submission to the Scottish Executive the university concluded:

> Licensing fees of the order we have calculated would at best mean high rents for students and at worst mean that a good deal of our own property could become nonviable for us to manage. Needless to say, both of these options are unpalatable and would have major repercussions for the University as a whole. (Edinburgh University, 2000)

A research agenda

The mandatory licensing regime, introduced in October 2000, is at an early stage of implementation. While the Executive collects statistical returns from local authorities on the operation of their local licensing schemes, no research or formal evaluation has yet been carried out by the Executive to gauge the efficiency and effectiveness of the scheme nationally or locally. The scheme also has wider implications for both the traditional private sector and for the diverse forms of shared provision in the non-profit sector. There is a clear need for an early evaluation of the scheme that would address a number of key themes including:

1. Is the scheme achieving the goals set by the Scottish Executive for its introduction, namely to ensure safe, good quality accommodation managed to acceptable tenancy management standards?
2. Have the changed operational parameters for the implementation of the scheme removed the weaknesses and inefficiencies found in the previous discretionary scheme?
3. Have authorities applied adequate staffing, training, IT and publicity resources to achieve the phased introduction timescale set out in the Order?
4. What is the rate of licence approval and refusal in relation to numbers of applications? How many refusals have arisen because of a failure to obtain planning consent?
5. What has the impact of the scheme been on the size of the private sector HMO market? Has there been a decline or growth in the sector? Is there evidence of new entrants of owners selling up, converting to single household/family renting or cutting occupancy numbers to avoid licensing controls?
6. What has the impact of the scheme been on the non-profit sector? Has the scheme pushed up rents or reduced provision in university and college owned accommodation? Have the number of student lodgings arrangements with private landlords reduced or remained stable? Have supported accommodation projects run by local authorities and registered social landlords been affected and if so in what ways? How has the scheme impacted on the management and costs of local authority owned hostels? Have the minimum notification measures designed to protect the location of Woman's Aid refuges been successful?
7. To what extent have local authorities approached mandatory licensing as essentially a regulatory and enforcement procedure or viewed it as a process designed as much to create a positive private renting environment that could stimulate growth of the private HMO sector?
8. Have local authorities incorporated the aims and objectives for licensing within a wider private rented sector housing strategy or have their schemes been implemented in isolation from an analysis of their contribution and impact on meeting housing need and demand?

Conclusion

Mandatory HMO licensing is a reality in Scotland but it is too early to draw conclusions about whether its form and procedures for implementation will prove effective in raising the physical and tenancy management standards in existing HMOs. It should be seen as an experiment and certainly one that should not be applied to the wider private rented sector until its benefits have been proved and shown to be worth the effort. At this stage there is no guarantee that mandatory licensing will achieve all its objectives nor that it will not have traded off achieving higher standards at the price of a smaller HMO private rented sector.

The Executive stated that licensing was "... not designed to drive HMO owners out of business" (Scottish Executive, 2000a, p 12) but much will depend on how the balance between regulation and sustainability will be achieved. Whether licensing will maintain or diminish the size of the private rented sector will depend on two crucial determinants: the total costs that landlords will incur to meet licensing conditions and the attitude of local authorities to the requirement in the statutory Order that applicants must obtain planning consent – a particularly contentious issue – before approval of a licence. As the scheme stands, it continues a historical culture towards HMOs of enforcement and control and is replete with sanctions but lacks tangible incentives that would be attractive to landlords. Initial arguments that having a licence will give successful landlords a market edge against competitors will have diminishing value as the scheme encompasses increasing numbers of smaller HMOs each year.

ELEVEN

Housing conditions in the private rented sector within a market framework

A.D.H. Crook

Introduction

The purpose of this chapter is to examine the evidence in England about the extent to which landlords respond to market signals when spending on repairs and improvements. The majority of this housing sector is now within the deregulated sub-sector and hence it is the market that sets rents for most dwellings, not the rent officer. In the past, grants have been available from local authorities to help fund improvements and repairs. Except in very limited circumstances, this is no longer the case. The government's view is that market rents should provide the resources for landlords to undertake maintenance and to make improvements. Conditions are thus now much more dependent than in the past upon the extent to which market signals (rents and capital values) provide incentives to landlords to undertake the work that is needed and also upon their willingness and ability to act upon these. Although local authorities have powers to enforce repairs, the successful use of these powers depends upon the market generating returns and the resources for landlords to respond.

The evidence is summarised in five sections:

- the policy framework, before and after rent deregulation;
- evidence about changing conditions;
- the extent to which spending on repairs and improvements is related to landlords' characteristics;
- the relationship between rents, capital values, investment returns, and conditions; and
- policy implications of this evidence.

Policy before and after deregulation

Until rent deregulation in 1989, post-war policy about conditions was framed within a context of rent control and regulation and the general acceptance that the private rented sector would continue to decline. The aims were to protect the health and safety of existing tenants, accepting implicitly that significant improvements would primarily result from the transfer of dwellings to other tenures.

Policy was directed towards achieving improvements through the statutory enforcement of repairs and other standards, the payment of grant aid to assist landlords with the costs of major repairs and (latterly) improvements, and with the purchase of the worst housing by local authorities and housing associations. These measures were needed because the majority of the sector was subject to rent regulation making it difficult for landlords to finance repairs and improvements. Even though many dwellings were let in ways that enabled landlords to charge de facto market rents, the generally low income of tenants did not produce quasi market rents sufficient to provide landlords with the rental income both to cover repair costs and give them a competitive rate of return.

Apart from slum clearance, government measures to secure improved conditions in existing dwellings were threefold (Crook and Sharp, 1989; Crook and Hughes, 2001).

First, rent control and rent regulation allowed landlords to raise rents when repairs or improvements were carried out, although not necessarily by amounts that gave competitive returns on the expenditure (Nevitt, 1966). After rent regulation in the mid-1960s, landlords were permitted to transfer unfit dwellings from rent control to regulation, provided they were made fit, tenants agreed to this, and rent increases were phased in.

Second, local authorities were empowered to secure repairs and improvements by a combination of enforcement powers (in both public health and housing legislation) and grant aid. Initially enforcement powers were restricted to repairs, but later included improvements. These powers are complex and few require mandatory action. Their use generally has been limited. They rely on tenants to complain and their willingness to do so depends on their knowledge of the system, their ability to withstand subsequent rent increases, and their security of tenure (Crook, 1989). Grant aid was initially limited to improvements, but was later widened to include repairs, as governments recognised that enforcement on its own had limited success. By 1980 landlords had the right to grant aid if served with repairs notices. Local authorities tended to use enforcement powers as a basis for non-coercive negotiations with landlords, either to obtain the much higher standards that could be achieved with discretionary grant aid or to transfer ownership to a social rented landlord (Burridge, 1987; Crook and Sharp, 1989).

Third, local authorities and non-profit housing associations were encouraged to acquire dwellings from landlords who were unable or unwilling to upgrade their dwellings. The main foci of such programmes were area improvement schemes, carried out in conjunction with local authorities' grant aid and enforcement powers. The greater emphasis within housing renewal policy given to improvement strategies from the mid-1970s onwards made it important for there to be significant improvements in private rented housing, since it made up a large proportion of dwellings within improvement areas. Hence, policy sought to address the negative externalities arising from the poor condition of the private rented stock that would counteract or prejudice improvements in other tenures (see Maclennan, 1985).

Evidence suggests that this grant and enforcement-led strategy did result in repairs and improvements being carried out – but not enough. The numbers of grants paid to landlords of pre-1919 dwellings between 1973 were substantially below what was needed, being less than half the proportion awarded to owner occupiers of equivalent aged dwellings (Crook and Sharp, 1989). Most of the work needed did not, in any case, fall within the ambit of the grant system, and had to be fully funded by landlords from rental income or from other sources. Fifteen percent of private rented dwellings experienced works of modernisation, repair or rehabilitation between 1976 and 1981, compared with 35 percent of owner occupied housing of the same age (DoE, 1983). Among pre-1919 houses, private landlords spent an average of £2,312 and owner occupiers spent £4,562 between 1981 and 1986 on repairs and improvements (DoE, 1988).

More detailed case study and other survey evidence showed that improvement spending and grant take up in the private rented sector before 1988 was strongly associated with new landlords entering the sector. These were property dealers and building contractors interested in capital gains, rather than with existing, long-standing landlords doing the repairs and maintenance that were needed. Their strategy was to buy property with sitting tenants at its (low) investment value, especially in improvement areas, to improve it with grant aid and then to sell with vacant possession upon vacancy. Local authorities' proactive enforcement strategies aimed to persuade long-term landlords to sell up to property dealers. The latter took advantage of grant availability to do up disrepaired property at low cost to themselves while providing building work for their firms (Crook and Martin, 1988; Crook and Sharp, 1989). Policy was much less successful in dealing with conditions in multiple occupied private rented dwellings, where local authorities' largely reactive strategies relied upon tenants' complaints and upon using unwieldy and complex enforcement powers (Thomas with Hedges, 1987; Crook, 1989).

Since 1988 government policy has changed significantly. Instead of managing the decline of the sector while seeking improvements to protect existing tenants and to reduce externalities, the Conservative government announced in 1987 that it wanted to see a revival of the private rented sector (DoE, 1987). The author, in Chapter Two of this volume, has already discussed this policy, its wider context, and its impact. The purpose of the rest of this section is to discuss the thrust of this policy change for achieving improved conditions.

The government was keen, not only to revive the sector, but also to change the structure of ownership and financing, in particular to draw in new corporate landlords backed with equity and debt funding from the main financial institutions. As the earlier chapter has shown, much of the recent research on the sector shows that it is very much a 'cottage industry', dominated by small-scale and individual landlords, most managing their properties in their spare time (Crook et all, 1995; Crook and Kemp, 1996a; 1996b; Crook et al, 2000). Landlords' portfolios are thus not large enough to generate economies of scale in management and maintenance of their stock, nor to spread market risk through regional and market segment diversification. The Conservative government was keen to attract new corporate landlords into the new market sector and to attract the major financial institutions to fund them. As a previous Conservative Minister put it: "to get new money to drive out the bad". The implications were clear: as new large-scale corporate landlords with good quality lettings emerged, existing landlords with poor property would either have to bring their properties up to standard or get out of the market altogether.

The overall policy was implemented by getting the market to work through the introduction of rent deregulation and changes to security of tenure. The government thought that rent deregulation and contractual security of tenure would result in more competitive returns since it would bring in higher rents, increased liquidity and improved confidence. In addition, two steps were taken, through the BES and HITs initiatives, to stimulate the development of new companies and to attract both new retail and institutional capital into these companies (Crook, this volume).

The new policy emphasis has made a profound difference to measures designed to achieve better physical conditions. Here again the emphasis is on getting the market to work, especially in the deregulated sector. The view of the past Conservative and the current Labour governments is that the prime responsibility for carrying out and financing repairs and improvements lies with landlords. Maintenance costs are thus part of the normal overhead of the running of the business of letting property and, as a general rule, landlords should not be subsidised from public funds for the costs of repairs (DoE, 1995). The expectation was that deregulation would lead to an improvement in conditions.

Market liberalisation has been pursued in the belief that the free market price of rented property will reflect the value of the housing services provided. The implied assumption is that tenants will be willing to pay higher rents for better conditions and that this competitive framework, allied where necessary to enforcement, will incentivise landlords to spend the funds to improve conditions. Hence, better maintained properties will attract higher rents and, therefore, reward those landlords who adequately maintain their properties. Rents in the deregulated sector should in principle provide landlords with the means of funding regular maintenance, while the backlog of capital repairs and any required improvements can be financed from loans secured on rental income and capital values. Moreover, as the market sector grows and becomes more competitive, and as this provides tenants with more choice, landlords letting poor condition property will find it difficult to attract tenants and this will provide them with incentives to bring their lettings up to better standards.

Until 1996, however, grants were still provided and they were mandatory where local authorities took enforcement action. All other grants became discretionary. Grants were no longer paid as fixed amounts and percentages of cost limits irrespective of total costs and rents, but were calculated on the extent to which costs could be funded through rent increases or increased capital values. Since 1996 mandatory grants have been wholly withdrawn and grants are only available at the discretion of the local authority, with the intention that they help finance essential work in the continuing regulated sector and are also targeted at (but not restricted to) renewal areas (See also Chapter Twelve in this volume). The amount of grant is also a matter for the discretion of local authorities (DoE, 1996). The government has recently consulted on changes to this regime (DETR, 2001a) (see Chapter Twelve in this volume for further detail).

Moreover, the role of local authorities in securing better conditions has also been changing. In the light of their 'enabling role', local authorities have begun to work increasingly with private landlords in partnership arrangements, including the setting up of joint accreditation and licensing schemes, as means of promoting improvements. Some of these schemes provide tangible financial benefits, for example cheaper insurance for lettings which match accreditation schemes' criteria with respect to matters like fire and gas safety (DETR, 1998b; 2001b). Again, as with grants, the government has been consulting on changes in these areas (DETR, 2000a; 2000b; DTLR, 2001).

The success of the new policy on achieving standards through market liberalisation rather than through enforcement and grants depends on the extent to which market rents provide landlords with adequate maintenance incentives in the deregulated sector. A successful policy outcome also depends upon the emergence of a more corporate and commercially oriented sector getting competitive returns from habitable dwellings. This means that the rents of dwellings in good conditions will need to be higher than for poor condition dwellings and by amounts that warrant additional spending if socially desirable standards which at least minimise negative externalities are to be achieved within a market framework. The emergence of larger scale landlords will also help, if they are able to achieve economies of scale in maintenance.

Evidence on conditions

The evidence in this chapter comes from two principal sources. First, from the regular quinquennial English House Condition Survey (EHCS) (DoE, 1993; DETR, 1998a). Second, from follow up surveys of the landlords owning the private rented part of the sample of dwellings included in the EHCS (Crook, Henneberry and Hughes, 1998; Crook et al, 2000). The second source enables EHCS data about dwellings, including condition, to be linked to data about landlords, including their expenditure on the dwellings included in the EHCS sample. This section focuses on three pieces of evidence: first, the relative state of conditions, compared with all other tenures; second, the extent to which conditions within the sector have improved between 1986 and 1996; third, the nature of differences within the sector in 1996, especially in terms of sub-sector, dwelling type and households (especially in terms of households' dependency on housing benefit).

Despite some recent improvement in conditions (see below), dwellings in the private rented sector are worse, on average, than conditions in other tenures. One measure of condition is disrepair. This itself can be defined in a number of ways. One is to identify those repairs, labelled as 'general repairs', in the 1996 EHCS (DETR, 1998, p 49), which need to be undertaken to prevent further significant deterioration in the short term, plus additional visible work that needs to be carried out in the medium term. These were identified in the survey and the cost of carrying them out then calculated (Table 11.1).

Table 11.1 confirms that private rented dwellings were in a worse condition than dwellings in all other tenures in 1996 and that this was true of all ages of construction, apart from those built since 1964. The latter dwellings were in as good a state of repair as owner occupied and nearly as good as registered social landlord dwellings of the same age. Since the figures in Table 11.1 assume economies of scale in the building costs applied to the repairs identified in the survey, they are likely to understate the actual costs of repair in the private rented (and owner occupied) sector, compared with other tenures. This is because the scale of private landlords' ownership (Crook, this volume) suggests that repair work in the private rented sector is likely to be undertaken on the basis of a contract covering only a few dwellings.

Although the evidence about the poor state of the private rented sector compared with other tenures in 1996 is clear, it is more difficult to reach exact conclusions about the extent to which conditions have improved over the years. Part of the sample of dwellings surveyed for the EHCS consists of a

Table 11.1: Standardised general repair costs by age and tenure, England, 1996 (£ per m²)

Age of dwelling	Private rented	Owner occupied	Local authority	Registered social landlord	All dwellings
Pre-1919	45	29	34	25	33
1919-1945	35	18	26	23	22
1945-1964	36	12	18	24	15
1964 and later	8	6	12	5	7
All	34	15	17	12	17

Note: Standardised general repair costs (expressed per square metre) are based on the assumption that the repairs identified in the survey are undertaken by a building contractor using a block contract to achieve economies of scale and using building prices for one region of England (the East Midlands).

Source: DETR (1998, interpolated from Figure 5.6)

panel of addresses included in both the 1991 and 1996 surveys, enabling longitudinal analysis to be undertaken. However, analysis of changes in repair costs and other measures of condition has to take account, not only of inflation in building costs, but also of changes in surveyor variability between surveys. In addition, analysis has to take account of the changing composition of the panel's tenure because some dwellings in the panel may move from one tenure to another between sample surveys. This movement between tenures is particularly marked within the private rented sector and, as a result, has a significant effect on changes in conditions.

This is well illustrated by evidence of changes between 1986 and 1991, when general repair costs fell by 24 per cent for all tenures. The largest proportionate reduction was in fact in the private rented sector where average repair costs fell by 36 per cent. However, this substantial fall is explained by the significant changes that took place in the composition of the stock. Only 62 per cent of that in the private rented sector in 1986 was still in that sector in 1991. Most importantly, the sector grew over this period and a significant number of dwellings (constituting a quarter of the total private rented stock in 1991) transferred from other tenures. Within that part of the stock which was privately rented in both 1986 and 1991, repair costs fell only 20 per cent between the two surveys, the smallest change among all tenures. This suggests that the significant reduction in average outstanding repairs in private renting between 1986 and 1991 were largely explained by better quality, especially owner occupied, stock entering the sector. Hence the reduction in repairs among 'continuing' dwellings was the least among all tenures.

The extent of absolute change between the 1991 and 1996 surveys is more difficult to gauge, because many building defects which surveyors thought warranted repairs being done in 1991 were not identified as needing repairs to the same extent in 1996 (DETR, 1998). Estimates have, however, shown that the condition of the private rented sector had improved relative to other tenures. As with the change between 1986 and 1991, this appears to be due to the transfer of substantial numbers of dwellings in good condition from the owner occupied sector, rather than from significant improvement of dwellings that were in the private rented sector in both 1991 and 1996. Only 65 per cent of private rented dwellings in 1996 had also been private rented in 1991. Those that were privately rented throughout the five years had general repair costs of £33.80 per square metre in 1996, compared with those that transferred from other tenures, which had £24.60 per square metre. This implies, therefore, that any improvement in the average conditions across the sector as a whole is due to a considerable extent to the transfer of dwellings between tenures.

This does not mean, of course, that there was no improvement at all between 1991 and 1996 among those dwellings that remained in the sector throughout that period. The data available from the longitudinal panel of the EHCS provide an opportunity to look at this. Two measures have been adopted. First, the extent to which addresses that were unfit in 1991 became fit by 1996. Second, the extent to which addresses changed their relative position within the distribution of repair costs from 1991 to 1996 (although, given the changes in surveyor behaviour between the two surveys, this cannot, even allowing for inflation, be used as a measure of absolute improvement).

Just over half the privately rented dwellings that were unfit in 1991 and that were still private rented in 1996 were fit by 1996. The proportion that became fit is smaller than among those dwellings which were owner occupied or vacant in 1991, but it does suggest some significant change has taken place within the sector. Dwellings which changed position (both in terms of being made fit and of changing relative ranking in the repair cost spectrum) can be related to information about the dwellings, tenants and landlords (the latter, as reported by tenants in the EHCS survey, not from data in the landlord survey). This shows that:

- Dwellings occupied by tenants on housing benefit in 1996 were as likely to be in addresses which had been unfit in 1991 and had been made fit and improved their relative repairs condition as were dwellings occupied by tenants not on housing benefit.
- Dwellings where there had been no change of tenants were similarly as likely to have been made fit and to have improved their relative repairs condition as dwellings where there had been a change of tenant between 1991 and 1996.
- Dwellings that were still regulated in 1996 were just as likely to have been made fit and improved their position as dwellings that were deregulated by 1996.
- Dwellings owned in 1996 by employers and relatives were not more likely to have been made fit than dwellings owned by other landlords, but were much more likely to have been in the best relative condition in 1996 and to have retained their position or improved it.
- Dwellings owned in 1996 by individuals and property companies were more likely than dwellings belonging to other landlords to be in the worst condition in 1991 and to have worsened their relative position between 1991 and 1996.

It is also possible to use the EHCS data to look more closely at the factors that are statistically associated with conditions (Crook et al, 2000). Regulated dwellings emerge as being in considerably worse condition, on a number of measures, than those in the deregulated sub-sector. Dwellings 'not available to the public' are in better condition than the rest, probably because two thirds of them have employers or relatives as landlords. In terms of policy formulation, however, it is the deregulated sub-sector that is of most interest because it represents the nearest approximation to the 'market'.

As might be expected, the age of a dwelling was statistically closely linked to repair condition. The older a dwelling, the higher the average value of outstanding repairs: post-1980 dwellings required repairs on average one sixth the value of those required by pre-1919 dwellings. Related to this was the association between the dwelling type and the value of outstanding repairs; there was a strong statistical relationship between these. Converted flats and terraced houses had significantly higher average outstanding repairs while semi-detached and detached houses and, in particular, purpose built flats required fewer repairs.

Dwelling location was also statistically related to outstanding repairs. Looking at the regional picture, it appears that property repair condition is poorer the further away it is from London and the South East. Moreover, urban and city centre properties along with rural dwellings in village centres and in non-residential locations also were in relatively poor repair.

There has been much concern about the extent to which dwellings in poor condition are occupied by tenants in receipt of housing benefit and about the policy implications that arise from this (DTLR, 2001). In 1996, however, there appeared to be no simple relationship between the mean value of outstanding repairs and tenants' receipt of housing benefit towards their rent. In general, those properties whose tenants were receiving housing benefit had average outstanding repairs which were not significantly different in amount from dwellings whose tenants paid the full rent out of their own pockets. However, when repair cost quartile groups were compared, a statistically significant relationship with housing benefit receipt did emerge. This suggested that households in receipt of it were more likely to be found in the dwellings with the greatest disrepair and less likely to be living in those with the least disrepair. In other words, housing benefit recipients were relatively concentrated in the poorer properties. This effect appeared to be more pronounced in relation to those dwellings whose tenants were on full, as opposed to partial, housing benefit. The fact that unemployment rates were higher and that average net household income was lower among tenants occupying dwellings in the worst condition than among tenants occupying dwellings in better condition is consistent with this finding about housing benefit. It should also be noted that among these dwellings in the worst condition, those that were occupied by tenants in receipt of housing benefit were more likely to be in urban (and city centre) locations than those occupied by tenants who did not receive housing benefit.

Types of landlord, condition, and spending

As we have already seen (Crook, this volume) landlords may be classified according to the proportion of their income they receive from private renting and how they view their dwellings, producing the fourfold classification into 'business', 'sideline investor', 'sideline non-investor', and 'institutional' landlords. Three fifths of addresses in the 1998 survey of landlords who owned private rented dwellings in the 1996 EHCS were let by owners who could be classified as sideline landlords; a similar proportion to the 1994 survey (Crook et al, 1998; 2000). Of these, about half were owned by sideline investor landlords and half by sideline non-investor landlords. About a fifth of addresses were owned by business landlords and a further fifth were owned by institutions. Taking business landlords and sideline investor landlords together, just over half of addresses in

The survey evidence confirmed that more is done (and more is spent) on property that is in good condition, not let to tenants on housing benefit, and not available for letting to the general public (including tied and service accommodation), and with a high market value. But the key determinants of both the likelihood of work being undertaken, and of the amount spent on the work, relate to the character and motivation of the landlord. Investment-oriented landlords are less likely to undertake repairs than those who let largely for non-commercial reasons. As Table 11.2 has shown, this is a particular problem, as the former landlords tend to be the owners of the worst condition dwellings.

Landlords can adopt one of two general approaches to the repair and physical maintenance and improvement of their dwellings: they can be proactive or reactive. The landlord survey evidence shows that less than half dwellings have landlords who regularly inspect their properties. Spending is therefore largely reactive with little evidence of planned maintenance or improvement. Where proactive policies are pursued, however, more work is done and more is spent. Such policies are more likely to be followed by landlords owning high-value dwellings and those giving low net rates of return. They are also more likely to be followed by business and institutional landlords, but they apply such approaches to two very different types of property and with very different outcomes. Business landlords have properties with high rents and high returns but which are in poor condition. Institutional landlords have properties with low rents and low returns but which are in good condition.

Rents, capital values, rental rates of return and conditions

The evidence discussed so far suggests that the worst conditions tend to be in shared dwellings, in urban areas, and occupied by tenants on low incomes, out of work, and in receipt of housing benefit. The dwellings owned in the worst conditions also tend to be owned by landlords who regard them as investments while those in better condition are regarded for non-commercial reasons. These ownership patterns also appear to be systematically related to spending on repairs and attitudes to maintenance.

In the light of this evidence it is important to understand the extent to which the market is generating both the rents and the capital values that provide competitive rates of return to landlords who do repair and improve poor condition dwellings.

Evidence for this comes from two sources. First, a multivariate statistical analysis undertaken on the relationship between rents and capital values and a wide range of variables related to property type and condition, using data from the 1991 English House Condition Survey (Crook and Hughes, 2001). Second, analysis of similar data in the 1996 survey which was linked to the subsequent survey of landlords (Crook et al, 2000).

Rents, capital values and conditions

Some of the results of the first analysis are shown in Tables 11.4 to 11.7. Each table shows the independent variables that the regression software found to be significantly related (at the 5 per cent level of probability) to the gross rent (or the dwelling value), the dependent variable. Alongside each variable is shown its coefficient value and its beta value.

Table 11.4 shows the results with respect to all dwellings in the sample, both those that, in 1991, were deregulated and those that were still regulated. As well as the constant, eight variables were significant in this model at the 5 per cent level but these explain only a relatively small proportion (25 per cent) of the variation in rents. One of the condition variables in the model – the cost of outstanding comprehensive repairs – is shown to be related to the rent level and that relationship is negative, which is to be expected. However, the influence on the rent level is not strong, being one of the weakest relationships in this model. Nevertheless, the coefficient suggests that for every £1,000 of outstanding comprehensive repairs, the rent of a dwelling will be reduced by £40 per year. The beta statistics show that furnished status and floor size have the greatest effect on the rent with the other variables all having broadly equal effects. The coefficient signs for furnished status and central heating are, as expected, positive. The negative sign for pensioner tenants possibly reflects that this is a surrogate for dwellings that are subject to rent regulation. The negative sign for detached dwellings is, as noted above, more difficult to interpret.

Although there is a relationship between rent and repair when the whole of the private rented sector is considered together, there appears to be none when only the deregulated part of the market is considered. The results in Table 11.5 exclude all dwellings in the regulated sector. They relate only to dwellings that were last let after deregulation in January 1989, but include lettings to all types

Table 11.4: Results of regression on 1991 dwelling annual gross rent (excluding charges) for all lettings by all landlords

Cases	522	
Adjusted R square	0.25	

Significant independent variables (5% level)

Variable name	Coefficient (B)	Beta
FURNDUM	1,381.3	.25
FLOOR91X	19.1	.22
OAPSDUM	−1,064.6	−.18
CHEATDUM	844.0	.16
DETDUM	−1,400.0	−.14
T1PRIX	-0.04	−.11
YHDUM	−943.7	−.11
PBFLDUM	684.3	.09
Constant	1,355.0	

Source: Crook and Hughes (2001)

Table 11.7: Results of regression on 1991 dwelling value ('as stands') for deregulated lettings by all landlords

Cases	190
Adjusted R square	0.61

Significant independent variables (5% level)

Variable name	Coefficient (B)	Beta
EMDUM	−50,666.7	−0.51
NWDUM	−36,575.5	−0.48
WMDUM	−37,028.2	−0.42
YHDUM	−36,166.4	−0.41
NDUM	−46,428.5	−0.40
EDUM	−31,088.8	−0.37
SWDUM	−25,983.8	−0.34
SEDUM	−23,602.0	−0.26
FLOOR91X	278.7	0.26
SEMIDUM	15,815.3	0.21
ADULTDUM	9872.1	0.18
VSATDUM	11,179.5	0.17
T1PRIX	−.78	−0.16
RUBDUM	−7,431.1	−0.14
ROADDUM	−6,282.1	−0.12
Constant	60,065.1	

Source: Crook and Hughes (2001)

market returns being generated for landlords who deal with poor dwelling conditions is only partial.

Newly deregulated markets take time to mature. Hence, 1991 may be too soon after deregulation in 1989 to expect a fully competitive market to be operating, such that market rents were systematically related to conditions. But five years later there was still no evidence of this. Table 11.8 examines the evidence from the 1996 EHCS to further explore the relationship between rent levels (per square metre of the dwelling) and a wide number of potentially linked factors relating to: dwelling characteristics, landlord characteristics, dwelling location and, most importantly, dwelling repair condition. The measure of outstanding repairs used was the standardised "general repair costs per square metre". The analysis focused solely on deregulated lettings.

The variables which multivariate regression analysis found to be statistically related to the level of rent are shown in Table 11.8. These were broadly in line with the results from the 1991 EHCS in that dwelling condition does not appear to have any relationship with the level of rent. Location and type of dwelling predominated and dwellings owned by 'other organisations' had lower rents than did others. This regression model had an adjusted R^2 statistic of 0.43, which indicates that just under half of the variation in rents could be explained by the factors, but half remained unexplained.

Table 11.8: Multivariate 1996 EHCS data analysis: variables significantly associated with the level of rent (per m² per annum). Deregulated lettings only, 1996 (in descending order of importance)

Variable	Coefficient (Effect on value of rent per m²)
Dwelling in South East	+£47.21
Dwelling size (per m²)	−£0.31
Dwelling in South West	+£23.38
Dwelling in rural location	−£34.63
Dwelling is detached house	+£18.71
Dwelling owned by 'other organisation'	−£13.65
Dwelling in city centre location	−£14.48
Constant Term	+£89.65
Cases	489

Source: Crook et al (2000)

Rental rates of return

Although analysis of the data on rents from the 1991 and 1996 EHCS provide no clear evidence that rents are related to conditions, analysis of the 1998 landlord survey shows that within the deregulated sector, especially that owned by investment motivated landlords, rental rates of return are related to conditions. The analysis uses an adjusted condition in order to compare data on rents, maintenance costs and capital values collected during the 1998 landlord survey with a measure of condition in the same year. This was done by adjusting the repair costs of the sample dwellings by the subsequent expenditure landlords had incurred (this can be only a proxy as it does not take account of deterioration between 1996 and 1998).

Table 11.9 shows the results for dwellings in the deregulated sector that are owned by business and sideline investor landlords. These results show that:

- Rents are not related to condition (although rent per square metre is higher in better than poorer properties, as a result of the fact that poorer condition properties are larger than better properties).
- Gross and net rental rates of return are related to condition, being higher among the poorer than the better condition properties. The relationships for the deregulated sector as a whole are not very strong, but are stronger and more significant among those addresses owned by business and sideline investor landlords. The relationships imply that annual net rental rates of return are 2.5 per cent lower among the best than the worst properties.
- The reason why returns, but not rents, are related to condition is because both annual spending on maintenance and minor repair and vacant possession market values are higher among the better than the poorer condition properties. Hence, at the 'top end' of the condition spectrum, the rents are

But, because capital values do reflect property conditions while rents do not, rental yields are higher at the bottom end of the market. Thus, landlords of the worst property have little short-term financial incentive to improve their property and to spend more on repairs as they will not be rewarded by higher rents. Spending more will instead lower their net rental yield. Although the evidence shows that conditions were related to capital values, this does not necessarily mean that landlords improving the worst properties will make a capital gain, even though they may not be able to increase rents. This is because there is evidence of capital losses among the worst condition properties. These are also where arrears and voids are highest. Although this suggests that investment in repairs and improvements may reduce voids and arrears, the 'neighbourhood' effect on both voids and on capital values inhibits what can be achieved by way of higher return. This suggests that the owners of the worst property were, in effect, 'milking' them for their rental income. Because neither rents nor capital values are likely to increase commensurately with improvement works, it may thus not be economically rational, even though it is socially desirable, for landlords of the worst property to undertake such action.

These findings imply that the market is not providing rational investors with sufficient incentives to undertake the work that is needed on the worst properties. In other words, this appears to be a case of market failure. It raises the question of whether intervention by central or local government could be effective in improving the condition of the worst property. This could involve enforcement action or financial assistance.

Various kinds of enforcement activity have been proposed as ways of ensuring that landlords carry improvements or repairs (for DETR, 2000a; DLTR, 2001). These include: a statutory duty on landlords to keep their property in a fit condition; the introduction of mandatory licensing for houses in multiple occupation; the introduction of licensing of all dwellings in low-demand areas; and the introduction of a restriction on housing benefit payments where a property is below some minimum standard.

However, the success of these enforcement strategies depends on landlords receiving a competitive rate of return (whether from rents or capital values) on the expenditure required to comply with these minimum standards. The evidence suggests that this will not happen and that investment-oriented landlords (who own the majority of the worst stock) will have difficulty in complying, with the result that enforcement action will be long drawn out, and eventually frustrated, or that landlords will withdraw from the market. Hence newer, tougher, enforcement measures would not, of themselves, address the fundamental economic and financial barriers to improvements and might lead to a reduction in overall supply.

Of course, enforcement action that leads to a reduction in the supply of the worst stock may not necessarily be a bad thing if it is accompanied by a replacement supply of good accommodation – available in the right locations to similar households and supplied by responsible landlords. This can include both existing good standard dwellings previously in the owner occupied market and new construction. The most effective way of ensuring that that happens may be to attract into the market corporate landlords funded by City institutions and with a long-term interest in the condition of their properties and a sufficiently large portfolio to achieve economies of scale and to take a proactive stance on repairs and maintenance. A number of obstacles would, however, need to be tackled before financial institutions could be persuaded to become large-scale investors in the residential lettings market (see Crook and Kemp, 1999; Crook, this volume).

But even if enforcement action were to be combined with measures to encourage new investment in the sector, it is unlikely to transform the bottom end of the market, especially as it will take time for these new and improved dwellings to come 'on stream'. Further action will be needed. This may include giving existing landlords financial assistance to afford minimum standards, subject to landlords meeting certain conditions regarding the management and maintenance of the dwellings and their availability for letting. Financial assistance is particularly needed in low-demand neighbourhoods where landlords do not have the prospects, under current conditions, of capital gains arising from investment in repairs and improvements. Financial assistance might take the form of grants, low interest loans, and equity sharing loans. There should be a recognition that loans will be less effective than grants in obtaining better conditions at the bottom end of the market because of the limited extent to which landlords can expect to achieve higher rents or enhanced capital values following improvement. While accepting, therefore, the general proposition that loans should have greater priority over grants in the future than in the past (DETR, 2001c), policy and practice about financial assistance should also recognise the particular circumstances in the deregulated private rented sector, which does not appear to be delivering higher rents for better conditions. Hence it cannot easily provide the basis for loan repayments. As a complement to financial assistance for existing landlords, a strategy to buy out landlords by registered social landlords (RSLs) could be introduced, with RSLs purchasing substandard properties from private landlords who are either unable or unwilling to undertake the necessary work and to comply with appropriate management standards.

It is unlikely that any one approach will work on its own. Wholesale reliance on the market is unlikely to address all the problems among the worst dwellings. But an enforcement strategy that does not take into account the workings of the market is equally unlikely to work. This suggests that a combination of approaches will be needed and that specific combinations will be required to meet local circumstances. It will take time before new corporate City-funded lettings companies emerge, able to provide high-quality accommodation to replace the worst dwellings. Hence, in the immediate future, an enforcement strategy, allied to financial assistance for prudent, competent and responsible landlords should be implemented together with the acquisition by RSLs of the worst dwellings owned by those landlords unable or unwilling to comply with appropriate physical and management standards.

Acknowledgements

The evidence and policy discussion in this chapter draws upon three pieces of research (Crook, Henneberry and Hughes, 1998; Crook et al, 2000; Crook and Hughes, 2001) undertaken with the author's colleagues, Professor John Henneberry and John Hughes (at the University of Sheffield) and Professor Peter Kemp (at the University of York). Their generous contribution to that work is hereby fully acknowledged The interpretations in this chapter are, however, those of the author alone and not necessarily of his collaborators in that research.

Appendix: list of variables used in the regression analyses

Dependent variables
NETYRENT   Annual gross rent (£), excluding service charges
VAL91AS   Dwelling value as stands in November 1991

Independent variables

Dwelling variables
CONVDUM   Dwelling is converted flat
DETDUM   Dwelling is detached house
PBFLDUM   Dwelling is purpose built flat
SEMIDUM   Dwelling is semi-detached house
P64DUM   Dwelling is post-1964
PWARDUM   Dwelling is 1945-1964
INWARDUM   Dwelling is 1919-1944
FLOOR91X   Total floor area to nearest square metre
ROOMS   Number of rooms occupied by tenants
BEDROOMS   Number of bedrooms in sole occupancy of tenants
CHEATDUM   Dwelling has part or full central heating
FURNDUM   Dwelling is furnished
GARAGDUM   Dwelling has garage

Regional variables
EMDUM   Dwelling in East Midlands region
EDUM   Dwelling in East region
NDUM   Dwelling in North region
NWDUM   Dwelling in North West region
SEDUM   Dwelling in South East region
SWDUM   Dwelling in South West region
WMDUM   Dwelling in West Midlands region
YHDUM   Dwelling in Yorkshire and Humberside region

Environmental variables
GRAFDUM   Graffiti problems in the neighbourhood
LITTDUM   Litter problem in the neighbourhood
NOISDUM   Noise problem in the neighbourhood
SHOPDUM   Shops conditions problems in neighbourhood
PARKDUM   Parking problems in the neighbourhood
PAVEDUM   Pavement disrepair problems in the neighbourhood
ROADDUM   Road disrepair problems in the neighbourhood
RUBBDUM   Rubbish problems in the neighbourhood
TRAFDUM   Traffic problems in the neighbourhood
VANDUM   Vandalism problems in the neighbourhood
VISDUM   Visually unattractive neighbourhood
AREADUM   Satisfactory external dwelling conditions in the neighbourhood

Land use variables
LATENDUM   Local authority housing predominates in the neighbourhood
AREASDUM   Non-residential land use in the neighbourhood
ODDUSDUM   Odd land uses in the neighbourhood
VACSDUM   Vacant dwellings in the neighbourhood

Tenant household variables

ASIANDUM	Asian tenant household
BLACKDUM	Black (not Asian) tenant household
FAMDUM	Tenant household with children (not lone parent)
ADULTDUM	Large adult tenant household
LOPARDUM	Lone parent tenant household
OAPSDUM	Retired tenant household
HBDUM	Tenants receive part or full housing benefit
HHSIZE	Number of persons in tenant household

Dwelling condition variables

UNFITDUM	Dwelling unfit
WST10DUM	Dwelling in worst 10% of all 1991 EHCS conditions
BST30DUM	Dwelling in best 30% of all 1991 EHCS conditions
TIPRIX	Cost of comprehensive repairs outstanding in 1991
TUPRIX	Cost of urgent repairs to dwelling needed in 1991
TAPRIX	Cost of general repairs to dwelling needed in 1991

Tenant satisfaction variables

VDISSDUM	Tenant very dissatisfied with dwelling
DISATDUM	Tenant dissatisfied with dwelling
VSATDUM	Tenant very satisfied with dwelling

Landlord variable

RESLLDUM	Dwelling has resident landlord

Source: Crook and Hughes (2001)

TWELVE

Room for improvement: the impact of the local authority grant system

Mike Ellison

Introduction

Local authority grant aid for the repair, improvement and adaptation of private rented dwellings is governed by the 1996 Housing Grants, Construction and Regeneration Act. While the worst housing conditions, in absolute terms, are still found in the private rented sector, local authority grant aid has not made a large-scale impact on conditions in the sector. This chapter focuses on the condition of the private rented sector, the provision for grant assistance, local authorities responses to their powers under the 1996 Act, based on a survey of local authorities in England in 1999, and the implication of the government's further reform of private sector renewal.

House conditions in the private rented sector

People living in the private rented sector experience the worst housing conditions. This has been a consistent finding of recent English House Condition Surveys. While the largest proportion of poor housing is now in the owner occupied sector the worst conditions in absolute terms are found in the smaller private rented sector.

The English House Condition Survey 1996 (DETR, 1998a), published May 1998, showed that the private rented sector is very fluid. Only 65 per cent of the private rented sector in 1996 had also been privately rented at the time of the previous survey, in 1991.

The large turnover in dwellings in the sector accounted for the overall improvement in housing conditions between 1991 and 1996 far more than any action to improve individual properties. The dwellings moving into the private rented sector had lower levels of disrepair than dwellings already in the sector.

Despite a general improvement in conditions in the sector, people living in private rented accommodation are still more likely to experience poor housing conditions and lack important facilities and services to provide a safe and warm living environment, compared to people living in the owner occupied, local

---

The definition of tenant for disabled facilities grants is set out in Section 19(5). This includes secure, introductory, statutory, agricultural, and employment related tenants and licences, which satisfy any conditions specified by the Secretary of State.

Tenant is again separately defined for the purposes of home repair assistance in Section 77(3). This includes secure, statutory, agricultural and employment related tenancies, except those of a number of public bodies. Home repair assistance is also available to people who are not tenants but who occupy a dwelling under a right of exclusive occupation granted for life or for a period of more than five years (Section 77(4)).

Tenants' applications for renovation grants, disabled facilities grants and common parts grants are means tested to determine what contribution, if any, the tenant will be required to make towards the cost of the grant aided works. The means test is detailed in the 1996 Housing Renewal Grants Regulations, as amended. The test has a similar structure to housing benefit/council tax benefit, but the regulations are not identical. The aim of the means test is to determine the value of a notional standard repayment loan over five years, at a given interest rate, that the tenant could afford to repay using a proportion of any 'excess income' that he or she has calculated under the regulations.

Landlords

The 1996 Act allows landlords to apply for renovation grants, HMO grants and disabled facilities grants for the benefit of a disabled occupant. Applications for grant aid have to be accompanied by one of a series of landlord's certificates. Landlords can also join a tenant's application for a common parts grant.

In relation to renovation grants the landlord must specify in a certificate of intended letting that he or she intends, for a period of five years following completion of the grant aid works, that the dwelling will be let or available for letting as a residence (not a holiday let) to a person who is not a member of his or her own family. In the case of personal representatives or trustees a person who is not a beneficiary.

The landlord's certificate for HMO grants is similar to that for renovation grants stating that the intention for the next five years is for the house or part of it to be residentially occupied, or available for residential occupation, under tenancies or licences by people who are not members of the landlord's family.

In relation to disabled facilities grants the landlord must specify that the intention is that the disabled occupant, for whose benefit the adaptations will be carried out, will live in the dwelling as the only or main residence for the next five years or for such shorter period as his or her health and other relevant circumstances permit.

There is no defined means test for landlords' grants. The local housing authority has a discretion in determining what level of grant aid, if any, to make available for each landlord's application. Section 31 of the 1996 Act requires the local authority, in determining the level of assistance, to have regard to the extent to which the landlord is able to charge a higher rent for the premises as a result of completing the works and that the local authority may seek and act upon the advice of rent officers.

Guidance by the then DoE states that "… an owner is primarily responsible for the upkeep of his property, and grant should only be an option where market forces are not operating effectively. Care should be taken to ensure an authority's grants policy does not leave the impression that grant has been used to reward poor management" (circular 17/96, para 51, annex J2).

This approach is illustrated by the policy of one Eastern district authority:

> We consider that landlords should be solely responsible for the repair and maintenance of their own properties and that it would be inappropriate to make grant aid available in these circumstances. However, in the case of unfit property which has been vacant for a long period, exceptions will be considered, subject to conditions. (July 1999)

The DoE's guidance goes on to suggest a number of factors that local authorities may consider in determining the amount of grant that should be awarded in landlord's applications:

- Whether the cost of the works should be affordable from the current rental income.
- Whether the works relate to safety improvements, which might be considered high priority for grant aid.
- The type of tenancy – regulated rents are less likely to provide surplus resources to fund improvements
- Current rent levels – where a landlord is charging a reasonable rent rather than one who charges higher rents than comparable rents locally.
- Age of the property.
- Strategic objectives of the authority in that locality.
- Any increase in the capital value of the property.
- Likelihood of the works proceeding without grant aid.
- Ability of the local authority to attach conditions over nomination rights.
- The landlord's record of keeping properties in good repair.

The guidance also reminds authorities that they must exercise their discretion under Section 31 reasonably and avoid a blanket approach, such as awarding grant of a certain percentage of the cost of works in every case.

Despite this guidance a number of local authorities have adopted blanket approaches to grants policies which appear to fetter their discretion either in relation to the amount of grant assistance available, as in the case of one North East district authority ("For landlords the grant is 25%, up to a maximum of £5,000" – August 1999), or in relation to the availability of grant aid at all, as in the case of a South East district authority ("During the severe financial restrictions on the grant budget 1997/98 Discretionary Grants for landlords were stopped. This was a difficult decision at the time with concern expressed about the potential knock on effect on innocent tenants" – July 1999).

Take up of tenants' and landlords' grants

There has never been widespread take up of grant aid by either tenants or landlords. The main reasons for this are a mixture of a lack of awareness of the availability of grant aid and the difficulty/complexity in applying for it.

In circular 17/96 the then DoE stated:

> The majority of landlords are not aware that local authorities can provide assistance in helping them improve the properties they own, and those that are aware of the grant system may lack information on what it can provide.

Due to financial constraints most local authorities have not advertised the availability of grants. One South East district authority saw the potential benefit of making grant aid available but considered that they did not have sufficient resources to do so:

> ... the Council wishes to use grant aid as an inducement to landlords to improve properties for letting ... the ability of the Council to fund such grant aid is unlikely to be available in the foreseeable future, due to capital resource constraints. (March 1997)

Some well-informed landlords and tenants will be able to seek grant aid but many will remain unaware that they may be able to receive financial assistance to improve and repair their properties.

Landlords who have considered applying for grant aid have often been unwilling to meet the five-year undertaking of future letting. The 1996 Act that introduced this condition also introduced another giving local authorities the power to reserve nomination rights over the property during the five-year grant condition period. Many authorities have exercised their discretion to introduce nomination rights as a grant condition, as did this Yorkshire district authority:

> ... a supplementary condition be applied to all grants given to landlords requiring Local Authority nomination rights to the property for a 5 year period. (June 1999)

The 1996 Act introduced a revised suite of housing renewal grants. Local authorities were given more discretionary powers to award renovation grants compared to the mandatory regime under the previous 1989 Local Government and Housing Act. Although the Act abolished mandatory renovation grants, Circular 17/96 stressed that, "... it is the intention of the Government that local authorities should still make use of discretionary grants ... for the improvement of private sector housing" (chapter 5, para 5.1.1). The circular also highlighted the need for local authorities to develop clear policies for dealing with future applications for grant aid,

The move to a mainly discretionary grant regime will highlight the need to have in place a clear strategy within which all grant applications can be considered. The application of the strategy will need to be:

• objective
• fair and reasonable
• open and transparent' (chapter 5, para 5.1.3).

Guidance reminded authorities that their criteria for grant aid "… should be agreed by the appropriate Council Committee and feature within an authority's housing strategy and implementation plan" (chapter 5, para 5.3.1).

Many local authorities took the opportunity of the move to a more discretionary grant regime and their fears over the lack of adequate central government subsidy for private sector renewal to draw up restrictive grant strategies. This approach is illustrated by the decline in the number of renovation grants paid under the two statutory regimes between 1995/96 and 1998/99. Figures published by the then DETR show that over 36,500 grants were paid by local authorities in England in 1995/96, the last full year of the 1989 Act regime. By 1998/99 the number of grants paid had fallen to just over 17,000.

Local authority grants strategies

With the implementation of the 1996 Act and its move to a more discretionary approach to grant aid, local authorities were required to review their grant strategies and determine priorities for future grant aid. Although the provisions of Part I of the Act came into effect from 17 December 1996 many authorities took some time to develop their new approach and to obtain approval from the appropriate council committee.

Analysis of over 140 local authority strategies, in place in 1999, highlights a wide discrepancy in approaches adopted by different local authorities. A number of factors appear as key influences on individual authorities' approaches to grant aid in the private sector. Fears over the lack of available resources to fund a comprehensive strategy is frequently cited in council committee reports for having to take a restrictive approach to private sector renewal.

Stock tenure profiles and particularly the number of houses in multiple occupation also can be seen to have a significant influence on an authority's strategy. To a lesser extent an authority's perception of private renting as a commercial activity on the one hand or the need to protect and assist vulnerable tenants on the other has influenced the development of policies on grant aid on private rented properties.

Some authorities misinterpreted their discretion to determine priorities for future grant aid as the power to withdraw grant aid from some types of applicants altogether. One example was subject to investigation by the Local Government Ombudsman in 1998. In this case a landlord applied for grant aid to help finance works subject to an improvement notice by the local authority prior to the implementation of the 1996 Act. The local authority wrote to the landlord in March 1997 stating:

> The City Council is no longer required to approve your application ... the Council's new discretionary grant policy under the 1996 Act was agreed by the Housing Committee on 4 March 1997. Under the new policy no provision is made for discretionary grants to landlords.

Following a complaint by the landlord, the ombudsman concluded that the council's policy, as expressed in their letter, fettered their discretion and prevented it from considering the exceptional circumstances of the grant applicant. Part of the ombudsman's recommendations to remedy the injustice suffered by the grant applicant as a result of the local authority's maladministration was that it should review its grants policy for landlords.

A number of other authorities appear to have taken a blanket approach to restricting the availability of grant aid to private sector landlords. The grants advice leaflet of one authority in the Home Counties, in July 1999 simply stated, "Landlords are not eligible". The committee report of an authority in the Midlands at the same time clearly stated that it was the policy of the council not to consider grants for houses in multiple occupation or common parts of buildings. Another Midlands district authority took the view that resources should be directed to other sectors:

> Renovation/HMO grant aid to HMO landlords is now withdrawn and diverted to funding improved housing conditions for needy owner occupiers.

Many other authorities developed very restricted approaches without completely removing the possibility of grant aid to landlords:

> There will be generally no grant aid for landlords/freeholders of property let in the private sector. (Midlands district authority, November 1996)

Many authorities determined a targeted approach to assisting private landlords with grant aid. Some policies were designed to target assistance at particular types of landlords. One Home Counties district authority's policy, in January 1999, stated that renovation would not normally be made available to landlords other than where the landlord was a registered charity or an almshouse trust. Meanwhile one neighbouring authority targeted assistance to small-scale landlords (excluding charities) owning no more than two properties other than their principal home.

Some authorities have sought to target assistance to particular types of repairs or improvements. Means of fire escape, thermal insulation and empty properties are frequently identified as works that are suitable for grant aid. Works required under Housing Act Notices, rather than other repairs, are often prioritised except in those authorities that took the view that these types of works should be funded by landlords in the ordinary course of events. For example, one East district authority's committee report, dated February 1997, included:

> I recommend that the council's policy be not to give grants to landlords for
> works required to meet their legal obligations.

Other criteria that have been developed have focused on private rented accommodation at less than market rent, where the landlord is less able to fund works from rental income, or to particular geographical areas especially in renewal areas, or to particular types of tenants. For example, one London borough, in June 1997, prioritised renovation grants for landlords to restore unfit properties and properties in substantial disrepair which are occupied by tenants aged 60 or over.

A Midlands district authority sought to include an additional condition to grant assistance to landlords that their tenants should have "a local connection through work or family ties".

Local authorities have also attempted to develop strategies to reward good landlords with a record of care for their tenants and their properties or those who are cooperative with the authority in undertaking repairs or improvements. Authorities have equally been anxious not to reward bad landlords who have poor standards and who are reluctant to remedy defects with their properties. A number of authorities' policies have aimed to make grant assistance available to landlords who cooperate without the need for formal enforcement action and exclude those landlords to whom statutory notices have been issued.

In June 1999, a South West district authority introduced a concept of a 'Good Landlord's Correction Factor' to the grant calculation in an effort to ensure that "good landlords obtain maximum grant aid". The Good Landlord Correction Factor includes an assessment of the standard of management/ maintenance of the property, any previous enforcement action required, and complaints from current tenants.

A South East district authority expressed their strategy in the following terms:

> The Council attaches importance to the level of co-operation received from
> landlords and will seek to reward those landlords who have consistently acted
> responsibly toward the maintenance of their properties. Conversely, the
> Council does not intend to reward those landlords who have consistently
> refused to co-operate with the Council and whose disregard for the welfare
> of their tenants and the maintenance of their properties has resulted in the
> need for enforcement activity. (December 1998)

A few local authorities have gone further in their attempts to marry the availability of grant aid to the promotion of good practice by landlords. Accreditation schemes give landlords a mark of approval in return for a and tenants to tackle poor conditions can make an impact on improving individual properties. However, at the current rate of assistance, grant aid is unlikely to make a large-scale impact on conditions in the private rented sector as a whole.

Local authorities have largely reacted to their increased discretion and the move away from mandatory renovation grants, introduced in the 1996 Act, to restrict availability of grant aid to the private rented sector. The main motivations for this are concerns over the availability of housing capital finance to fund the grants system and the need to balance the use of public money to improve poor conditions in the sector with the responsibility landlords should bear for their commercial activity.

The proposed replacement of the current grant regime with a general power for local authorities to assist with repairs, improvements and adaptations by way of grants, loans and other measures is unlikely to make a significant difference unless it leads to an increase in the overall resources available for private sector renewal and local authorities view the private rented sector as a priority for assistance.

Payment of housing benefit is a more significant factor in poor condition private rented tenancies than grant aid is likely to be. There is, therefore, a logical approach in creating penalties within the housing benefit system, even where there are incentives through grant aid for landlords to improve conditions in their properties. The challenge will be to visit the penalties within housing benefit upon the landlords of properties in poor condition and not the innocent tenants, many of whom are older people in long term tenancies, younger households and unemployed people, who have little or no access to alternative housing options.

THIRTEEN

New law, new policy

David Hughes and Stuart Lowe

In April 2000 the Government issued its Green Paper on housing, *Quality and Choice: A decent home for all* (DETR, 2000a). The majority of this was taken up with proposals for social housing; only one chapter (chapter 5) dealt with the private rented sector. Perhaps significantly this was headed 'Promoting a healthy private rented sector', evidence that the continuance and viability of this sector is part of central policy, not least in so far as it provides extra housing choices for those who are not willing – or who are not *yet* willing – to buy their own home, especially younger households. A secondary function is the flexibility private renting provides for the economy by enabling people who need to move to find work to obtain accommodation, while enabling those who are away from home for some time to let out their properties. The Green Paper therefore declared a policy of wishing to see the sector grow and prosper with no major legislative changes intended that could have an inhibiting effect; rather the declared objectives were to raise the standards of management among the majority of private landlords, particularly those who rent only a few properties who, arguably, lack management skills and experience. The Green Paper here stressed that encouragement, support and education largely provided at a local level by authorities and professional and voluntary organisations would be the preferred way forward, though central government accepted it would have a role in spreading best practice and in giving support generally.

The features of a system based on encouragement, support and education were identified as use of local accreditation systems for landlords and development of a National Approved Lettings Scheme (NALS) by relevant trade bodies so that small landlords may be able to identify reliable agents through whom to let, while in some cases registered social landlords might be able to provide low-cost management services for landlords.

With regard to landlords who provide bad accommodation or a poor service or both, the import of the Green Paper was that they should either improve or get out of letting altogether. With regard to poor physical conditions, proposals to replace the existing housing fitness standard with a new health and safety rating scale were argued to be the best way forward, enabling authorities to have a clearer idea of which properties need the most urgent intervention, while targeting the use of existing financial resources for home improvement more efficiently. Significantly, no mention was made of an increase in funding for home improvement.

students to be accredited in some way to ensure acceptable standards of accommodation and management? It will not be easy to replace the current complex warp and weft of housing tenures that has grown up as a system of individual responses to perceived problems with a new model that meets all needs and satisfies all interests.

Following on from the initial modernisation proposal the scoping paper envisaged that the law reform exercise would consist of two phases. The first would be the issue of reforming housing status as outlined above, and would have two 'limbs', the long-term tenancy and its short-term counterpart. The former would consider: the definition and scope of such a tenancy; its creation and terms including, *inter alia*, information about tenancy terms, rules for amending a tenancy and for consulting tenants, creation of joint tenancies and sub-letting; security of tenure, termination and possession issues, including grounds for possession, the variety of court orders available in tenancy proceedings and their effects, use of possession proceedings in rent arrears cases, and the effect of various notices given by either landlord or tenant, including the effect of notice to quit given by one joint tenant on the rights of the other. The 'short-term tenancy limb' was envisaged as dealing with: the definition and scope of such a tenancy, including its applicability to social housing; the creation of such a tenancy, including the issues of what information should be given to tenants and that of whether there should be a power to vary the level of rent charged; the terms of such a tenancy, including the question of whether there should be a statutory requirement for all such tenancies to be written, with a default position for landlords and tenants who do not have written agreements that a set of statutory terms should automatically apply; and access to rent fixing mechanisms and the questions of termination and possession. The second phase of reform would consider the issues of harassment and unlawful eviction, and succession. At a later stage consideration would have to be given to integrating the work done on the foregoing issues with other matters such as revision of the law relating to repairing obligations and fitness standards.

The Law Commission proposals, though quite extensive from a lawyer's point of view, would not be so radical in their effect as that great change in the balance of interests between landlords and tenants which came about under the Thatcher and Major governments. Before 1980 the pattern of the legislation, despite occasional changes of course such as the short-lived alterations made by the 1957 Rent Act (see Chapter One), had been, for the better part of the 20th century, one of favouring private sector tenants. The long-term interest of tenants in maintaining their *homes* was allowed to trump the interests of landlords in their *houses*. At the same time it is true that no parallel security existed for public sector tenants, but the assumption seems to have been that de facto they had security, which was only to be disturbed in exceptional circumstances. The 1980 Housing Act was a major turning point not only in granting security of tenure to public sector tenants – although sceptics might argue only so as to create a class of people able to enjoy the right to buy and so cease to be tenants – but also by the introduction of limited security in the private sector by the new creations of protected shortholds and the 'Mark I' assured tenancy. The 'Mark II' assured tenancy and the assured shorthold tenancy introduced in 1988 brought a significant change in the balance of interests of landlords and tenants, and that change was confirmed by the 1996 Housing Act, which effectively made the assured shorthold the 'normal' tenancy for private sector lettings, with assured tenancies being the exception reserved primarily for use by registered social landlords.

The Law Commission issued its Consultation Paper No 162, *Renting homes 1: Status and security* (Law Commission, 2002), on 10 April 2002, dealing with the legal framework for regulating the provision of homes by all landlords. The proposals built on the earlier work of the Commission by continuing to argue for a reduction in the number of housing statuses and the removal of as many as possible of the differences between them, with a view to new legislation being included in the government's programme for 2003/04. The basic principles underpinning the proposals were declared to be: a continuing guarantee in law of security of tenure for tenants in appropriate circumstances; repossession of dwellings only after due process of law; the incorporation of a consumer-based perspective into housing law, and compatibility with human rights under the 1998 Human Rights Act.

Briefly, the outline of the proposals follows the initial scoping document in arguing for two basic statutory housing statuses – 'Type I' having considerable security of tenure and being principally used by 'social' landlords and 'Type II' having much less security and principally used by private landlords. Each of these types would be based on a written contract that should contain the obligations and rights of both landlord and tenant. The duty to provide the written agreement would fall on the landlord. In all cases the written contract would contain 'core' terms relating to the property to be let and the rent, 'compulsory' terms that would include any terms implied by law – for example as to repairs – and terms defining the circumstances entitling the landlord to seek possession, and 'default/negotiable' terms setting out a detailed statement of the other rights and obligations of the parties. The terms here would be those on a prescribed list laid down by ministerially made regulations. In default of particular agreement by the parties the terms in the regulations would apply. These regulations would be made only after consultation with relevant interests in the housing industry to ensure the fairness and clarity of the terms.

One important proposed feature is that not only would a court order be required before possession could be obtained but also that the landlord would need to give warning in writing that proceedings for possession are contemplated. In addition to such formal proceedings, however, it is proposed that the use of alternative dispute resolution proceedings should be encouraged to deal with issues arising between the parties, for example where an allegation of anti-social behaviour is made against a tenant. Such mechanisms could serve to solve disputes and give a chance for behaviour to be amended without putting the tenancy at risk.

It was further proposed that the rationalised structure of housing statuses should apply not only to tenancies and licences coming into existence after the commencement of the new legislation but also to those currently in existence.

The issues in greater detail

Fair contracts

The relationship of landlord and tenant is essentially a contractual one and the Law Commission's proposals reflected consumerist thinking on the law of contract which stresses that bargains should be fair and transparent. This is in considerable contrast to the historic conception of the common law which stressed freedom of contract and the argument that parties to a contract are able to conclude any terms they wish – a notion which, of course, entirely ignores any disparity of bargaining power between the parties. Consumerist theories seek to redress any such imbalance.

Thus, a central theme of the proposals is that the law should be based on the notion of initially fair and balanced contractual terms rather than the current position whereby statutory rules are required to override unbalanced agreements. These fair terms would be contained in a single document to which both parties could refer for their rights and obligations rather than having to look to external statutory intervention. Interestingly, however, the proposals stress that one object of the 'new' contractual approach would be to ensure an understanding by landlords that becoming a landlord is concerned as much with providing a service to customers as it is about temporarily granting a right to occupy land. This emphasis on a new 'ethos' for landlords may be hard to achieve in practice given the background and nature of many small landlords in the 'pure' private rented sector.

Several authors in this volume allude to this issue. Hector Currie, for example, in his discussion of the licensing of HMOs in Scotland (Chapter Ten) makes the point that in reality it remains at best uncertain whether HMO licensing will improve the standard of management in the PRS. Regulation may simply drive landlords from the market because essentially their interest is commercial not ethical. Similarly Diane Lister (Chapter Seven) points out that one feature of small landlords' attitude to letting is *their* ability to control their property(ies). All this casts some doubt on the idea that landlords might come to see their investments as providing a service rather than a commercial return on capital. Better landlords no doubt, and justifiably, consider that there is an element of public service in what they do but whether the majority of run-of-the-mill landlords might be persuaded to adopt an ethic of public service, possibly against their own perceived interest, is questionable.

The emphasis on 'fairness' and transparency would apply throughout the contract of letting according to the proposals, including those open to negotiation, it being the hope of the Law Commission that the consultation process would itself produce a set of terms which would command widespread acceptance as representing a fair balance between the interests of the parties. To this end a series of model agreements to be made widely available in hard copy and electronic forms was also proposed.

To give 'teeth' to the fairness and transparency philosophy the Law Commission proposed a 'rent sanction' whereby landlords would be liable to suffer deductions in rent (on a daily basis up to a maximum of two months' rent) for each day's delay in providing an appropriate written contract after the expiry of the initial two weeks after possession has been assumed. Whether further criminal sanctions against defaulting landlords should be provided for was left as an open issue for consultation, but it was proposed that there should be a further right for tenants and licensees to go either to the court or to a rent assessment committee to obtain an order to make the landlord commit the terms of any oral agreement to writing accurately or to correct any inaccuracy in a written agreement. Here, however, it may be questioned whether, given the reluctance of some tenants to challenge the activities of some landlords, this remedy might not be anything more than cosmetic in reality. Diane Lister's research (Chapter Seven) shows clearly that in many cases, especially in dealings between landlords and younger tenants, the parties are ill equipped to negotiate let alone commit an agreement to paper. The notion of a clearly written, idealised statement may be, as it stands, an unrealistic expectation.

The Law Commission further addressed the need for ensuring respect for agreements. This particularly arises in the context of the proposed 'Type II', under which landlords would be able to seek possession simply by giving notice of their intention to do so. The issue arises whether such a course of action would be adopted as a way of avoiding contractual obligations on which a tenant or licensee sought to rely. The proposals, however, left open the question of whether such action could be dealt with either by allowing the dispossessed person to claim compensation after eviction on proof that this arose as a reaction to his or her assertion of contractual or statutory rights, or whether a system of prior accreditation of landlords would be a better method of ensuring that such reactions do not occur. Our conclusion is that many small private landlords do need help and education in fulfilling their role and hence an accreditation scheme has its attractions. On the other hand it has to be asked whether the imposition of an accreditation requirement would drive many such landlords out of the market as an extra bureaucratic burden beyond toleration. Hector Currie's evidence on the licensing of HMOs in Scotland indicates that this is particularly likely with smaller HMO landlords, so that the imposition of new layers of regulation might well have the effect of diminishing the size of the sector.

The 'Type II' contract

We shall concentrate our attention on this contract as it is clearly the one proposed principally for use by the private rented sector, which is, of course, the prime concern of this book.

This contract would be a short-term agreement with minimal security of tenure replacing the current assured shorthold tenancy. It would be used primarily by private landlords and, indeed, in the absence of other agreement between the parties it would be the 'default' agreement for such landlords. It would, however, be able to be created on both a periodic and a fixed term basis. Though security of tenure under this type of contract would be minimal there would be some, for the court would have jurisdiction to award possession on both mandatory or discretionary grounds. The former, which would relate to circumstances in which a landlord is entitled to possession and where the court would be required to grant the necessary order, would be (a) the 'notice only' ground and (b) the 'serious rent arrears' ground. It was proposed that the 'notice only' ground would provide that a landlord would be entitled to a possession order simply on the basis that the correct notice of intention to seek an order had been given in accordance with the terms of the contract of letting. There would be no need to demonstrate any fault on the part of the tenant or licensee. A further provisional proposal is that where a landlord could seek possession on the basis of notice only, that is in relation to a periodic Type II agreement, the landlord should be able to utilise an accelerated procedure which would not involve a hearing. However, this type of procedure would not be available where the letting had been for a fixed term. The 'serious rent arrears' ground would be available where two months' arrears of rent had accumulated both at the date of the notice of intention to take proceedings and which remained outstanding at the date of the possession hearing. This ground of possession would be available with regard to both fixed term and periodic lettings. As a supplement to this proposal the Law Commission further provisionally proposed that in the absence in a contract of any system for recording rent payments there should be a statutory, but rebuttable, presumption that rent has been paid. Furthermore, they also provisionally proposed that it should be a term of all relevant contracts of letting that the landlord should provide a documented system of payment records.

There would be, according to the Law Commission proposals, no other mandatory grounds for possession; any other ground, for example acts of nuisance or annoyance by a tenant, would be discretionary. It was also proposed that at the expiry of a fixed term Type II agreement where no other agreement had been reached that a periodic agreement should automatically arise.

Although the Type II contract would provide only minimal security of tenure the Law Commission proposals argued that where market conditions demanded it landlords would be encouraged to enhance the level of protection by contractual agreement, either by granting fixed terms of 21 years or by opting to use Type I contracts.

One major development of existing law would arise if the proposal from the Commission to introduce 'structured discretion' with regard to discretionary grounds of possession were to be introduced. Under existing law where such discretion exists it is a matter for the court to decide how to exercise that discretion, and superior courts such as the Court of Appeal have been loath to interfere greatly in the exercise of that discretion. The Law Commission, however, have proposed an explicit list of factors to be taken into account by courts in future, including:

- whether the eviction of the household concerned would be proportional to the benefit to be gained, clearly reflecting the need for courts to comply with the 1998 Human Rights Act which demands such an exercise;
- the effects of granting or not granting an order, not only on the tenant and his/her household but also on the landlord;
- the landlord's interests;
- the interests of the landlord's other tenants;
- the interests of the general public.

Clearly, many of the factors outlined above would be particularly relevant in relation to Type I contracts utilised by local authorities and registered social landlords, but they cannot be entirely ignored with regard to Type II contracts and represent an interesting refocusing of the way in which courts would be expected to go about exercising discretionary powers.

The conversion of existing assured shorthold tenancies into 'Type II'

The Law Commission's initial proposal in general here is that legislation could convert current assured shortholds into Type II agreements with any specific terms of the existing tenancy, for example a fixed term agreement, becoming part of the new agreement. This could be done 'at a stroke' and not by means of phasing, and would need to be accompanied by a major public information and advice campaign. Given the low levels of knowledge of rights and obligations common among both landlords and tenants in the current private rented sector such a campaign would clearly be more than needed. Jill Morgan notes in Chapter Eight, for example, the need for education of landlords in relation to the harassment issue.

Assessment of the proposals

It is not easy to assess the proposals, or to predict the final outcome of events, as so many of them are in outline form, while the overall exercise itself is only a consultative one. Even so the degree of continuity between the initial scoping paper and the consultation exercise gives rise to indication of the general way in which both law and policy are likely to move, particularly with regard to the private rented sector.

In practice under the current law the majority of tenants have only very limited rights as they occupy under the terms of assured shorthold tenancies. This would be confirmed if the broad thrust of the consultative proposals is followed through into legislation. Indeed the concept of a 'notice only' mandatory ground of possession in respect of periodic Type II agreements would finally lay to rest almost a century of law and policy in which the status of residential tenancies has generally attracted a considerable degree of legislative protection. In its place would be a frank recognition of the fundamentally commercial and contractual nature of private sector tenancies. As the current legal position is hardly far removed from this it is really rather hollow to debate whether the final loss of security of tenure would be balanced by the enhanced clarity of contractual obligations to be brought about by the proposals.

No doubt tenants would be grateful for clear and unambiguous statements of their rights and obligations, as, no doubt, would some landlords. However, it is debatable to what extent small private landlords could be persuaded to regard their activities as a true service industry. As Tony Crook points out in Chapter Two the sector is dominated by individual landlords, many of whom have no qualifications in the lettings business and think of their one or two properties mainly as investments. The idea that they might come to have a public service view of this seems rather far removed from the reality.

On 18th July 2001 the government introduced the Home Energy Conservation Bill into Parliament, which was considerably amended during its passage. It is odd that the Bill should have been given a title relating to energy conservation, for much of it is concerned with amending the law relating to houses in multiple occupation (HMOs). Such properties have been at the centre of much of the debate over the future of the private rented sector in housing for many years for frequently, though not inevitably, they are in poor physical or unsafe condition, with a considerable lack of amenities for occupants. Particular problems have arisen over the definition of what constitutes a HMO: clearly the existing control powers of local authorities can only be applied to properties that are within the legal definition.

A particularly contentious issue has been whether property occupied by students will automatically fall within the definition of HMO. For many years local authority practice in many areas was to treat student accommodation in the private rented sector as falling within control. This was upset by the decision in *Barnes v Sheffield City Council* (1995) 27 HLR 719, which stressed that it is the way in which people occupy a dwelling that is the determining factor, not their educational status. If a group of students occupy a house they rent in a way that is analogous to family occupation – by sharing the chores of daily living, they form a single household and their house is not a HMO.

The current proposals could change that, but in a somewhat roundabout way. The Secretary of State would be given extensive powers to adapt and modify the definition of what constitutes 'multiple occupation'. It is likely that these powers would be used to bring student lettings generally with HMO control. However, the initial proposal of July 2001 would have been a much more radical innovation which would have classified any property as a HMO where it was "occupied by adult members of more than two families". This would have caught flat sharers and would have resulted in nearly all property let to three or more people being classified as a HMO. That met with strong opposition from organisations representing small landlords.

Similar examples of a retreat from quite draconian initial proposals can be encountered when other provisions are examined. Thus, under the existing law, local authorities have powers to make registration schemes which can lead to the imposition of particular controls on HMOs. The parallel legislation in Scotland has been criticised by landlords' organisations as heavy handed in practice, with, it was alleged, authorities attempting to use their powers to exercise control not only over property but also over the wording of tenancy agreements (*The Times*, Money Section, 23 February 2002) (see also Chapter Ten). The proposed provisions for England give the Secretary of State considerable powers to make regulations to modify the working in practice of the registration provisions, and it appears that opposition from landlords in Scotland to the law north of the Border has led to second thoughts on new law south of it.

This is not, of course, to say that tenants' rights have been abandoned. What it does mean, however, is that the locus of debate over those rights will shift from Parliament, the assembly of the elected representatives of all the people, to Whitehall. There it might be supposed debate will take place between ministers and civil servants on the one hand and representatives of local housing authorities, landlord organisations and tenants' groups on the other. In such a context there is room for trade-offs and compromise between the parties.

Arguably the fact that the legislative provisions now contain fewer explicit safeguards for the rights of the occupants of HMOs means that their interests have been somewhat sacrificed to those of landlords as ministers have sought to maintain a large and diverse private rented sector and not to frighten some landlords from the lettings pool. The final shape of the regulations may, of course, tell a very different story, but time alone can tell on that point.

The story of the HMO provisions may be a pointer to the future of the private rented sector in housing. The changing nature of that sector in terms of both property and clientele may justify a considerable shift in policy terms away from the protection of tenants' interests. In legal terms this would be represented by preferring a contract-based mode of relationships between tenants and landlords over one based on statutorily created statuses. However, such a change in law and policy marks an historical discontinuity and the real question remains whether the actual state of the private rented sector as examined by our contributors justifies such a major upheaval.

How far changes in the law have influenced the revival of the private rented sector is open to debate — just as how far the legal regime from 1915 to 1980 influenced its decline. Historically other factors, such as the decline in the constituency for private renting (as people found it easier to obtain council housing or to buy their own homes), or the physical impact on the private rented stock of slum clearance programmes certainly had more influence than purely legal issues. As Steve Wilcox points out in Chapter Three a very large part of the growth in the early 1990s can be attributed to the availability of housing benefit, albeit in the context of the newly deregulated market. Arguably, it is these other factors that have influenced the growth of the sector more than the increasingly favourable legal regime that has come into being over the last 20 years. There is a new constituency for private renting, a constituency where, it can be contended, youth and mobility render the desire for security and permanence of less account than in the past. Furthermore there are more 'new players' coming into the sector in the form of those who are seeking an income from properties specifically purchased on 'mortgage to let' terms. Other 'new players' include entrepreneurs who see opportunities to utilise city centre properties in reconfigured residential forms. This latter phenomenon as Hughes and Davis describe, is easily observed in university towns where the growth in the student population has done much to help transform the private sector. Student lettings in many places had become the last refuge of many private landlords.

The new pattern of student lettings, however, appears to indicate that new money and new entrants are coming into the rental sector as providers of accommodation. Parents of students, as well as institutional investors, increasingly seek to finance their children's costly further education through buy-to-let. In this context the 'new' private rented sector is not just acting as the provider of accommodation for students, but also as a force in urban regeneration by creating central urban residential units appropriate for other sections of the population who wish to live near their work and/or their leisure opportunities, and who do not wish for the suburban pattern of family homes and gardens.

Conclusion

The environmental, demographic, financial and legal conditions are thus favourable to the re-emergence of private renting as an accommodation option – for at least some sectors of the population. But it is an option that is primarily commercial in nature, with few, if any, long-term prospects of security. There is a new constituency for private renting. It is a diverse constituency though among its features are youth and transience. But not everyone in that constituency can strike a good commercial bargain, and while the Law Commission's overall notion of modernising the tenurial pattern of private renting is undoubtedly sound, and indeed desirable, there is a need for the other mechanisms envisaged by the Green Paper, such as accreditation and selective controls for particular areas, property type and certain landlords, to be put in place as well. Tenurial change alone without protection for the vulnerable and exploitable is not desirable.

Finally, we should remind ourselves that the PRS does not operate in a vacuum. If the aim of housing policy is to meet housing need, awareness of the wider context is vital. Recent decline in PRS lettings especially in the South of England reflects the sharp increase in house prices. As in other areas of high demand, increased house prices reduce the number of households leaving the social housing sector to buy into owner occupation. The number of social housing re-lets available thus reduces considerably and in combination with reduced private sector supply creates pressure on low-income households, especially those newly forming.

Keeping our collective eye on this wider story is a point to emerge from a number of contributors. The government's idea that the revived PRS permitted a reduced need to build new social housing (implicit, as Steve Wilcox describes in Chapter Three, in at least one influential housing needs model) has to be treated with some scepticism. What is manifestly clear from these pages is the shifting sands that underpin the PRS market. As the recent decline in supply in some areas shows, and in the absence of new social rental supply, Steve Wilcox's statement that there has been "... a resurgence in the numbers of households needing to be placed in bed and breakfast and other forms of unsatisfactory temporary accommodation" is a salutary warning. Such a situation is a recipe for sustaining the worst practices in the private rental market, making accreditation and a 'better managed' sector much more difficult to achieve.

References

Allen, J. and McDowell, L. (1989) *Landlords and Property – social relations in the private rented sector*, Cambridge: Cambridge University Press.

Anderson, I. (1999) 'Young single people and access to social housing' in J.Rugg, (ed) *Young people, housing and social policy*, London: Routledge.

Armstrong, H. (1997) 'Speech by minister for housing at the annual conference of the association of residential letting agents', *Agreement: the Journal of ARLA*, vol 4, p 5.

Ashworth, A. (1978) 'Protecting the home through criminal law', *Journal of Social Welfare Law*, pp 76–85.

Bailey, N. (1996) *The deregulated private rented sector in four Scottish cities 1987-1994*, Edinburgh: Scottish Homes.

Bailey, N. (1999) 'Deregulated private renting: A decade of change in Scotland', *Netherlands Journal of Housing and the Built Environment*, vol 14, no 4, pp 363–84.

Benjamin A. (2001) 'What works: New trends in social housing practice No 14, student housing', *Roof*, Jan/Feb, pp 33-6.

Best, R., Kemp, P.A., Coleman, D., Merrett, S. and Crook, A.D.H. (1992) *The future of private renting: Consensus and action*, York: Joseph Rowntree Foundation.

Bevan, M., Kemp, P.A. and Rhodes, D. (1995) *Private landlords and housing benefit*, York: Centre for Housing Policy, University of York.

Bevan, M. and Sanderling, L. (1996) *Private renting in rural areas*, York: Centre for Housing Policy, University of York.

Brown, T. (2000) 'Government continues to ignore the particular problems of rural housing in England', *Housing*, p 37, June.

Burridge, R. (1987) *The role of discretion in the regulation of housing standards,* Paper presented to Institute of Environmental Health Officers Conference, London.

Burrows, L. and Hunter, N. (1990) *Forced out!*, London: Shelter.

Burrows, R. (1997) *Contemporary patterns of residential mobility in relation to social housing in England*, York: Centre for Housing Policy, University of York.

Cabinet Office (2000) *Sharing the nation's prosperity – economic, social and environmental conditions in the countryside*, London: The Stationery Office.

Carter, D. and Dymond, A. (1998) *Quiet enjoyment*, London: Legal Action Group.

Chapman, P., Phimister, E., Shucksmith, M., Upward, R. and Vera-Toscano, E. (1998) *Poverty and exclusion in rural Britain: The dynamics of low income and employment*, York: Joseph Rowntree Foundation.

Clark, D. (1990) *Affordable rural housing – A national survey of needs and supply*, Salisbury: Rural Development Commission.

Conley, J.M. and O'Barr, W.M. (1990) *Rules versus relationships: The ethnography of legal discourse*, Chicago, IL: University of Chicago Press.

Coopers and Lybrand (1993) *Fiscal incentives to regenerate the private rented sector*, London: Coopers and Lybrand.

Coopers and Lybrand (1996) *The outlook for housing investment trusts*, London: Coopers and Lybrand.

Countryside Agency (2000) *The state of the countryside*, Cheltenham: Countryside Agency.

Cowan, D. (1999) *Housing law and policy*, Basingstoke: Macmillan Press.

Cowan, D. (2001) 'Harassment and unlawful eviction in the private rented sector: a study of law in(-)action', *The Conveyancer and Property Lawyer*, no 65, pp 249-64.

Crace, J. (2000) 'Flat Earth', *Guardian Education*, 19 September.

Crook, A.D.H. (1989) 'Multi-occupied housing standards: the application of discretionary powers by local authorities', *Policy & Politics*, vol 17, no 1, pp 41-58.

Crook, A.D.H. and Hughes, J.E.T. (2001) 'Market signals and disrepair in privately rented housing', *Journal of Property Research,* vol 18, no 1, pp 21-50.

Crook, A.D.H. and Kemp, P.A. (1996a) *Private landlords in England*, London: HMSO.

Crook, A.D.H. and Kemp, P.A. (1996b) 'The Revival of Private Rented Housing in Britain', *Housing Studies*, vol 11, pp 51-68.

Crook A.D.H. and Kemp, P.A. (1999) *Financial institutions and private rented housing*, York: York Publishing Services.

Crook, A.D.H. and Martin, G.J. (1988) 'Property speculators, local authority policy and the decline of private rented housing in the 1980s', in P.A. Kemp (ed) *The private provision of rented housing*, Aldershot: Avebury.

Crook, A.D.H. with Sharp, C.B. (1989) *Property dealers, local authority policy and the repair and improvement of unfurnished private rented housing,* Occasional Paper, TRP 89, Sheffield: Dept of Town and Regional Planning, University of Sheffield.

Crook, A.D.H., Henneberry, J.M. and Hughes, J.E.T. (1998) *Repairs and improvements to private rented dwellings in the 1990s*, London: DETR.

Crook, A.D.H., Hughes, J. and Kemp, P.A. (1995) *The supply of privately rented homes: Today and tomorrow*, York: Joseph Rowntree Foundation.

Crook, A.D.H., Hughes, J. and Kemp, P.A. (1998) 'Housing investment trusts and the returns from residential lettings', *Journal of Property Research*, vol 15, pp 229-48.

Crook, A.D.H., Henneberry, J.M., Hughes, J.E.T. and Kemp, P A. (2000) *Repairs and maintenance by private landlords*, London: DETR.

Crook, A.D.H., Kemp, P.A., Anderson, I. and Bowman, S. (1991) *The business expansion scheme and rented housing*, York: Cloister Press.

Crook, A.D.H. and Kemp, P.A., with Barnes, Y. and Ward, J. (2002) *Investment returns in the private rented sector*, London: British Property Federation.

Currie, H. and Miller, B. (1987) *A home of my own: A survey and review of multiple occupancy in Scotland*, Edinburgh: Scottish Council for Single Homeless.

Currie, H., Third, H., Satsangi, M. and Brown, A. (1998) *Good practice in the use of licensing schemes for houses in multiple occupation in Scotland*, Edinburgh: Scottish Office Central Research Unit.

David Couttie Associates (2001) *Ryedale Housing Needs Study*: available from Ryedale District Council.

Dearing (1997) *Report of the national committee of inquiry into higher education*, chapter 1, pp 14-15, London: HMSO.

DEFRA (Department for the Environment, Food and Rural Affairs) (2001) *The rural white paper, implementation plan*, London: The Stationery Office.

Department of Applied Economics, University of Cambridge (1997) *An economic model of the demand and need for social housing*, London: DETR.

Departments of Geography and Land Economy, University of Aberdeen (1996) *Scottish rural life update*, Edinburgh: Scottish Office.

DETR (Department of the Environment Transport and the Regions) (1998a) *English house condition survey 1996*, London: The Stationery Office.

DETR (1998b) *How local authorities used the private rented sector prior to the Housing Act 1996*, Housing Research Summary No 86, London: DETR.

DETR (1999 and 2001) *Rent officer statistics, quarters 1 to 4*, London: DETR.

DETR (2000a) *Quality and choice: A decent home for all, the Housing Green Paper*, London: DETR.

DETR (2000b) *Quality and choice: A decent home for all: A housing policy for England*, London: DETR.

DETR (2001a) *Private sector housing renewal, reform of the housing grant, Construction and Regeneration Act 1996, Local Government and Housing Act 1989 and Housing Act 1985*, Consultation Paper, London: DETR.

DETR (2001b) *Developing a voluntary accreditation scheme for private landlords, a good practice guide,* London: DETR.

DETR (2001c) *Private sector housing renewal: A consultation paper,* London: DETR.

DETR and DSS (Department of Social Security) (2000) *The way forward for housing,* London: DETR.

Ditch, J., Lewis, A. and Wilcox, S. (2001) *Social housing, tenure and housing allowance: An international review*, London: DWP.

DoE (Department for the Environment) (1983) *English house condition survey 1981*, London: HMSO.

DoE (1987) *Housing: The government's proposals*, Cmnd 214, London: HMSO.

DoE (1993), *Housing in England*, London: HMSO.

DoE (1995) *Our future homes: Opportunity, choice, responsibility*, Cmnd 2901, London: HMSO.

DoE (1996a) *Private sector renewal: A strategic approach*, London: The Stationery Office.

DoE (1996b) *Code of guidance on parts VI and VII of the Housing Act 1996: Allocation of housing accommodation, homelessness,* London: HMSO.

Doling, J. (1983) 'How much protection do the Rent Acts provide?', *Journal of Planning and Environmental Law*, pp 713-23.

DSS (Department of Social Security) (1997) *Social security departmental report*, Cmnd 3613, London: The Stationary Office.

DTLR (Department for Transport, Local Government and the Regions) (2001) *Selective licensing of private landlords: A consultation paper*, London: DTLR.

DTZ Pieda Consulting (1998) *The nature and demand for housing in rural areas*, London: HMSO.

DWP (Department for Work and Pensions) (2001) *Housing benefit and council tax benefit, quarterly summary statistics August 2001*, London: DWP.

Dyer, S. (1996) *The use of additional capital allocations for homelessness projects*, Edinburgh: Scottish Office.

Edinburgh University (2000) *Response to mandatory licensing of houses in multiple occupation (HMOs) Civic Government (Scotland) Act 1982 (licensing of houses in multiple occupation) Order 200: Guidance on implementation*, June. [Letter to Mr Richard Grant, Scottish Executive].

Elsmore, K. (1998) *Minding the gap: Shortfalls between private rents and housing benefit in one London borough*, London: London Housing Unit.

Elsmore, K. (2000) *Market of desperation: Housing benefit shortfall and private tenants in Brent*, London: London Housing Unit.

Englander, D. (1983) *Landlord and tenant in urban Britain 1838-1918*, Oxford: Clarendon Press.

Flemming, M.C. and Nellis J.G. (1984) *The Halifax house price index: Technical details*, Halifax: Halifax Building Society.

Ford, J. (1999) 'Young adults and owner occupation: A changing goal?' in J. Rugg, (ed) *Young people, housing and social policy*, London: Routledge.

Ford, J., Quilgars, D., Burrows, R. and Pleace, N. (1997) *Young people and housing*, Salisbury: Rural Development Commission.

Forrest, R. and Murie, A. (1994) 'Home ownership in recession', *Housing Studies*, vol 8, no 4, pp 227-40.

Francis, H. (1971) *Report of the committee on the Rent Acts*, Cmnd 4609, London: HMSO.

Furlong, A. and Cartmel, F. (1997) *Young people and social change: Individualisation and risk in late modernity*, Buckingham: Open University Press.

Gibb, K. (1994) 'Before and after deregulation: market renting in Glasgow and Edinburgh', *Urban Studies*, vol 31, no 9, pp 1481-95.

Green, H. and Hansbro, J. (1995) *Housing in England 1993/94*, London: OPCS, HMSO.

Green, H., Bumpstead, R., Thomas, M. and Grove, J. (1999) *Housing in England 1997/98*, London: Office for National Statistics, The Stationery Office.

Hamnett, C. (1999) *Winners and losers: Home ownership in modern Britain*, London: Taylor and Francis.

Hamnett, C. and Randolph, B. (1988) *Cities, housing and profits*, London: Hutchinson.

Hancock, P. (1999): *Lone parent households in the rural private rented sector*, MA in housing studies dissertation, York: Department of Social Policy and Social Work, University of York.

Hansard (1974a) Parliamentary Debates: House of Commons, vol 878, cols 671-2

Hansard (1974b) Parliamentary Debates: House of Commons, vol 876, cols 1028-30.

Hansard (1974c) Parliamentary Debates: House of Commons, vol 878, cols 655-71.

Hansard (1974d) Parliamentary Debates: House of Commons, vol 878, cols 657-58.

Hansard (1974e) Parliamentary Debates: House of Commons, vol 878, cols 658-61.

Hansard (1974f) Parliamentary Debates: House of Commons, vol 878, cols 663-64.

Hansard (1974g) Parliamentary Debates: House of Commons, vol 878, cols 669-70.

Hansard (1988) House of Lords, vol 499, cols 1343, 24 October, London: HMSO.

Hansard (1988) House of Lords, vol 499, cols 1529-31, 21 July, London: HMSO.

Harloe, M. (1985) 'Landlord/tenant relationships in Europe and America – the limits & functions of the legal framework', *Urban Law & Policy*, vol 7, pp 359-83.

Harvey, A. (1964) *Tenants in danger*, Harmondsworth: Penguin Books.

Hawkins, K. (1983) 'Bargain and bluff: Compliance strategy and deterrence in the enforcement of regulation', *Law and Policy Quarterly*, vol 5, pp 35-73.

Hedges, B. and Clemens, C. (1994) *Housing attitudes survey*, London: HMSO.

Henderson, M., Holland, C. and Shucksmith, M. with Rogers, A. (1991) *Agricultural tied housing in Scotland - A report to the Rural Forum,* Perth: Rural Forum Scotland.

Holland, Sir Milner (1965) *Report of the committee on housing in Greater London*, Cmnd 2605, London: HMSO.

Holmans, A.E. (1987) *Housing policy in Britain*, London: Croom Helm.

Holmans, A.E. (1995) *Housing demand and need in England 1991-2001*, York: Joseph Rowntree Foundation.

Holmans, A.E. (2000) 'British housing in the twentieth century: An end-of-century overview' in *Housing Finance Review 1999-2000*, York: Chartered Institute of Housing and the Council of Mortgage Lenders for the Joseph Rowntree Foundation.

Housing Corporation (1995) *Housing policy in rural areas*, London: Housing Corporation.

Hutter, B.M. (1988) *The reasonable arm of the law*, Oxford: Clarendon Press.

Inside Housing (2000) 'Housing Corporation set to extend rural housing programme', 3 November.

Inside Housing (2001) 'Byers promises HMO licensing review', 3 August.

Investment Property Databank (2000) *Glossary of terms*, London: IPD.

Jew, P. (1994) *Law and order in private rented housing*, London: Campaign for Bedsit Rights.

Jones, G, and Gilliland, L. (1993) 'I would hate to be young again', *Biographies of risk and its avoidance, young people in and out of the housing market,* Working Paper 4, Edinburgh: University of Edinburgh.

Kass, G. (1980) 'An exploratory technique for investigating large quantities of categorical data', *Applied Statistics*, vol 29, pp 119-27.

Keenan, P. (1998) 'Residential mobility and low demand : A case history from Newcastle', in S. Lowe, S. Spencer and P. Keenan (eds) *Housing abandonment in Britain: Studies in the causes and effects of low demand housing,* York: Centre for Housing Policy, University of York.

Kemp, P.A. (ed) (1988) *The private provision of rented housing,* Aldershot: Avebury.

Kemp, P.A. (1990) 'Deregulation, markets and the 1988 Housing Act', *Social Policy and Administration*, vol 24, no 2, p 145.

Kemp, P.A. (1992) 'The ghost of Rachman' in C. Grant (ed) *Built to last? Reflections on British housing policy*, London: Roof.

Kemp, P.A. (1993) 'Rebuilding the private rented sector', in P. Malpass and R. Means (eds) *Implementing housing policy*, Buckingham: Open University Press.

Kemp, P.A. (1997) 'Ideology, public policy and private rental housing since the war' in P. Williams (ed) *Directions in housing policy – towards sustainable housing policies for the UK*, London: Paul Chapman.

Kemp, P.A. (1998a) *Housing benefit : Time for reform*, York: Joseph Rowntree Foundation.

Kemp, P.A. (1998b) 'Private renting in England', *Netherlands Journal of Housing and the Built Environment*, vol 13, no 3, pp 233-53.

Kemp, P.A. and Keoghan, M. (2001) 'Movement into and out of the private rented sector in England', *Housing Studies*, vol 16, no 1, pp 21-7.

Kemp, P.A. and McLaverty, P. (1993) *Rent officers and housing benefit,* York: Centre for Housing Policy.

Kemp, P.A. and Rhodes, D. (1994) *Private landlords in Scotland,* Edinburgh: Scottish Homes.

Kemp, P.A. and Rhodes, D. (1997) 'The motivations and attitudes to letting of private landlords in Scotland', *Journal of Property Research*, vol 14, pp 117-32.

Kemp, P.A. and Rugg, J. (1998) *The single room rent: Its impact on young people*, York: Centre for Housing Policy, University of York.

King, C. (2000) 'No quick fix for HMOs', *Roof*, p 14, September/October.

Kleinman, M., Whitehead, C. and Scanlon, K. (1996) *The Private rented sector*, London: National Federation of Housing Associations.

Law Commission (2001) *Reform of housing law: A coping paper*, London: Law Commission.

Law Commission (2002) *Renting homes: Status and security*, London: Law Commission.

Lister, D. (2000) 'Constructing tenancy relations – young people and their experiences of the private rented sector in England', unpublished paper presented at European Network for Housing Research Conference, 'Housing in the 21st century: Fragmentation and reorientation', Gavle, Sweden, 26-30 June.

Lister, D. (2001) 'Constructing pre-tenancy relations in the private rented sector – the experiences of young people and landlords', unpublished paper presented at the Socio-Legal Studies Association Conference, University of Bristol, 4-6 April.

Llewelyn-Davies and the University of Westminster, (2000) *Conversion and redevelopment: Process and potential*, London: DETR.

London Research Centre (1999) *Housing benefit and the private rented sector*, London: DETR.

Lloyd, M.G. and Danson M.W. (2000) 'The land reform policy group in Scotland: Institutional sponsorship for land reform', *Local Economy*, vol 15, no 3, pp 214-24.

Lowe, S., Keenan, P. and Spencer, S. (1999) 'Housing abandonment in inner cities: The politics of low demand for housing', *Housing Studies*, vol 14, no 5.

Lyons, T.J. (1984) 'The meaning of holiday under the Rent Acts', *The Conveyancer and Property Lawyer*, pp 286-95.

McConaghy, M., Foster, K., Thomas, M. [ONS], Grove, J. and Oliver, R. [DETR] (2000) *Survey of English housing 1998/9*, London: The Stationery Office.

MacGregor, B.D. (1993) *Land tenure in Scotland*, the John McEwen Memorial Lecture, Perth: Rural Forum.

Maclennan, D. (1985) 'Urban housing rehabilitation: an encouraging British example', *Policy & Politics*, vol 13, no 4, pp 413-29.

Market Research UK Ltd (1999) *Eden district housing needs study*, Newcastle: available from Eden District Council.

Marsh, A., Niner, P., Cowan, D., Forrest, R. and Kennett, P. (2000) *Harassment and unlawful eviction of private rented sector tenants and park home residents*, London: DETR.

Morgan, J. (1996) 'The casualization of housing', *Journal of Social Welfare and Family Law*, vol 18, pp 445-60.

Morrell, G.D. (1991) 'Property performance analysis and performance indices: A review', *Journal of Property Research*, no 8, pp 29-57.

Morrell, G.D. (1995) 'Property Indices: A coming of age?', *Journal of Property Valuation & Investment*, vol 13, no 3, pp 8-21.

Mulholland, H. (2000) 'Held captive', *Guardian Education*, 23 May.

Murie, A. (1996) 'Reflections and conclusions' in H. Currie and M. Murie (eds) *Housing in Scotland*, Coventry: Chartered Institute of Housing.

Murie, A., Leather, P., Caffyn, A., Phillimore, J., Revell, K. and Appleton, N. (1999) *East Lindsey district council: Housing needs study*, Birmingham: Centre for Urban and Regional Studies, University of Birmingham.

Nash, D. and Reeder, D. (eds) (1993) *Leicester in the twentieth century*, Stroud: Alan Sutton Publishing.

National Housing Federation (2001) news release, 15 June.

National Union of Students (2001) *Housing survey*, London: NUS.

Nelken, D. (1983) *The limits of the legal process: A study of landlords, law and crime*, London: Academic Press.

Nevitt, A.A. (1966) *Housing, taxation and subsidies*, London: Nelson.

ONS (Office for National Statistics) (2000) *Social trends*, no 31, 2001 edn, London: The Stationery Office.

ONS (2001) *Housing benefit and council tax benefit quarterly summary statistics*, London: The Stationery Office.

Paley, B. (1978) *Attitudes to letting in 1976*, London: HMSO.

Parker, R (1967) *The rents of council houses*, London: G Bell and Sons.

Pavis, S., Platt S. and Hubbard G. (2000) *Young people in rural Scotland: Pathways to social inclusion and exclusion*, York: York Publishing Services.

Phillips (1993) 'Rural gentrification and the processes of class colonisation' *Journal of Rural Studies*, vol 9, no 2, pp 123-40.

Report on an investigation into complaint No 96/B/0644 against Leicester City Council, 12 February 1998.

Rhodes, D. (1993) 'The state of the private rented sector', *Housing Research Findings,* no 90, York: Joseph Rowntree Foundation.

Rhodes, D. and Bevan, M. (1997) *Can the private rented sector house the homeless,* York: Centre for Housing Policy, University of York.

Rhodes, D. and Kemp, P.A. (1996) *The Joseph Rowntree Foundation index of private rents and yields: Technical specification,* York: Centre for Housing Policy, University of York.

Robbins (1963) *Report of the committee on higher education* (appointed by the prime minister under the chairmanship of Lord Robbins 1961-1963), Cmnd 2154-1, London: HMSO.

Robinson, G.M. (1998) *Conflict and change in the countryside,* Chichester: John Wiley & Sons.

Rowan-Robinson, J., Watchman, P. and Barker, C. (1990) *Crime and regulation,* Edinburgh: T & T Clark.

Rugg, J, (1999) 'The use and "abuse" of private renting and help with rental costs' in J. Rugg, (ed) *Young people, housing and social policy,* London: Routledge.

Rugg, J. and Burrows, R. (1999) 'Setting the context – young people, housing and social policy', in J. Rugg, (ed) *Young people, housing and social policy,* London: Routledge.

Rugg, J. and Jones, A. (1999) *Getting a job, finding a home: Rural youth transitions,* Bristol: The Policy Press.

Rugg, J., Rhodes D. and Jones, A. (2000) *The nature and impact of student demand on housing markets,* York: York Publishing Services Ltd.

Rural Development Commission (1998) *A home in the country? Affordable housing in rural England,* Salisbury: Rural Development Commission.

Ryan, A. (1982) 'The romantic theory of ownership' in P. Hollowell, (ed) *Property and social relations,* London: Heinemann Educational Books Ltd.

Satsangi, M., Hague C., Higgins M., Pawson H., Rosenburg L., Bramley G. and Storey C. (2001) *Factors affecting land supply for affordable housing in rural areas,* Edinburgh: Scottish Executive Central Research Unit.

Satsangi, M., Storey C. and Bramley G. with Dunmore K. (2000) *Selling and developing land and buildings for rent and low-cost home ownership: The views of landowners,* Edinburgh: Scottish Homes/Scottish Landowners' Federation.

Scottish Council for Single Homeless (1987) *Draft code of guidance for houses in multiple occupation,* Edinburgh: SCSH.

Scottish Executive (1999) *News release: Alexander plans increased safety for tenants*, 30 September, Edinburgh: Scottish Executive Information Directorate.

Scottish Executive (2000a) *Guidance on the mandatory licensing of houses in multiple occupation*, Edinburgh: Scottish Executive.

Scottish Executive (2000b) *The Civic Government (Scotland) Act 1982 (licensing of houses in multiple occupation) Order 2000*, Scottish Statutory Instrument 2000, No 177, Edinburgh: Scottish Executive.

Scottish Executive (2001) *Land reform: The draft bill*, Edinburgh: The Stationery Office.

Scottish Homes (1997) *The Scottish house condition survey 1996: Main report*, Edinburgh: Scottish Homes.

Scottish Homes, (1998a) *Regional plans 1998-2001 for Highlands and Islands Region, Glasgow and North Clyde Region, South and West Region, Lothian, Borders and Forth Valley Region, and North and East Region*, various: Scottish Homes.

Scottish Homes (1998b) *Tackling rural housing*, Scottish Homes' policy statement, Edinburgh: Scottish Homes.

Scottish Labour Party (1997) *Scottish Labour Manifesto 1997*, Glasgow: Scottish Labour Party.

Scottish Landowners' Federation (1998) *Rural housing in Scotland: A new initiative*, Edinburgh: Scottish Landowners' Federation.

Scottish Office (1988) *Houses in multiple occupation: Possible changes in the law*, Edinburgh: Scottish Development Department.

Scottish Office (1998) *Towards a development strategy for rural Scotland: The framework*, Edinburgh: Scottish Office.

Scottish Office (1999) *Investing in modernisation – an agenda for Scotland's housing*, Green Paper cmmd 4272, Edinburgh: The Stationery Office.

Scottish Office Environment Department (1991) 'Housing in multiple occupation guidance notes', Circular Env,20/1991, Edinburgh: Scottish Office.

Scottish Office Land Reform Policy Group (1998a) *Identifying the problems*, Edinburgh: The Stationery Office.

Scottish Parliament Information Centre (1999), *Employment, housing and poverty in rural areas, research note 99/29*, Edinburgh: Scottish Parliament Information Centre.

Shelter Scotland (1998) *Land reform and housing: Identifying the problems*, Edinburgh: Shelter Scotland.

Shucksmith, M. (1990) *The definition of rural areas and rural deprivation*, Research Report No 2, Edinburgh: Scottish Homes.

Index

References to figures and tables are in *italics*